A Comprehensive Patent Practice Form Book

A Practitioner's Guide to Administrative Domestic and International Application Procedure

David M. Gorzo

ABA
AMERICAN BAR ASSOCIATION
Intellectual Property Law Section

Cover design by Jill Tedhams/ABA Design

The materials contained herein represent the opinions of the authors and/or the editors and should not be construed to be the views or opinions of the law firms or companies that such persons are in partnership with, associated with, or employed by, nor of the American Bar Association or the Section of Intellectual Property Law, unless adopted pursuant to the bylaws of the Association.

Nothing contained in this book is to be considered as the rendering of legal advice for specific cases, and readers are responsible for obtaining such advice from their own legal counsel. This book is intended for educational and informational purposes only.

Printed in the United States of America.

27 26 25 24 23 5 4 3 2 1

A catalog record for this book is available from the Library of Congress.

In tribute to Thomas Edison, who once said
"I make more mistakes than anyone else I know,
and sooner or later, I patent most of them."

Contents

The following documents can be found at
https://ambar.org/PPFB

Domestic Practice Sample Document Files

Pre-Filing

D-01 Initial invention disclosure form/questionnaire

Filing

D-02 Transmittal cover letter for new application
D-03 Fee transmittal letter
D-04 Declaration (37 CFR 1.63) for utility or design application using an Application Data Sheet (37 CFR 1.76) and assignment for single assignee
D-05 Design application specification appendix
D-06 Assignment agreement
D-07 Petition under 37 CFR 1.84 to accept color drawings
D-08 IDS cover letter (before NF OA)
D-09 IDS statement under 37 CFR 1.97(e) or fee required (after first OA, but before final OA or allowance)
D-10 IDS statement under 37 CFR 1.97(e) and fee required (after final OA or Allowance, but before issue fee payment)
D-11 Preliminary amendment (Util)
D-12 Preliminary amendment (Des)
D-13 Response to Notice of Noncompliant Amendment
D-14 Claim for priority under 35 USC 119 and transmittal of priority document under 37 CFR 1.55
D-15 Communication re. co-pending applications (Des)
D-16 Authorization to incorporate extension of time with reply
D-17 Rescission of prior disclaimer/request to revisit art

Post-Filing, Pre-Exam

D-18 Certificate of transmission
D-19 Transmittal letter
D-20 Request for corrected official filing receipt
D-21 Response to informational notice to applicant

Post-Exam

Post-Allowance

Post-Grant

Foreign Practice Sample Document Files

PCT

PCT

EPC

Disclaimer

The content provided in this manual is for informational and reference purposes only, and is neither intended to be, nor should it be, regarded or relied upon as legal advice. The inclusion in this manual of a link to any published background reading article should not necessarily be construed as an endorsement by the author and/or publisher of this manual of any views or opinions expressed therein. The author and/or publisher make no vouchment regarding the factual accuracy of the reading articles referenced herein. Any errors or inaccuracies in the original text of this manual are the sole responsibility of the author.

Text Plan

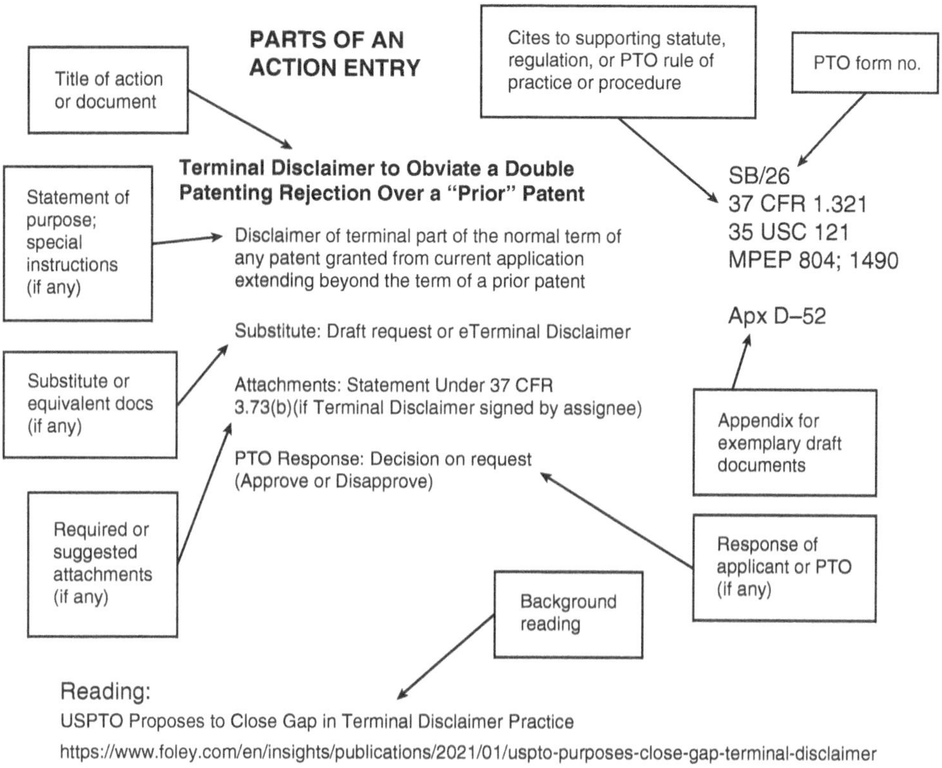

The schematic shows the layout and elements of an example "action." Not all parts depicted may occur in every action.

In **Part One: Domestic Application Practice**, actions for provisional, utility, and design applications are combined into a single sequence in order to reduce redundancy. Text pertaining exclusively to certain application types is designated by the appropriate symbol, as follows:

(P) Text pertains to provisional applications only.

[U] Text pertains to utility applications only.

(D) Text pertains to design applications only.

Unmarked text pertains to utility and design applications, or all three.

Introduction

Attorney malpractice claims have been rising in recent years according to published reports from the American Bar Association. Patent practitioners have not been spared the ire of disgruntled clients. Malpractice claims against patent firms jumped 30 percent from 2007 to 2011,[1] and continue to rise. Analysts attribute the problem to the rising complexity of patent practice, as well as a surge in patent filing activity. Total applications filed in the U.S. Patent Office (USPTO) have increased 24 percent since 2010 and more than doubled since 2000.[2] It is evident that patent applicants are wary of attorney negligence, stressing the need for practitioners to use uttermost care in preparing and prosecuting applications.

What This Book Is

In light of malpractice risk and increasing workload, it is vital for practitioners to work effectively and efficiently. This manual and form book provides a tool for promoting the quality of application conduct by enhancing mindfulness of the practitioner to procedural options available at any given point during the application protocol. It will aid the practitioner in anticipating the Patent Office's actions, as well as elevate the practitioner's awareness of options available in prosecuting an application.

This book is a comprehensive guide to patent application administrative (non-substantive) procedure. It will cover the patenting process from initial invention disclosure by the inventor/applicant through post-grant proceedings. Patent application procedure is a rule-driven, stepwise process. With some variation within established bounds, applications follow a prescribed, substantially predictable, trajectory. Beginning with the premise that patent application practice is primarily an exchange of documents between applicant and the Patent Office, each transmittal of documents represents a discrete

1. ABA, Profile of Legal Malpractice Claims: 2008–2011 (2012); *see also* 4 Ronald E. Mallen with AllisonMartin Rhodes, Legal Malpractice § 31:2 (2015).
2. Source: USPTO.

"action" or step in the patenting process, usually pursuant to encoded patent rules of practice (i.e., 37 CFR; MPEP). Accordingly, this practice guide will feature the steps or actions comprising the application process, and the documents used to implement them. A compendium was assembled of practically every possible action by the applicant or the Patent Office, both initiated and in response. The text addressing application procedure consists mostly of a series of entries, with each entry representing a specific action. The actions are arranged in the text in sequential order as they would normally occur during application pendency.

Entries are composed of the title of the action, usually with a brief description, the appropriate response from the applicant if the action is office initiated, along with requisite attachments if necessary. Accompanying each action entry, when possible, are sample documents and citations to supporting rules and regulations of patent practice (i.e., 35 USC, 37 CFR, and MPEP). The sample docs are a catalog of actual as-filed documents that the reader can use as exemplars in drafting requests, petitions, responses, and other non-form transmittals to the Patent Office. Cites to rules of practice allow the reader to consult the legal basis of a specific action. Links (URLs) for a selection of supplemental background readings are furnished for most actions and related topics.

The manual will allow the reader to be mindful of all established administrative procedural actions that can occur at any point in the course of a patent application, enabling vigorous administrative management of an application. Accordingly, the reader will be aware of the customary actions that can be issued by the Patent Office, as well as all acceptable actions, both mandatory and elective, that are at the practitioner's disposal. Applicant-initiated actions can ordinarily be implemented via standard forms, or drafted documents, or either. Most of the listed applicant actions that can be administered with a drafted document are accompanied by as-filed document submittals as examples of how to initiate an action or respond to the Patent Office. By providing documentary examples of applicant-initiated actions, as well as responses to Patent Office communications, the practitioner can quickly and easily deal with most any issue that might arise without spending valuable time researching or drafting administrative documents *ex nihilo*. In most instances, multiple specimens of a document type are provided, giving the user a choice of styles or versions of the document. If appropriate, the exemplary documents can be used as is, or can be modified with language that suits the practitioner's needs or preferences.

It should be emphasized that this manual will focus on administrative actions of the application process, as distinguished from substantive or prosecutorial actions where specialized scientific or technical knowledge is applied. This guide will not instruct the reader how to prepare invention disclosures (i.e., specification/claims) or responses to examination-related office actions. Instead, it will present an inclusive register of extant non-substantive administrative actions available to the practitioner during the course of application, along with model documents for accomplishing such actions. It is intended that this manual will enable the practitioner to leverage all appropriate actions to result in a disposition most favorable to the applicant.

Scope

The content is divided broadly into domestic and foreign application practice, covering provisional, nonprovisional, and design applications domestically, and foreign applications under the Paris Convention, the European Patent Convention (EPC), Patent Cooperation Treaty (PCT), and the Hague Agreement. Additionally, Part Three concentrates on biotechnology applications. The application process is divided into four principal phases: (1) re-application activities, (2) filing, (3) cost-filing/prosecution, and (4) post-grant. Pre-application deals largely with matters of patentability and eligibility for patent, vis-à-vis the subject invention. Filing covers assembling the application package and submitting it to the Patent Office. The post-filing phase includes the period between submittal and examination, followed by prosecution, which is the interaction between the Patent Office and the applicant during which the application is examined for patentability and ultimately rejected or allowed. Finally, the post-grant period deals with activities after the patent issues.

Please note that, in order to reduce redundancy, material for provisional, utility, and design applications has been combined into a single sequence in Part One: Domestic Application Practice. Material pertinent to each application type is designated with an appropriate indicator. (*See* Text Plan at p. xix.)

How to Use This Manual

In order to be an effective practice aid, this guide should be regularly consulted at all stages of the patenting process in order to: orient an application in the procedure, chart a course for managing an application, inform the practitioner of the available options at any given point by being aware of what should be done and what can be done, and also to plan ahead. Before committing time and resources to initiate a new application, the manual can be used to evaluate patentability of the asserted invention. For applications in the assembly and post-filing stages, the manual can act as a checklist for ensuring that all necessary and discretionary elements are included in the filing package before examination. After examination, the manual can act as a guide for a robust and effective prosecution. In sum, it will permit the practitioner to make full use of the administrative tool box. It is hoped that the information presented will make the administration of patent applications more efficient and effective, and reduce procedural oversights that may result from inadvertently overlooking available actions.

Who Should Use This Manual

This manual is targeted mainly to practitioners, but will be useful to anyone engaged in or contemplating patent application. It will be an informative reference for patent law practitioners of all experience levels, but beginning associates, as well as patent law students, will find it especially helpful for familiarizing themselves with the patenting details they will encounter on the job, and to which they may not have been exposed during their formal course of legal study. It will be particularly beneficial for sole practitioners and patent agents who are engaged in all aspects of application practice, as well as paralegals, patent legal secretaries, and others managing the administrative aspects of patent application. The manual can also serve as a study guide for those preparing to sit for the Patent Bar. Although it is not directed to the nonpractitioner, inventors who are considering applying for patent and are somewhat familiar with application procedure may find it helpful in dealing with the Patent Office in a more competent and professional manner. The Patent Office will appreciate *pro se* applicant submittals that are proper, precise, and well crafted. Also, inventors who are filing an application through an attorney or patent agent may find it beneficial in dealing with their practitioner in a more effective fashion and knowing what to anticipate during the application process.

PART ONE
Domestic Application Practice

"The issue for patents for new discovers has given a spring to invention beyond my conception."

— Thomas Jefferson

I. Introduction: Patents, Weak and Strong

The objective of applying for patent is not to just get a patent, but to get the strongest patent possible. All patents are not created equal. A stronger patent has greater commercial value, is more enforceable against infringement, and is better able to survive novelty challenges and post-grant reviews. It can also earnhigher licensing fees and demand a higher price if offered for sale.

A strong patent starts with a quality application. Naturally, the novelty or inventiveness of the claimed subject matter has a substantial impact on the strength of the application and subsequent patent. Nonetheless, even a significant innovation can fall victim to a poorly executed application that is ineffectively managed, and a well-crafted application can be squandered if clumsily administered. To avoid these potential pitfalls it is essential to begin witha skillfully executed application and then follow through with a robust prosecutionafter filing. This requires awareness of practice rules, as well as how to file the proper supporting documents for the most effective disposition of an application.

Reading:

Practical Considerations and Strategies in Prosecuting U.S. Patent Applications
https://www.finnegan.com/en/insights/articles/practical-considerations-and-strategies-in-prosecu ting-u-s.html

How to Create a Bulletproof Patent
https://www.forbes.com/sites/stephenkey/2021/01/19/how-to-create-a-bullet proof-patent/?sh=8a e0623ceb65

3 Ingredients of High-Quality Patent Application
https://triangleip.com/high-quality-patent-application/#

How to Own Higher Quality Patents
https://henry.law/blog/own-higher-quality-patents/

How to Measure the Quality of a Patent – and a Patent Law Firm
https://www.chiplawgroup.com/how-to-measure-the-quality-of-a-patent-and-a-patent-law-firm/

Striking a Balance Between Quality and Value in a Patent Portfolio
https://ipwatchdog.com/2022/10/27/striking-balance-quality-value-patent-portfolio/id=152350/

II. Sources of Domestic Patent Law

Statutes controlling patent procedure are codified at U.S. Code Title 35 (Patent Act) and U.S. Code of Federal Regulations Title 37, Part 1. Agency rules and regulations covering patenting practices at the USPTO are collected in the *Manual of Patent Examining Procedure* (MPEP, 9th ed., Oct. 2019, last revised June 2020). The Leahy-Smith America Invents Act (AIA) of 2011 is the most recent significant modification of patent law. The AIA converted the United States from a first-to-invent to a first-to-file patent system for applications filed on or after March 16, 2013, bringing the United States into accord with much of the rest of the world. The American first-to-file system differs, however, by allowing an inventor a one-year grace period for filing an application after public disclosure of the subject matter. Public disclosure bars an inventor from obtaining patent in many other countries.

A. Federal Statutes

1. U.S. Constitution, Article 1, Section 8, Clause 8
2. Patent Acts (Statutes): U.S. Patent Act: Title 35 of U.S. Code (USC) §§ 1 *et seq.*
3. America Invents Act (AIA): enacted September 2011;f irst-to-file system initiated March 2013

Reading:
First to File: Everything You Need to Know
https://www.upcounsel.com/first-to-file

When Should a Patent Application Be Filed?
https://www.bitlaw.com/guidance/patent/when-to-file-a-patent
-application.html

What Is Patent Law?
https://www.jdsupra.com/legalnews/what-is-patent-law-76144/

First to File Means File First! The Risk of Not Immediately Filing a Patent Application
https://www.ipwatchdog.com/2016/01/09/first-to-file-means-file-first-filing-a-patent-application/id=64809/

Online Resources:
Aside from uspto.gov (https://www-aws.uspto.gov/patents/laws), patent statutes and regulations can be found at a number of sites, such as bitlaw.com, law.justia.com, and law.cornell.edu, among others.

B. Federal Rules/Regulations

1. PTO Rules of Practice (37 CFR 1.1 *et seq.*)
   - Part 1: Rules of Practice in Patent Cases
   - Part 42: Trial Practice before the Patent Trial and Appeal Board
2. Manual of Patent Examination Procedure (MPEP)
   Pertinent MPEP chapters:
   - Ch. 600—Parts, Form, & Content of Applications
   - Ch. 700—Examination, Prosecution
   - Ch. 800—Applications filed under 35 USC 111
   - Ch. 900—Prior Art, Classification
   - Ch. 1300—Allowance and Issue
   - Ch. 1400—Correction of Patents
   - Ch. 1500—Design Patents
   - Ch. 2100—Patentability

C. Case Law

1. U.S. Supreme Court
2. Federal Courts of Appeals
   - Courts of Appeals for the Federal Circuit (CAFC)
3. Agency Decisions (USPTO)
   - Patent Trial and Appeal Board (PTAB)

Patent Law Updates:
https://www.ipwatchdog.com/
https://patentlyo.com/
https://www.jdsupra.com/law-news/ip-law/

https://www.bitlaw.com/source/cases/patent/index.html
https://www.natlawreview.com/article/patent-case-law-updates-august-2021
https://www.patentdocs.org/
https://www.ipupdate.com/

III. Pre-Filing Activities and Considerations

Activities prior to application preparation and filing consist mainly of patentability assessment of the subject invention and eligibility of the applicant and invention for patent. Patentability is an initial evaluation of whether the subject invention meets threshold prerequisites for patent with respect to statutory requirements and prior art. Eligibility for patent determines if any statutory bars exist to preclude the applicant, or the invention itself, from legitimately entering the application process. This is also a good time to consider the pros and cons of applying for patent.

Reading:
Before Applying for a Patent: 3 Questions to Ask Yourself
https://www.legalzoom.com/articles/before-applying-for-a-patent

Seven Steps to Take Before Applying for a Patent
https://www.ownmyinvention.com/learn/Seven-Steps-To-Take-Before-Applying-For-A-Patent

How to Apply for a Patent
https://patentrebel.com/how-to-apply-for-a-patent/

Patent Process
https://www.lambertpatentlaw.com/patents/patent-process/

10 Things to Consider Before Applying for a Patent
https://ttconsultants.com/10-things-to-consider-before-applying-for-a-patent/

What to Do Before Filing
https://www.fillun.com/what-to-do-before-filing

A. Initial Invention Disclosure

- transmittal of invention information from inventor/applicant to practitioner as a prelude to patentability assessment and application preparation

- before submitting a patent application, prospective applicants should disclose invention to others only if a Non-Disclosure Agreement (NDA) is in effect

Provisional/Utility

- information may be gathered from various sources, including disclosure form/questionnaire, descriptions, illustrations, photographs/videos, sketches, drawings, prototypes, mockups, models, inventor(s) interview, inventor publications, notebooks, and the like
- include structure, function, method of use, method of manufacture/assembly, inventive step, advantages over prior art, problem solved

Design

- disclosure information can include images, representations, specimens, or models exhibiting external, surface appearance, ornamental or aesthetic features, shape, form, design, or configuration, showing the novel or inventive features

Initial Invention Disclosure Apx D-01

Invention Disclosure Form (IDF)/Record (IDR)

- questionnaire for invention description and related information
- often used by law firms, corporations, and universities for new matter intake

Reading:

Fields in an Invention Disclosure Form: The Master List
https://triangleip.com/fields-in-an-invention-disclosure-form/

How to Write an Invention Disclosure Record
https://henry.law/blog/write-idr/

Invention Disclosure Form: Why Does It Matter?
https://www.jdsupra.com/legalnews/invention-disclosure-form-why-does-it-2229222/

Writing the Invention Disclosure
http://bayareaip.com/forms/Writing_the_Invention_Disclosure.pdf

Joint Applicants Statement of Respective Contributions 35 USC 116; 37 CFR 1.324, 1.45 MPEP 602.09, 2109

Lists co-inventors and their respective inventive contributions to the invention (executed by all co-inventors)

Reading:
Inventorship: Navigating the Muddy Waters of Inventorship Determination and Correction
https://www.kilpatricktownsend.com/-/media/2019/IP-Desk-Reference-2015/Navigating-the-Muddy-Waters-of-Inventorship

When Do Collaborators Become Co-Inventors?
https://www.finnegan.com/en/insights/articles/when-do-collaborators-become-coinventors.html

Whose Invention Is It Anyway? 5 Questions on Patent Ownership That Inventors and Patent Owners Should Always Be Prepared to Answer
https://www.spruson.com/patents/whose-invention-is-it-anyway-5-questions-on-patent-ownership-that-inventors-and-patent-owners-should-always-be-prepared-to-answer/

B. Advantages and Disadvantages of Patent Application and Patent

- applicants should weigh various strategic factors involved in patenting, such as cost, risks, benefits, and alternatives. Patents are valuable only if they are enforced.

Inventions in certain fast-developing areas of technology may become obsolete before the patent expires.

Reading:
Should You File a Patent Application?
https://www.bitlaw.com/guidance/patent/why-file-a-patent-application.html

Why Are Patents Important? (Advantages of Patents)
https://patentrebel.com/why-are-patents-important-advantages-disadvantages-pros-cons/

Advantages and Disadvantages of Patents
https://www.upcounsel.com/advantages-and-disadvantages-of-patents

Advantages and Drawbacks of Patents
https://www.hartdavidcarson.com/news/advantages-and-drawbacks-of-patents/

Protecting Your Intellectual Property with Patent Alternatives
https://www.industryweek.com/the-economy/regulations/article/21947672/protecting-your-intellectual-property-with-patent-alternatives

Patent Pending Alternatives: Your Next Best Option
https://www.forbes.com/sites/theyec/2019/08/19/patent-pending-alternatives-your-next-best-option/?sh=5cdefe9147d2

How to Protect Your Invention Without a Patent
https://ocpatentlawyer.com/how-to-protect-invention-without-patent/

The Top 3 Advantages and Disadvantages of Patents
https://boldip.com/advantages-disadvantages-patents/

Pros and Cons of Patents
https://prosancons.com/business/pros-and-cons-of-patents/

Advantages and Disadvantages of Obtaining a Patent
http://trademarkspatentslawyer.com/the-advantages-and-disadvantages-of-obtaining-a-patent/

C. Patentability Assessment [MPEP Chap. 2100]

- a preliminary evaluation of the likelihood that the subject invention is patentable on its merits; at this point, it should be determined whether the candidate invention satisfies the *prima facie* conditions of patentability; namely, new, useful, nonobvious, and statutory class

Reading:
Basics of Patentability
https://blog.juristat.com/basics-of-patentability

Patentability: Everything You Need to Know
https://www.upcounsel.com/patentability

Utility Patent Requirements: Everything You Need to Know
https://www.upcounsel.com/utility-patent-requirements

1. Provisional/Utility

The subject matter must satisfy the following patentability requirements:

a. Statutory Class	35 USC 101
- subject matter must fall within a statutory category eligible for patent	MPEP 2106

Reading:
Patentable Subject Matter: Everything You Need to Know
https://www.upcounsel.com/patentable-subject-matter#

Evaluating the Evaluation: Breaking Down New USPTO Guidance for Patent-Eligible Subject Matter
https://www.pillsburylaw.com/en/news-and-insights/uspto-guidance-patent.html

What Is Patentable Subject Matter?
https://www.fr.com/what-is-patentable-subject-matter/

Patentable Subject Matter for a Utility Patent—Explained
https://thebusinessprofessor.com/en_US/property-law/patentable-subject-matter-for-a-utility-patent

Patentable Subject Matter under Section 101
https://cardinal-ip.com/patentable-subject-matter-under-section-101/

USPTO Releases New Guidance on Patent Subject Matter Eligibility
https://www.jonesday.com/en/insights/2019/01/uspto-releases-new-guidance-on-patent-subject-matt

Section 101 (Patentable Subject Matter Eligibility) Index
https://www.bitlaw.com/patent/section-101-index.html#pto

Statutory Classes

1. Process or Method
   a. Conventional Processes (e.g., heat treatments, chemical reactions for making/changing something, ways of making products/chemicals)
   b. Software
      - must be hardware-based (*Bilski v. Kappos*, 561 U.S. 593 (2010))
      - more difficult after *Alice Corp. v. CLS Bank International*, 573 U.S. 208 (2014)
      - ok if it solves technological problem or limitation in a general-purpose computer
      - ok if use is unconventional
      - see *Mayo* test, which follows
   c. Business Methods
      - must be more than merely mental steps or algorithm (*Bilski* (2010))
2. Machines
   - devices/things used for accomplishing a task
   - can be software if used to improve computer operation

3. Manufactures
   - articles of manufacture made by hand or machine
4. Compositions of Matter
   - chemicals, conglomerates, aggregates, etc.
   - usually supplied in bulk (solid-particulate), liquid, or gaseous form
5. New Uses
   - new/nonobvious processes for using known invention
   - must be claimed as process (35 USC 100(b))
6. Judicial Exceptions MPEP 2106.04-05
   - laws of nature, natural phenomena, abstract ideas do not, themselves, qualify for patent
     - inventions incorporating exceptions into a practical application may be eligible

   use two-step "Mayo test" analysis (*Alice Corp. v. CLS Bank*, 573 U.S. 110 (2014) (citing *Mayo v. Prometheus*, 566 U.S. 66, 101 (2012))
     - Step 1: determine if invention embodies exception; if yes, proceed to Step 2
     - Step 2: determine if invention integrates exception into practical application (inventive concept; i.e., implementation of the idea must not be generic, conventional, or obvious); if yes, invention may be patent eligible
   - *Mayo* analysis especially relevant in software applications

Reading:
Patentable Subject Matter and Judicial Exceptions
https://www.brettoniplaw.com/patentable%20subject%20matter%20and%20judicial%20exceptions.html

Patentable Subject Matter After Alice: Best Practices for Responding to 35 U.S.C. § 101 Rejections
https://www.mbhb.com/intelligence/snippets/patentable-subject-matter-after-alice-best-practices-for-responding/

Determining the Patent Eligibility of Inventions Under the New USPTO Guidelines
https://www.natlawreview.com/article/determining-patent-eligibility-inventions-under-newuspto-guidelines

b. New (novel) — 35 USC 102

- subject matter must be unanticipated, original, and unknown in public domain before filing date — MPEP 2131-33

Reading:

Novelty Patent: Everything You Need to Know
https://www.upcounsel.com/novelty-patent

Patentability: The Novelty Requirement of 35 U.S.C. 102
https://ipwatchdog.com/2017/06/10/patentability-novelty-requirement-102/id=84321

Novel Invention? What Is a Section 201 Novelty Rejection?
https://www.patenttrademarkblog.com/novel-invention-section-102-rejection/

Anticipation (Sec. 201)
https://klarquist.com/patent-defenses/anticipation-sec-102/

1. Prior Art—any knowledge publicly available prior to filing date (anticipation), unless such knowledge came from inventor and was not disclosed more than one year before filing — MPEP 2120-28
   - any U.S. patent with earlier filing date
     - exception: common assignee or joint research agreement (PTO Rule 104(c)(4))
2. Any Physical/Method Step Difference
   - any novel feature
     - physical differences
     - new combinations of known components
3. New Usefulness

c. Usefulness (utility) — 35 USC 101

- functional usefulness; useful purpose — MPEP 2107
- operability (theoretical; "on paper")
- demonstrable, current use or some social benefit
- usefulness must be specific, substantial, and credible
- in practice, usefulness is a relatively low bar; a *de minimis* showing is usually sufficient

Reading:
Understanding the Patent Law Utility Requirement
https://www.ipwatchdog.com/2015/11/07/understanding-the-patent-law-utility-requirement/id=63007/

Can You Patent Something That Doesn't Work?
https://www.jdsupra.com/legalnews/can-you-patent-something-that-doesn-t-5519121/

d. Nonobviousness — 35 USC 103
  - measure of inventiveness or innovation — MPEP 2112, 2141-42, 2158
  - often called "inventive step" outside U.S.
  - sufficient difference from what has been previously described; or unexpected results for one with ordinary skill in the art
  - physical or method step difference over all prior developments (prior art; 35 USC 102) available to public
  - Graham Factors (*Graham v. John Deere*, 383 U.S. 1, 148 (1966)); USPO 459); MPEP 2141
    - scope/content of prior art
    - novelty of invention
    - skill level or artisans in the art (person of ordinary skill in the field of your invention would not have been able to think of or make the invention by looking at the available public information)
      - determine obviousness of invention on basis of #1-3
      - consider secondary/objective factors
  - General Arguments
      - unexpected/new/surprising results (must be more than marginal);
      - commercial success; long-felt need; failure of others; etc.

Reading:
Patent Obviousness: Everything You Need to Know
https://www.upcounsel.com/patent-obviousness

What Is an Obvious Invention (Section 103 Rejection)?
https://www.patenttrademarkblog.com/obvious-invention-section-103-rejection/

Non-Obvious Obviousness Arguments (to Overcome 35 USC 103 Rejections)
https://www.vonbriesen.com/legal-news/5995/non-obvious-obviousness-arguments-to-overcome-35-usc-103-rejections

What Is an Obvious Invention (Section 103 Rejection)?
https://ttconsultants.com/what-is-an-obvious-invention-section-103-rejection/

How Do I Know If My Invention Is "Nonobvious" When Applying for a Patent?
https://www.nolo.com/legal-encyclopedia/how-do-i-know-if-my-invention-is-nonobvious-when-applying-for-a-patent.html

Inherency in the Prior Art: The Rules Are Becoming Clearer
https://corporate.findlaw.com/intellectual-property/inherency-in-the-prior-art-the-rules-are-becoming-clearer.html

e. Enablement	35 USC 112(a)
- how to make/practice invention	MPEP 2164
- the subject invention must be adequately developed such that its structure/function/operation is well defined	*see also* MPEP 608.01(p)
- disclosure (written description; specification) must contain detail of sufficient particularity to allow one skilled in the art to make and practice the invention	

Reading:
Patent Enablement: What Level of Detail Do I Need for a Patent?
https://piersonpatentlaw.com/patent-enablement-what-level-of-detail-do-i-need-for-a-patent/

Patent Enablement
http://www.the-business-of-patents.com/patent-enablement.html

Enablement (Sec. 112(1/a))
https://klarquist.com/patent-defenses/enablement-sec-1121a/

Patent Drafting: Understanding the Enablement Requirement
https://ipwatchdog.com/2017/10/28/patentability-drafting-enablement-requirement/id=89721/

Supreme Court to Revisit the Patent Enablement Standard
https://www.law.com/newyorklawjournal/2023/01/24/supreme-court-to-revisit-the-patent-enablement-standard/?slreturn=20230227133710

2. Design [What Is Patent Eligible or Can Be Claimed in a Design Application] [MPEP 1502]

- new, original, ornamental design, ornamentality, nonobvious in ornamental or aesthetic sense; must be article of manufacture (35 USC 171)
- usefulness or functional utility under 35 USC 101 need not be demonstrated (35 USC 101)
- the subject matter that is claimed is the design embodied in or applied to an article of manufacture (or portion thereof) and not the article itself. *Ex parte Cady*, 1916 C.D. 62, 232 O.G. 621 (Comm'r Pat. 1916). "35 U.S.C. 171 refers, not to the design of an article, but to the design for an article, and is inclusive of ornamental designs of all kinds including surface ornamentation as well as configuration of goods." *In re Zahn*, 617 F.2d 261, 204 USPQ 988 (CCPA 1980)
- the design for an article consists of the visual characteristics embodied in or applied to an article
- since a design is manifested in appearance, the subject matter of a design patent application may relate to the configuration or shape of an article, to the surface ornamentation applied to an article, or to the combination of configuration and surface ornamentation
- design is inseparable from the article to which it is applied and cannot exist alone merely as a scheme of surface ornamentation. It must be a definite, preconceived thing, capable of reproduction and not merely the chance result of a method
- a design patent protects the overall visual appearance of a design. Design patent applications are limited to ornamental features and cannot include functional elements

Ineligible Subject Matter [MPEP 1504.01]

- a design for an article of manufacture that is dictated primarily by the function of the article lacks ornamentality and is not proper statutory subject matter under 35 USC 171
- specifically, if at the time the design was created, there was no unique or distinctive shape or appearance to the article not dictated by the function that it performs, the design lacks ornamentality and is not proper subject matter
- a design that simulates a well-known or naturally occurring object or person is not original as required by the statute
- subject matter that could be considered offensive to any race, religion, sex, ethnic group, or nationality is not proper subject matter for a design patent application (35 USC 171 and 37 CFR 1.3)

Reading:
Design Patents: Novelty and Nonobviousness
https://malloylaw.com/federal-circuit-provides-guidance-on-patentability-test-for-design-patents/

Utility vs. Design Patents: Which 1 Is Right for You?
https://builtin.com/operations/design-vs-utility-patents

D. Prior Art Search

[MPEP 904; Rule 56 (37 CFR 1.56): Duty of candor and good faith; duty to disclose]

Although not compulsory, it is generally advisable to conduct, at least, a precursory novelty search before committing resources toward filing in order to determine if prior art exists that could clearly result in application rejection from anticipation. Knowledge of prior art can also assist in drafting a more effective specification and claims. In accordance with Rule 56, applicants are also obligated to disclose to the PTO any prior art they are aware of that may bear on the patentability of a pending application.

Resources for searching prior art include patent, patent application, and utility model, and design databases (both domestic and foreign), non-patent literature, including popular, industrial, and scientific publications.

U.S. Patent Classification System (USPC)
Manual of Classification
Cooperative Patent Classification (CPC) System
U.S. Design Classes
Locarno International Classification of Designs

Reading:
Prior Art Search: Everything You Need to Know
https://www.upcounsel.com/prior-art-search

How to Do a Prior Art Search Yourself
https://henry.law/blog/how-to-do-prior-art-search-yourself

Prior Art Search—An Overview
https://sagaciousresearch.com/blog/prior-art-search-overview/

Prior Art Search: Is It Necessary Before Filing a Patent Application?
https://www.goodmanallen.com/blog/should-you-do-a-prior-art-search-before-filing-a-patent-application

7 Unconventional Ways to Perform a Design Patent Search
https://www.greyb.com/design-patent-search/

How to Do a Prior Art Search Yourself
https://henry.law/blog/how-to-do-prior-art-search-yourself/

Summary of Prior Art [MPEP 2120–29, 2153–54]
- any published writing (including patents) available before filing
- any U.S. patent (or PPA) filed earlier than filing date
- any relevant invention or development existing before filing date
- any public/commercial use, sale, or knowledge of invention before filing date, unless activity came from actual inventor

E. Statutory Bars to Patent

- an assessment of statutory criteria that may preclude application

Reading:
Statutory Bar
https://smithhopen.com/glossary/statutory-bar/

Statutory Bars and Patent Rights
https://alloypatentlaw.com/alloy-patent-law-ip-legal-blog/statutory-bars/

Watch Out for Statutory Bars: Don't Lose Patent Rights Before You Even File the Application
https://corporate.findlaw.com/intellectual-property/watch-out-for-statutory-bars-don-t-lose-patentrights-before-you.html

1. Prior public disclosure (35 USC 102; MPEP 2133.03, 2152)
   102(a): invention described in publicly available disclosure prior to filing
   102(b): One Year Rule: disclosures made within one year of filing by inventor/applicant or another who obtained information from inventor/applicant are permitted
   - if international filing is contemplated, any public disclosure should be avoided, as many foreign jurisdictions demand "absolute novelty" before filing an application

Reading:
Is It O.K. to Publish Your Life Sciences Invention Before Filing for a Patent?
https://www.finnegan.com/en/insights/articles/is-it-o.k.-to-publish-your-life-sciences-invention-before-filing-for-a-patent.html

File a Patent Application Before Telling Others About the Invention
https://ocpatentlawyer.com/beware-of-marketing-an-invention-before-filing-a-patent-application/

Tips to Help Keep Your Disclosure From Becoming Prior Art, Part 1: What Constitutes Disclosure?
https://www.nutter.com/ip-law-bulletin/Tips-to-Help-Keep-Your-Disclosure-from-Becoming-Prior-Art-Pt1

On-Sale Bar: Everything You Need to Know
https://www.upcounsel.com/on-sale-bar

Protecting Patent Rights From the On-Sale Bar After Helsinn
https://www.venable.com/insights/publications/2019/02/protecting-patent-rights-from-the-on-sale-bar

2. Eligibility of Inventor/Applicant (35 USC 116, 118; 37 CFR 1.42; MPEP 605.01, 2109)
   - is applicant eligible to apply for patent?
     - applicant must have contributed at least one inventive concept (37 CFR 1.45)
   - is applicant true inventor or *bona fide* owner of rights?
     - consider circumstances of invention (independent, within employment)
     - employer-applicant must have legitimate legal rights to employee invention
   - any co-inventors (contributor to whole) or joint inventors (contributor in part) involved?

Reading:
The Who's Who and What's What of a Patent Application: An Overview of Inventors, Assignees, and Applicants
https://www.wnlaw.com/blog/whos-whats-patent-application-overview-inventors-assignees-applicants/

Inventorship in U.S. Patent Applications
https://www.stoel.com/legal-insights/article/inventorship-in-u-s-patent-applications

The Complete Guide to Inventorship: Inventors, Joint Inventors, and Co-Inventors
https://revisionlegal.com/patent/the-complete-guide-to-inventorship-inventors-joint-inventors-and-co-inventors/#:~:text=To%20be%20considered%20joint%20and%20co-inventors%2C%20the%20inventors,the%20claims%20being%20made%20in%20the%20patent%20application

When Do Collaborators Become Co-Inventors?
https://www.finnegan.com/en/insights/articles/when-do-collaborators-become-coinventors.html

Conception for Joint Inventors
https://patentlyo.com/patent/2021/07/conception-joint-inventors.html

It All Starts With Inventorship
https://www.finnegan.com/en/insights/blogs/prosecution-first/it-all-starts-with-inventorship.html

F. Alternatives in IP Protection

- consideration of options in patent and other forms of IP protection

1. Design versus Utility Patent Application (MPEP 1502.01)

Applicants/practitioners should consider whether it is more advantageous to apply for design or utility patent, or both. Design patents are normally cheaper and faster to obtain, but offer comparatively limited protection. Design patent may be appropriate if the function of the inventive article is defined largely by exterior or surface morphology.

Reading:
Utility Patent vs. Design Patent: Everything You Must Know
https://www.upcounsel.com/utility-patent-vs-design-patent

Utility vs. Design Patents: Which 1 Is Right for You?
https://builtin.com/operations/design-vs-utility-patents

Patent Types: Design Patent vs. Utility Patent
https://www.kaufholdpatentgroup.com/patent-types-design-patent-vs-utility-patent/

Utility vs. Design Patents: Ultimate Guide
https://www.linkedin.com/pulse/utility-vs-design-patent-ultimate-guide-j-d-houvener

Design Patents
https://www.goodmanallen.com/blog/design-patents

Utility Patent or Design Patent?
https://www.alotechinc.com/utility-patent-design-patent/

U

2. Utility Patent versus Trade Secret

Applicants should consider patent application and post-grant expenses, plus the risk that patent does not issue, against maintaining proprietary technology as trade secret. Trade secrets can theoretically last in perpetuity and are typically less expensive to protect. However, only limited kinds of technology are amenable to being kept as trade secret (e.g., processes, methods of manufacture, formulas, among others), and trade secrets are generally more difficult to enforce than patents. Stronger protection afforded under the Defend Trade Secrets Act of 2016 (DTSA) may render trade secret a more attractive alternative to patent.

Reading:

Patent vs. Trade Secret: Everything You Need to Know
https://www.upcounsel.com/patent-vs-trade-secret

Trade Secrets vs. Patents: Pros & Cons
https://www.obrienpatents.com/trade-secrets-vs-patents-pros-cons/

Trade Secrets vs. Patents: Which Is Right for You?
https://www.morningtrans.com/trade-secrets-vs-patents-which-approach-is-right-for-you/

Secret to a Patent Fight? Managing the Conflicts between Patents and Trade Secret Rights
https://www.americanbar.org/groups/intellectual_property_law/publications/landslide/2018-19/july-august/so-you-want-take-trade-secret-patent-fight/

Patents or Trade Secrets? Deciding How Best to Protect Your Invention Part I: Can the Invention Be Kept Secret?
https://www.nutter.com/ip-law-bulletin/patents-or-trade-secrets-deciding-how-best

Patents vs. Trade Secrets: Which Way to Go?
https://triangleip.com/patents-vs-trade-secrets/

Trade Secret or Patent?
https://www.theiplawblog.com/2022/01/articles/ip/trade-secret-or-patent/

Trade Secret v. Patent: Why the Differences in Valuing Matter?
https://builtin.com/founders-entrepreneurship/intellectual-property-patents-trade-secrets

Patent vs. Trade Secret Strategy: A Four Factor Decision Framework
https://www.foley.com/en/insights/publications/2021/12/patent-vs-trade-secret-strategy-4-factordecision

Patents and Trade Secrets: A Dual Strategy for Protecting Innovations
https://www.gtlaw.com/en/insights/2023/4/published-articles/patents-and-trade-secrets-a-dual-strategy-for-protecting-innovations?utm_content=buffer8d5da&utm_medium=social&utm_source=linkedin.com&utm_campaign=buffer

The Changing Trade Secret and Patent Equilibrium
https://techcrunch.com/2016/06/20/the-changing-trade-secret-and-patent-equilibrium/

The Defend Trade Secrets Act of 2016
https://davidiplaw.com/the-defend-trade-secret-act-of-2016/#:~:text=Prior%20to%20the%20Defend%20Trade%20Secret%20Act%20of,to%20them%20that%20they%20did%20not%20have%20before

3. Design Patent versus Copyright and Trademark

Before filing, applicants should decide whether copyright and/or trademark protection would be more suitable for their subject matter than patent. Copyright is quicker and more economical to obtain than patent, and may be favored in cases where the inventive article is artistic in nature and can be considered a work of authorship.

Trademark protection may be appropriate when images of the article (or the article itself in the case of trade dress) have value as a recognized source identifier, business symbol, or logo.

Reading:

Design Patent vs. Copyright Protection
https://patentrebel.com/design-patent-vs-copyright-protection/

How to Protect Your Design? Design Patent vs. Copyright
https://studentorgs.kentlaw.iit.edu/ckjip/protect-design-design-patent-vs-copyright/

Choosing Between Design Patent and Copyright Protection? Sometimes You Don't Have To
https://mabr.com/choosing-between-design-patent-and-copyright-protection-sometimes-you-dont-have-to/

Design Patent vs. Trademark: Comparing Differences and Finding the Best IP to Protect Your Products
https://www.patenttrademarkblog.com/design-patent-trademark/

The Differences Between Patents and Trademarks
https://patentrebel.com/difference-between-patent-and-vs-trademark/

Trademark vs. Patent: Everything You Need to Know
https://www.upcounsel.com/trademark-vs-patent

IV. Filing

Overview

The application process begins with preparation of an assembly of application documents in accordance with prescribed procedures. The package consists of the invention disclosure and accompanying papers. The application package can be submitted to the USPTO via mail or, more commonly, using the PTO's online filing system, EFS-Web.

Categories of Patent Applications

United States patent law provides for two main classes of patent applications, namely provisional and nonprovisional. Provisional applications (PPA) are relatively informal in format and are used to establish a priority filing date for a later-filed utility application. Provisionals are not examined and do not issue into patent. Nonprovisional applications (NP or RPA) must adhere to a prescribed format and are of three principal kinds: utility, design, and plant. Plant patents are rare and highly specialized and will not be considered in this manual.

The application procedure for Letters Patent is an intricate, rule-driven process consisting predominantly of an exchange of documents between the applicant and the PTO. The procedure can be divided into three broad phases: re-filing, filing, and post-filing. During the re-filing period, information is gathered and evaluated regarding an invention's patentability and eligibility for application.

Should the invention satisfy this assessment, an application package can then be prepared and submitted to the Patent Office. As an initial matter, the PTO conducts a formalities review which verifies that the application papers are in proper order for examination. If defects exist, the applicant is given an opportunity to correct them. Eventually, the nonprovisional application disclosure is reviewed substantively for patentability by an examiner in accordance with established protocols and guidelines. Typically, the examiner will find that the invention violates one or more conditions of patentability and does not qualify for patent. The applicant is given an opportunity to rebut the examiner's arguments and support the patent eligibility of the invention. This interaction between applicant and examiner continues until the examiner is either convinced to advance the application to grant, or else reject the application and close prosecution. The Patent Office is obligated to grant Letters Patent for an invention unless it can set forth a legitimate reason not to.

Reading:
How to Apply for a Patent: Everything You Need to Know
https://www.upcounsel.com/how-to-apply-for-a-patent

Different Types of Patent Applications
https://www.effectualservices.com/different-types-of-patent-applications/

Steps in the Patent Process
https://ocpatentlawyer.com/steps-patent-process/

Patent Process, Overall Steps and Procedures
https://ocpatentlawyer.com/patent-process-overall-steps-and-procedures/

Patent Process
https://www.lambertpatentlaw.com/patents/patent-process/

Patent Pending Process: Everything You Need to Know
https://www.upcounsel.com/patent-pending-process

Patent Application Process
https://patentgc.com/patent-application-process/

Provisional Patent Application (PPA)
35 USC 111(b); 37 CFR 1.53(c); MPEP 201.04, 601.01(b)

Overview
A provisional application is used primarily to establish an early priority date, which can be claimed if a corresponding nonprovisional application is filed within one year. A PPA is not subjected to substantive examination and can be a relatively informal, preliminary version of a regular nonprovisional utility application.

Nevertheless, it should still contain a complete description of how to make and practice the invention in order to effectively establish a valid priority filing date. If desired, additional PPAs can be filed within the one-year pendency of the initial PPA, covering improvements to the original disclosure. A subsequent corresponding RPA, if filed within one year after the original PPA, can claim priority to all the preceding provisionals.

Reading:

When Should You File a Provisional Patent Application?
https://www.linkedin.com/pulse/should-i-file-provisional-patent-application-john-storella#:~:text=Expect%20a%20thin%20provisional%20application%20to%20cost%20between,application%20is%20just%20a%20stake%20in%20the%20ground

Frequently Asked Questions: Provisional Patent Applications
https://www.cooleygo.com/provisional-patent-applications-faq/

What Is a Provisional Patent Application?
https://www.heerlaw.com/provisional-patent-application

Considerations for Protecting Your Inventions with Provisional Patent Applications
https://www.jdsupra.com/legalnews/considerations-for-protecting-your-8111775/

Pros and Cons of Filing a Provisional Patent Application
https://www.hrfmlaw.com/pros-and-cons-of-filing-a-provisional-patent-application/

The Problem with Provisionals: Part 1
https://gapatents.org/2019/03/12/the-problem-with-provisionals-part-1/

Adding Claims to Provisional Patent Applications
https://www.ip-firm.com/adding-claims-to-provisional-patent-applications/

Provisional Patent Applications Are Crucial amid COVID-19
https://www.finnegan.com/en/insights/articles/provisional-patent-applications-are-crucial-amid-covid-19.html

Provisional Patent Applications—Frequently Asked Questions
https://www.bpmlegal.com/content/provapp

Start with a Provisional or a Non-Provisional Patent Application?
http://www.ericksonlawgroup.com/law/patents/patentfaq/start-with-a-provisional-or-a-non-provisional-patent-application/

Provisional vs. Non Provisional Patent: Everything You Need to Know
https://www.upcounsel.com/provisional-vs-non-provisional-patent

Differences between a Provisional and Nonprovisional Patent Application
https://ocpatentlawyer.com/file-provisional-nonprovisional-patent-application/

Nonprovisional (Utility) Patent Application (RPA)

35 USC 111(a); 37 CFR 1.53(b); MPEP 201.01, 601.01(a)

Overview

A utility patent provides protection for the novel or inventive function of new and useful machines, processes, manufactures, or compositions of matter, and any new and useful improvements thereof. A utility nonprovisional patent application is subjected to substantive examination and will issue as Letters Patent should it satisfy the conditions of patentability.

Reading:

Utility Nonprovisional Patent Application
https://patentandtrademarklaw.com/utlitlty-nonprovisional-patent-application

What Is a Utility Patent?
https://www.callahan-law.com/what-is-a-utility-patent/

Protect Your Inventions with Non-provisional Patent Applications
https://thepatentprofessor.com/services/non-provisional-patent-applications/

Design Patent Application

35 USC Ch. 16; 37 CFR 1.151 *et seq.*; MPEP Ch. 1500

Overview

A design patent provides protection for the novel or inventive outward or surface appearance of an article of manufacture, but not for functional or structural features. Appearance encompasses the ornamental configuration or shape of an article, surface ornamentation, or a combination thereof. Design patents can also be granted for novel, nonobvious aesthetic improvements to the shape of an article.

Reading:

Idiosyncrasies of Prosecuting U.S. Design Patents
https://www.jdsupra.com/legalnews/idiosyncrasies-of-prosecuting-u-s-58054/

Design Patent Application Process
https://lloydmousilli.com/design-patent-application-process/

Design Patents 101—Part 1 of 2
https://lewisbrisbois.com/blog/category/intellectual-property-technology/design-patents-101-part-1-of-2

Design Patents 101—Part 2 of 2
https://lewisbrisbois.com/blog/category/intellectual-property-technology/design-patents-101-part-2-of-2

Design Patents: Common and Costly Mistakes to Avoid
https://isb.idaho.gov/blog/design-patents-common-and-costly-mistakes-to-avoid/

Design Patent
https://www.cohnpatents.com/design-patent/

Design Patents—Design Patent Prosecution: It's Not the Same
https://casetext.com/analysis/design-patents-design-patent-prosecution-its-not-the-same

Are Design Patents Worth It? Perhaps Yes
https://www.coloradoiplaw.com/are-design-patents-worth-it-perhaps-yes/

A. Application Prep/Assembly

1. *Required Parts*

Ⓟ 35 USC 111(b); 37 CFR 1.53(c); MPEP 601.01(b); 35 USC 111(a); 37 CFR 1.53(b), Ⓓ 37 CFR 1.154; MPEP 601.01(a)

a. *Associated Docs/Elements*

Transmittal of New Application	Ⓟ SB/16
Transmittal Cover Sheet	AIA/15
- indicate additional included papers in appropriate boxes	Ⓓ AIA/18
Substitute: Cover letter for initial application filing	Apx D-02
Attachments: Application package documents	
Application Fee Payment	MPEP 509, 607
- fees can be submitted via EFS-Web at time of application submittal	
- use debit deposit account or credit card	
- if filing by mail, use check or credit card (include Credit Card Payment Form (PTO-2038))	
Fee Transmittal Sheet	
Accounting of application fees tendered	SB/17
Substitute: fee transmittal letter	Apx D-03
- if filed via U.S. Mail: include Credit Card Payment Form (PTO-2038)	
Specify Entity Status:	

Reading:
How the Wrong Applicant Entity Status Can Doom Your Patent
https://harrityllp.com/how-the-wrong-applicant-entity-status-can-doom-your-patent/

Am I Entitled to Small Entity or Micro Entity Fee Status?
https://www.bpmlegal.com/content/howsmall

1. Assertion of Small Entity (SE) status	37 CFR 1.27(a)
Asserting SE Status	35 USC 41(h)(1)
- determining Small-Entity: individual, small biz (500 employees max), university, or 501(c)(3) non-profit	MPEP 509.02-03
(P) - indicate SE status on PPA cover sheet (SB/16) and ADS	

Reading:
Small Entity Status: What Does It Mean and What Is It Worth?
http://www.the-business-of-patents.com/small-entity.html

United States: Small Entity Status in the USA
https://www.mondaq.com/unitedstates/patent/746084/small-entity-status-in-the-usa

2. Certification of Micro Entity (ME) status	37 CFR 1.29
(P) - also specify ME status on PPA Cover Sheet and ADS	35 USC 123 MPEP 509.04

Certification of Micro Entity Status

- determination of Micro Entity: must meet SE criteria (37 CFR 1.27(a)), and (1) applicant has not been named as inventor on more than four utility, design, or plant patents; (2) applicant (or assignee) had gross income in previous year of less than 3x median household income (ca. 57K; 3x = ca. 170K); or (3) majority of applicant's employment income is from institution of higher learning, or applicant has assigned, or is obligated to assign, rights to institution of higher learning

Reading:
Micro Entity Patent: Everything You Need to Know
https://www.upcounsel.com/micro-entity-patent

Micro Entity Status in Patent Applications
https://www.yospinlaw.com/2016/02/01/micro-entity-status

Implementing the New Micro Entity Status at the U.S. Patent Office
https://www.mbhb.com/intelligence/snippets/implementing-the-new-micro-entity-status-at-the-u-s-patent-office

a. Certification of Micro Entity—Income-based	SB/15A
Asserts eligibility for fee discount based on gross income of inventor(s)	37 CFR 1.29(a) MPEP 509.04(a)
b. Certification of Micro Entity—Employment-based	SB/15B
Asserts eligibility for fee discount based on employment by institution of higher education or being independent inventor	37 CFR 1.29(d) MPEP 509.04(b)
Attachments: SB/15A (income) SB/15B (higher ed. employment)	
(P) **Certification and Request for COVID-19 Provisional Patent Application Program**	SB/452

Deferred-fee provisional application pilot program and collaborative database to encourage inventions related to Covid-19

- payment of filing fee deferred until corresponding nonprovisional application filed
- subject matter made public in searchable database

Application Data Sheet (ADS)	AIA/14
Inventorship bibliographic, representative, correspondence address, and other application information	37 CFR 1.76 MPEP 601.05

- via EFS, can be prepared before filing (optional) or will be generated automatically upon e-filing

Reading:

Provisional Patent Application Data Sheet: Everything to Know
https://www.upcounsel.com/provisional-patent-application-data-sheet

Patent Application Declaration (PAD)	AIA/08
- Inventor(s) attest to be true and original inventors of subject matter	37 CFR 1.45, 1.63 35 USC 115
- each joint inventor must have contributed to at least one claim (37 CFR 1.45(c))	MPEP 602
- can be submitted after initial filing	
- Use AIA/01 if including ADS	
- Use AIA/10 (Supp. Data Sheet for Declaration) if including additional inventors	
Attachments: substitute statements or assignments	37 CFR 1.63(e), 1.64
[U] - Substitute Statement in Lieu of an Oath or Declaration for Utility or Design Patent Application (35 U.S.C. 115(d) and 37 CFR 1.64)	AIA/02

Reading:
Patent Application Declarations for Unavailable or Uncooperative Inventors
https://www.mintz.com/insights-center/viewpoints/2231/2020-09-14-patent-application-declarations-unavailable-or

I Do Declare: Inventor Declarations in AIA Applications
https://www.finnegan.com/en/insights/blogs/prosecution-first/i-do-declare-inventor-declarations-in-aia-applications.html

False Declaration Leads to Unenforceable Patent, Reinforces Importance of Accurate Inventorship Claims
https://www.bipc.com/false-declaration-leads-to-unenforceable-patent,-reinforces-importance-of-inventorship-claims

Declaration (37 CFR 1.63) for Utility/Des Application Using ADS (37 CFR 1.76) and Assignment — Apx D-04

- declaration of inventorship

Attachments: patent application, proof of assignment

b. Disclosure — 37 CFR 1.153

- written description (Specification) — Ⓓ MPEP 1503; Ⓟ MPEP 608

(P) PPA Disclosure

- although recommended, the PPA disclosure need not follow the formal RPA format
- the PPA disclosure must be complete to allow enablement in order to establish a valid priority date; it should be kept in mind that completeness is also critical if the option to convert to an RPA is to be preserved

Reading:
Provisional Applications: The Good, the Bad and the Ugly
https://www.ipwatchdog.com/2018/01/20/provisional-applications-good-bad-ugly/id=92623/

- the disclosures of PPA and RPA should be a detailed and complete description of how to make and practice the invention

(P) Provisional Disclosure — 37 CFR 1.51(c); 35 USC 112(a); MPEP 601.01(b)

(1) Title

(2) Detailed Description of the Invention

(3) Claim(s)

- optional; but at least one claim should be included if foreign filing is considered in order to ensure valid priority date

Reading:
Should Provisional Patent Applications Have Claims?
https://ipo.org/wp-content/uploads/2013/04/JuneauProvisionalPracticeII.pdf

(4) Drawings

- not required, but should be included if necessary to comprehend the invention

[U] RPA Disclosure — 37 CFR 1.71; 35 USC 112(a); MPEP 608.01

[Note: Beginning 30 June 2023, the specification, claims, abstract, and drawings sections of new nonprovisional (RPA) applications filed pursuant to 35 USC 111(a) not submitted in DOCX format will incur a $400 surcharge (See https://www.uspto.gov/patents/docx for information.)]

Reading:
Patent Disclosure: Everything You Need to Know
https://www.upcounsel.com/patent-disclosure#:~:text=A%20formal%20patent%20disclosure%20is,unique%20nature%20of%20the%20product

BEST MODE: Noncompliance with the Duty of Disclosure Is Not an Option
https://www.iptechblog.com/2021/06/best-mode-noncompliance-with-the-duty-of-disclosure-is-not-an-option/

How to Write a Patent Application
https://www.ipwatchdog.com/2018/08/11/how-to-write-a-patent-application/id=97223/

Tips for Writing a Patent Application
https://www.thoughtco.com/writing-descriptions-for-patent-application-1992255

The specification should include the following sections in order:

(1) Title of the Invention, which may be accompanied by an introductory portion stating the name, citizenship, and residence of the applicant (unless included in the application data sheet)	MPEP 606
(2) Cross-Reference to Related Applications (e.g., PPA)	37 CFR 1.78 MPEP 211
(3) Statement Regarding Federally Sponsored Research or Development - acknowledgment should be made of federal sponsorship where necessary	MPEP 310

Sample Statements:

STATEMENT AS TO RIGHTS TO INVENTIONS MADE UNDER FEDERALLY SPONSORED RESEARCH AND DEVELOPMENT

This invention was made with government support under Grant #8602787 awarded by the National Science Foundation. The government has certain rights in the present invention.

STATEMENT OF RIGHTS TO INVENTIONS MADE UNDER FEDERALLY SPONSORED RESEARCH

Not applicable.

(4) The names of the parties to a joint research agreement - a joint-research agreement allows the parties to avoid each other's prior-art patent disclosures as if they were commonly owned, without assigning their patent rights to the same entity - particular attention should be paid to any existing research agreements, as R&D is often a collaborative effort between entities, such as industrial-academic partnerships	35 USC 100(h), 102(c) 37 CFR 1.71(g), 1.9(e) MPEP 804.03, 2156

Sample reference language to a joint research agreement:

JOINT RESEARCH AGREEMENT

The presently claimed invention was made by or on behalf of the below listed parties to a joint research agreement. The joint research agreement was in effect on or before the date the claimed invention was made and the claimed invention was made as a result of activities undertaken within the scope of the joint research agreement. The parties to the joint research agreement are 1) The ABC Corporation and 2) The Regents of XYZ University.

Reading:

US Patent Law and Cross-Border R&D

https://www.chinabusinessreview.com/us-patent-law-and-cross-border-rd/

U (5) Reference to a "Sequence Listing," a table, or a computer program listing appendix submitted on a compact disc and an incorporation-by-reference of the material on the compact disc (*see* 37 CFR 1.52(e)(5)).	37 CFR 1.77 MPEP 608.05
The total number of compact discs including duplicates and the files on each compact disc shall be specified.	
(6) Statement regarding prior disclosures by the inventor or a joint inventor.	
Technical Field (optional) (omit, or include in Background section)	
(7) Background of the Invention (problem to be solved)	MPEP 608.01(c)
(8) Brief Summary of the Invention	MPEP 608.01(d)
(optional; summary of independent claims only)	
(9) Brief Description of the Several Views of the Drawings	37 CFR 1.74 MPEP 608.01(f)
- if color drawings submitted, reference should be made in Description (see 37 CFR 1.84(a)(2)(iii))	
(10) Table of Reference Numerals (optional)	
(11) Detailed description of the invention	MPEP 608.01(g), 2164
- main embodiment; operation	
- additional embodiment; operation	
- see MPEP 724.02 for preventing trade secrets, proprietary, and other confidential information from appearing in the public file record	
(12) A claim or claims	37 CFR 1.75
- particularly pointing out and distinctly claiming	35 USC 112(b) MPEP 608.01(i)-(p)

Reading:
Basics of Writing a Patent Claim for a Patent Application
https://ocpatentlawyer.com/basics-writing-claim-patent-application/

(12) Abstract (of the Disclosure) (150 words max)	37 CFR 1.72 MPEP 608.01(b)
(13) Drawing Sheets	35 USC 113 37 CFR 1.81 MPEP 608.02

Reading:
Using Photographs in a Patent Application
http://articles.ampatentdrawings.com/photographs/using-photographs-in-a-patent-application/

(D) Design Disclosure — 35 USC 112(a); 37 CFR 1.153-154; MPEP 1503.01

- Preamble (optional)
  - should state the name of the applicant, the title of the design, and a brief description of the nature and intended use of the article in which the design is embodied
- Title (500 characters max)
- must designate particular article
- Cross-reference to related applications
- Statement regarding federally sponsored research or development
- Description
  - reference to drawing(s) only
  - if color drawings submitted, reference should be made in Description (see 37 CFR 1.84(a)(2)(iii))
- Feature description
  - a "characteristic features" statement describing a particular feature of novelty or nonobviousness in the claimed design may be permissible in the specification
- Claim (single claim only)
  - in formal terms to the ornamental design for the article (specifying name) as shown, or as shown and described
- Drawing Sheets — 35 USC 113
  - photographs and color drawings permitted under certain conditions — 37 CFR 1.152; MPEP 1503.02

Reading:
Can You Use Photographs in Design Patent Applications?
https://www.ilnipinsider.com/2018/08/can-you-use-photographs-in-design-patent-applications/

Permissible Drawing Amendments for U.S. Design Applications
https://www.quarles.com/publications/recent-ptab-guidance-on-permissible-drawing-amendments-for-u-s-design-applications/

Practice Note: Avoid Multiple Embodiments in Design Patent Applications
https://www.bakerdonelson.com/webfiles/Bios/Practice%20Note%20Chaloner.pdf

Defining a Claim: How Design Patent Drawings Can Strengthen or Spoil Your Application
https://www.aipla.org/list/innovate-articles/defining-a-claim-how-design-patent-drawings-can-strengthen-or-spoil-your-application

Federal Court Clarifies the Scope of Drawings in a Design Patent
https://www.lewisrice.com/publications/federal-court-clarifies-the-scope-of-drawings-in-a-design-patent/

Appendix (if appropriate)	MPEP 1503.01(II)(B)(2)
- include statements describing or suggesting other embodiments of the claimed design which are not illustrated in the drawing disclosure, and which are not permitted in the specification of an issued design patent. Such statements may be included in the design application as originally filed to provide antecedent basis for a future amendment.	Apx D-05

2. *Additional Documents*

a. *Accompanying Papers as Needed/Appropriate*

Assignment Recordation Cover Sheet	PTO-1595
Cover sheet for written assignment	MPEP 302.07
- file via Electronic Patent Assignment System (EPAS)	
Attachments: Executed Assignment Agreement	Apx D-06
- specify on Utility Application Transmittal (AIA/15, Box #10)	

Reading:

Who Owns What: Assignment and Ownership of Patents and Applications
https://www.cooleygo.com/assignment-and-ownership-of-patents-and-applications/

Procuring U.S. Patents without a Signed Assignment of Patent Rights
https://www.mintz.com/insights-center/viewpoints/2231/2020-10-27-procuring-us-patents-without-signed-assignment-patent

Employee Inventors and Patent Ownership: Whose Rights Are They Anyway?
https://www.americanbar.org/groups/intellectual_property_law/publications/landslide/2020-21/march-april/employee-inventors-patent-ownership-whose-rights-are-they-anyway/

How to Transfer Ownership of Patents
https://www.patenttrademarkblog.com/transfer-ownership-patents/

Patent Assignment: A Basic Guide
https://www.inquartik.com/blog/basic-patent-assignments-guide/

What Is a Patent Assignment?
https://patentrebel.com/what-is-a-patent-assignment/

Patent Ownership Basics
https://www.neustel.com/patent-ownership-basics/

Assignment of Patent Rights
https://www.inhousecommunity.com/article/assignment-patent-rights/

Power of Attorney (POA)

Authorization of practitioner to represent applicant before the USPTO during application activities	37 CFR 1.32 MPEP 402.02(a)
- indicate on Utility Application Transmittal (AIA/15, Box #11)	
1. Authorization by assignee who wishes to become applicant (*see* 37 CFR 1.46(c)) to appoint practitioner as representative	AIA/80
Attachments: Statement under 37 CFR 3.73(c)	
2. Authorization by *pro se* inventors who are the applicantfor patent to appoint one or more of the joint inventors as having power of attorney in the application file	AIA/81
3. POA and Revocation of POA with new POA	AIA/81A 37 CFR 1.36(a) MPEP 402.05, 2560
Attachments: petition fee (37 CFR 1.17(f))	AIA/17p
- for revocation of POA by fewer than all applicants	
4. Authorization by applicant to appoint practitioner as representative	AIA/82A & B
PTO Response: Notice of Acceptance (or Denial)	PTOL-308

Reading:

Is a Power of Attorney Required to File a Patent Office Action Response?
https://www.patenttrademarkblog.com/power-attorney-required-file-patent-office-action-response/

Who Has the Power? Granting Power of Attorney in AIA Applications
https://www.finnegan.com/en/insights/blogs/prosecution-first/who-has-the-power-granting-power-of-attorney-in-aia-applications.html

Understanding Post-AIA Power of Attorney Procedures
https://www.mintz.com/insights-center/viewpoints/2015-03-19-understanding-post-aia-power-attorney-procedures

Why It Is Super-Important to Get a Power of Attorney Filed in Absolutely Every Patent File
https://blog.oppedahl.com/?p=1586

Statement Under 37 CFR 3.73(c)	
Establishes assignee's ownership rights in patent application	AIA/96 37 CFR 3.73(c)
- used by legal/obligatory assignee to establish ownership of invention/application	MPEP 325
- indicate on Utility Application Transmittal (AIA/15, Box #11)	
Attachments: executed assignment if not yet recorded	

Reading:

Applicants These Days: Who Are They? And How Can They Be Changed?
https://www.finnegan.com/en/insights/blogs/prosecution-first/applicants-these-days-who-are-they-and-how-can-they-be-changed.html

Petition Under 37 CFR 1.84 to Accept Color Drawings	Apx D-07
Request to submit color drawings	37 CFR 1.84(a)(2),
- briefly explain why color drawings are necessary	1.84(b)(2)
- petition not required for provisional and design applications	
Attachments: petition fee (37 CFR 1.17(h))	AIA/17p
- proposed color drawing sheets	
- if submitted by mail, include three (3) sets of drawings	

Reading:

How to File Color Drawings Electronically Via EFS-Web
https://patentablydefined.com/2011/01/19/how-to-file-color-drawings-electronically-via-efs-web/

Are Photos or Color Drawings Acceptable in US Patent Applications?
https://www.patenttrademarkblog.com/photos-color-drawings-us-patent-application/

Petition Drawing: Everything You Need to Know
https://www.upcounsel.com/petition-drawing

Color Drawings
http://foundpersuasive.com/color_drawings.aspx

Patent Drawings: How to Show Color without Using Color
https://www.waltmire.com/2018/01/20/patent-drawings-show-color-without-using-color/

Information Disclosure Statement (IDS)	SB/08(a) & (b)
Fulfills Duty of Disclosure, Candor and Good Faith (*see* 37 CFR 1.56(a))	35 USC 301 37 CFR 1.97 *et seq.*
- file with RPA/Des	MPEP 609
- specify on Utility Application Transmittal (AIA/15, Box #13)	
Content Requirements	37 CFR 1.98
- must include a list of all patents, publications, U.S. applications, or other information that may bear on the patentability of subject invention	MPEP 609.04(a)
Timing Requirements for Filing:	MPEP 609.04(b)
(1) can be filed with initial application, through pendency	
- file within 3 months of application filing date, or before mailing date of first OA on merits, whichever is later; or before first OA on merits after filing RCE; otherwise statement under 1.97(e) and fee required	
- cover letter optional	Apx D-08

(1)(a) for national applications (not including CPAs), within three months of filing or before first Office action on the merits, whichever is later; (b) for national stage applications, within three months of entry into national stage or before first Office action on the merits, whichever is later; (c) for RCEs and CPAs before the first Office action on the merits; or (d) for international design applications, within three months of the date of publication of the international registration under Hague Agreement Article 10(3) or before first Office action on the merits, whichever is later.

- no 37 CFR 1.97(e) statement or fee

(2) after the period in (1), but prior to the close of application prosecution, i.e., before mailing of final OA, a Notice of Allowance, or an *Ex Parte Quayle* action, whichever is earlier.

- 37 CFR 1.97(e) statement *or* fee required — Apx D-09

(3) after the period in (2) but on or before the date issue fee is paid.

- 37 CFR 1.97(e) statement *and* fee required — Apx D-10
- without statement, RCE required for IDS to be considered

(4) after the period in (3) and up to the time the patent application can be effectively withdrawn from issue under 37 CFR 1.313(c).

- after payment of issue fee, IDS will not be considered

Attachments: Cover Letter

- Copies of foreign patents and non-pat literature (NPL)(use SB/08(b))(per 37 CFR 1.98(a)(2))
- may require statement under CFR 1.97(e) and fee, depending on when filed (e.g., after Allowance)
- may be filed online via e-IDS — MPEP 609.07
  - PTO response: Notice of Noncompliant IDS issued if irregularities exist
  - if requested, copy of SB/08, initialed by examiner as considered (per MPEP 609)

Reading:

What Is an Information Disclosure Statement or IDS?
https://www.patenttrademarkblog.com/what-is-an-ids/

Information Disclosure Statements: When and How to File
https://www.mintz.com/insights-center/viewpoints/2231/2018-01-information-disclosure-statements-when-and-how-file

Information Disclosure: Avoiding Common Pitfalls
https://www.sternekessler.com/news-insights/publications/information-disclosure-avoiding-common-pitfalls

Ten Mistakes to Avoid When Drafting Information Disclosure Statements
https://ipwatchdog.com/2022/02/12/ten-mistakes-avoid-drafting-information-disclosure-statements/id=145743/

What Is an Information Disclosure Statement (IDS) and How to File One?
https://ocpatentlawyer.com/what-is-an-information-disclosure-statement-ids/

Best Mode: Noncompliance With the Duty of Disclosure Is Not an Option
https://www.iptechblog.com/2021/06/best-mode-noncompliance-with-the-duty-of-disclosure-is-not-an-option/

Information Disclosure Statement: Everything You Need to Know
https://www.upcounsel.com/information-disclosure-statement

Information Disclosure Statement in Patent Applications
https://www.yospinlaw.com/2021/02/16/information-disclosure-statement

IDS Fees and Deadlines: When to File and How Much
https://www.patenttrademarkblog.com/ids-due-fees/

Preliminary Amendment	37 CFR 1.115
- revise disclosure before examination	*see also* 37 CFR 1.121
- often filed to avoid possible adverse action in U.S application suggested by prior PCT patentability opinion	MPEP 714.01(e)
- may be filed with initial application or at any time before first Office Action	
- should be submitted within 3 months of application filing date to avoid possible disapproval	
- no new matter permitted per 37 CFR 1.121(f) if filed after initial application submittal	
- file with RPA/Des	
- indicate on Utility Application Transmittal (AIA/15, Box #14)	
[U] **Utility**	Apx D-11
[D] **Design**	Apx D-12

Reading:

When Can You Amend a Patent Application?
https://www.mriplaw.com/blog/9k90q9fxim97rngq5b9tgllyc4kf5y

What Is a Preliminary Amendment?
https://www.patenttrademarkblog.com/preliminary-amendment/

Notice of Noncompliant (Non-Responsive) Amendment	PTOL-324 37 CFR 1.121
- issued when amendment submitted fails to comply	MPEP 714(II)(F) with 37 CFR 1.121
Applicant Response: submit corrections per Notice	Apx D-13
Claim for Priority Under 35 USC 119 and Transmittal of Priority Document	Apx D-14 35 USC 119(a)&(b)
- if claiming priority to foreign application	37 CFR 1.55
- MPEP 213.06; 215	
- specify on Utility Application Transmittal (AIA/15, Box #16)	
Attachments: Certified Copy of Foreign Priority Document(s)	
- file with RPA/Des	
PTO Response: acknowledgment of receipt of priority document	

Reading:

Understanding Priority Claims for U.S. Patent Applications: Part 1
https://www.mintz.com/insights-center/viewpoints/2231/2018-07-22-understanding-priority-claims-us-patent-applications

Claim of Priority to an Earlier Filed Patent Application
https://ocpatentlawyer.com/priority-claim-patent-application/

[U] **Nonpublication Request (NPR)**	SB/35
- if not foreign filing, direct that application not be published during pendency (usually 18 months from filing)	37 CFR 1.213(a) 35 USC 122(b)(2)(B)(i)
- indicate on Utility Application Transmittal (AIA/15, Box #17)	MPEP 1122
Substitute: enter information on ADS	AIA/14

Reading:
Nonpublication Requests for Patent Applications Part 1: Benefits
https://www.kilpatricktownsend.com/en/Blog/MEMO/2021/1/Nonpublication-Requests-For-Patent-Applications-Part-1-Benefits

Nonpublication Requests for Patent Applications Part 2: Disadvantages
https://www.jdsupra.com/legalnews/nonpublication-requests-for-patent-1163850/

Nonpublication Requests for Patent Applications Part 3: Pitfalls
https://www.jdsupra.com/legalnews/nonpublication-requests-for-patent-5017796/

Should We Request Non-Publication of Our Patent Applications?
https://henry.law/blog/should-we-request-non-publication-of-our-patent-applications/

Nonpublication Requests of U.S. Patent Applications: Proceed with Caution
https://www.mmviplaw.com/nonpublication-requests-of-u-s-patent-applications-proceed-with-caution/

Can Publishing Your U.S. Patent Application Reveal Confidential Information?
https://www.tms.org/pubs/journals/JOM/matters/matters-0109.html

The Pros and Cons of Non-Publication Requests
https://www.iam-media.com/the-pros-and-cons-of-non-publication-requests

Biotechnology Disclosures [37 CFR Subpart G; MPEP Chapter 2400] [See Part Three, Biotechnology Applications.]	
Transmittal of Sequence Listing	
- nucleotide and/or amino acid sequence subject matter	37 CFR 1.52, 1.821-25 MPEP 608.05, 2420-26
Deposit of Living Biological Material	37 CFR 1.801-09
- required when access to biological subject matter necessary to make/practice the invention	MPEP 2402-11
Disclosures Involving Computer Code [*see* MPEP 2161.01 for patentability]	
Submission of Computer Program Code	37 CFR 1.96 MPEP 608.05(a)

Request for a Transfer of a Computer Readable Form	SB/93
- for computer code applications	MPEP 608.05
Communication re. Co-Pending Applications	Apx D-15
- informs examiner of other applications that may have bearing on present application	37 CFR 1.56 MPEP 2001.06(b)
- may be submitted with or after initial filing	

b. *Optional Accompanying Papers*

Expedited Examination (available for RPA/Des applications only)	
Petition to Make Special (PTMS) Under Accelerated Examination Program (AEP)	SB/28 (via EFS) 37 CFR 1.102(c)(2)
Expedited examination based on evidence that that the invention will enhance quality of the environment, contribute to conservation of energy, aid in counterterrorism	MPEP 708.02(III, IV, V)
- explain relevance of subject matter	
- only small entities eligible	
- no fee required petitions based on grounds other than those stipulated require fee	AIA/17p
Attachments: Pre-examination Search Statement and Accelerated Examination Support Document per SB/28	
PTO response: decision to grant or deny	

Reading:

Expedited Examination of U.S. Patent Applications
https://www.neustel.com/expedited-examination-patent-applications/

How to Speed Up Patent Prosecution at the USPTO
https://henry.law/blog/speed-up-patent-prosecution/

Fast Track Patent Examination
https://www.sternekessler.com/news-insights/publications/fast-track-patent-examination

Accelerating the Acquisition of an Enforceable Patent: Bypassing the USPTO's Backlog
https://www.martindale.com/matter/asr-1265974.Acquisition.pdf

How to Slow Down Patent Prosecution with the USPTO
https://henry.law/blog/slow-down-patent-prosecution/
(Slowing down prosecution)

Certification and Petition to Make Special Under the Cancer Moonshot Expedited Examination Pilot Program	
- expedited processing of applications disclosing inventions in the field of oncology and smoking cessation	SB/465
Petition to Make Special Based on Age for Advancement of Examination Under 37 CFR 1.102(c)(1)	e-Petition; SB/130 37 CFR 1.102(c)(1)
Expedited examination where at least one named applicant is 65 or older - no fee required	MPEP 708.02(II)
Attachments: evidence that applicant is 65 or older (e.g., birth certificate) - Supporting Declaration	
PTO Response: decision on request	
Substitute: can be filed as e-Petition	

Reading:

Accelerating U.S. Patent Examination Based on Inventor Age
https://www.mmviplaw.com/accelerating-u-s-patent-examination-based-on-inventor-age/

Expediting Examination Based on Age & Health
https://freship.com/expediting-examination-based-on-age-health/

Petition to Make Special Based on Health for Advancement of Examination Under 37 CFR 1.102(c)(1)	37 CFR 1.102(c)(1) MPEP 708.02(I)
Expedited examination where at least one named applicant is of ill health - file petition per 37 CFR 1.181 - no fee required	
Attachments: evidence of applicant's ill health (e.g., medical certificate) - see MPEP 724.02 for preventing confidential information from appearing in the public file record	
PTO Response: decision on request	

U	**Certification and Request for Prioritized Examination Under 37 CFR 1.102(e) (TrackOne Request)**	AIA/424 37 CFR 1.102(e)
	- fee-based request for expedited examination	MPEP 708.02(b)
	Attachments: petition fee and other requisite fees	AIA/17i
	PTO Response: grant of request	

Reading:

Timing Considerations for Concurrent PCT and Track One Applications
https://www.nixonpeabody.com/insights/alerts/2021/01/05/timing-considerations-for-concurrent-track-one-and-pct-applications

Track One USPTO Examination for Patent Applications
https://patentlawip.com/practice-areas/patents/track-one-examination/

The USPTO's Track One Program Offers Many Inventors a Quicker Path to Obtaining a Patent
https://patentco.com/the-usptos-track-one-program-offers-many-inventors-a-quicker-path-to-obtaining-a-patent/

How to Get Prioritized Patent Examination in the US
https://www.two-ip.com/how-to-get-prioritized-patent-examination-in-the-us/

A Practitioner's Perspective: The USPTO's Track 1 Prioritized Patent Examination Process
https://www.law.com/thelegalintelligencer/2022/11/28/a-practitioners-perspective-usptos-track-1-prioritized-patent-examination-process/?sl return=20230305135053

USPTO's Track One vs. Patent Prosecution Highway
https://blueironip.com/usptos-track-one-vs-patent-prosecution-highway/

Request for Participation in the Global/IP5 Patent Prosecution Highway (PPH) Pilot Program in the USPTO	SB/20GLBL 37 CFR 1.102 MPEP 708.02(c)
Expedited application prosecution for corresponding applications filed in participating IP offices	
- available for RPA/Des	

Attachments: OEE Work Product/Translation and references cited therein

PTO Response: decision to grant or deny request

Reading:

Patent Prosecution Highway
https://www.ssmp.com/wp-content/uploads/2017/02/CT_1308_Patent-Prosecution-Highway.pdf

What Is PPH (Patent Prosecution Highway)?
https://www.patenttrademarkblog.com/what-is-pph/

Effective Utilization of the Patent Prosecution Highway
https://www.vorys.com/publications-2016.html

Patent Prosecution Highway: Is It the Promised Expressway or Is It a Roadblock?
https://www.fredlaw.com/news media/2016/11/08/1372/patent_prosecution_highway_is_it_the_promised_expressway_or_is_it_a_roadblock/

The PPH Program at the USPTO: Favorable Stats Don't Alleviate Big Risks
https://www.ipwatchdog.com/2019/10/30/pph-program-uspto-favorable-stats-dont-alleviate-big-risks/id=115477/

D

Request for Expedited Examination (Rocket Docket) — SB/27; 37 CFR 1.155; MPEP 1504.30

- prioritized processing for design applications

Reading:

Rocket Docket for Design Patents
https://patentrebel.com/rocket-docket-design-patents/

"Rocket Docket" for US Designs
https://blog.oppedahl.com/?p=4541

Fight Back against Counterfeits: Design Patent Rocket Docket
https://www.hea-ip.com/new-blog/https/wwwhea-ipcom/blog

Design Patent Rocket Docket
https://galvanilegal.com/design-patent-rocket-docket/?cn-reloaded=1

Attachments: processing fee (37 CFR 1.17(k))

PTO Response: Deny or Approve

Authorization to Incorporate Extension of Time with Reply	Apx D-16 37 CFR 1.136(a)(3)
Avoids potential loss of patent rights for applicants who inadvertently omit petition for extension of time	MPEP 710.02(e)
Rescission of Prior Disclaimer/Request to Revisit Art	Apx D-17

- affirmative rescission of any prior subject matter disclaimer in parent application
- use to recapture disclaimed subject matter in parent application, allowing broader claim construction in child (divisional, continuation) application

Sample Language:

"Regarding any characterizations of claims or referenced art in parent application that could be construed as a disclaimer of any subject matter supported by present disclosure, such disclaimers are retracted"

- preferably filed with application package or soon thereafter

Reading:

Rescinding Estoppel: The Most Overlooked Means to a Broader Claim Construction
https://www.carterdeluca.com/news/rescinding-estoppel-overlooked-means-broader-claim-construction/

Recapture: Disclaimer in Parent Must Be Rescinded in Continuation
https://patentlyo.com/patent/2007/02/recapture_discl.html

Classic Prosecution Disclaimer
https://patentlyo.com/patent/2021/06/classic-prosecution-disclaimer.html

B. Application Submittal

1. E-Filing (EFS-Web)	MPEP 502.05

Reading:

What to Do If You Omit a Document or File the Wrong Document in a New, Electronically Filed Application
https://patentablydefined.com/2010/06/04/what-to-do-if-you-omit-a-document-or-file-the-wrong-document-in-a-new-electronically-filed-application/

Your USPTO: DOCX Streamlines Patent Filing Process
https://www.inventorsdigest.com/articles/docx-streamlines-patent-filing-process/

Electronic Patent Filing: Everything You Need to Know
https://www.upcounsel.com/electronic-patent-filing

2. Paper Filing via U.S. Mail	MPEP 513
- surcharge for mail utility application submittal; $200 for ME, $400 for SE (37 CFR 1.16)	
Attachments: include Certificate of Mailing or Transmission Under 37 CFR 1.8	SB/92

Reading:
How to Get Your $400 Paper-Filing Penalty Refunded
https://blog.oppedahl.com/?p=3665

V. Post-Filing

From initial application filing, it can typically be 16 to 20 months until the PTO takes up the case for examination. During this period, the applicant may submit additional documents related to the application and, if required, respond to notices from the PTO regarding completeness of the application and other pre-examination formalities. In due course, the application is reviewed for patentability, commencing the prosecution phase of the application process.

First Office Action Estimator (check how long until first OA is issued),
https://www.uspto.gov/learning-and-resources/statistics/first-office-action-estimator

(P) Provisional applications are not substantively examined and, therefore, no formal prosecution is conducted. After filing, informalities may be corrected, such as submitting missing parts, correcting inventor names, and the like. Amendments can also be filed, but must only correct minor, non-substantive defects. If the applicant wishes to introduce additional new matter, a new provisional must be filed. Applicants have the option of converting a PPA into an RPA at any time during pendency. Provisional applications are disclosed on Patent Center only when an RPA claiming priority therefrom is granted or published. After filing, marketed subject matter may be marked as "Patent Pending" or "Patent Applied For."

Reading:
Are Provisional Patent Applications Published?
https://www.neustel.com/provisional-patent-applications-published/

Are Provisional Patent Applications Published?
https://www.kaufholdpatentgroup.com/patent-search-are-provisional-patents-published/

A. Pre-Examination

NOTE: After initial application submittal, subsequent document transmittals to the PTO should be accompanied by a Certificate of Transmission and Transmittal Form or Letter.

Certificate of Transmission	Apx D-18
Establishes that correspondence has been sent to PTO as of date thereon	37 CFR 1.8 MPEP 512
For suggested formats, *see* MPEP 512	
Substitute: Certificate of Mailing or Transmission Under 37 CFR 1.8	SB/92
Transmittal Form (Letter)	SB/21
Cover sheet/letter for transmittal of correspondence to PTO after initial filing	
Substitute: Transmittal Letter	Apx D-19

1. Routine Office Communications

- EFS Acknowledgment Receipt (issued online immediately after e-filing submittal) RESPONSE: none	
- Electronic Patent Application Fee Transmittal	SB/06
- Fee Worksheet (EFS-generated)	
- (immediate after e-filing submittal)	
- Official Filing Receipt (within about 2 weeks after filing)	
RESPONSE: if inaccurate, request Corrected Filing Receipt	

Request for Corrected Filing Receipt	Apx D-20
Requests correction and replacement of erroneous Official Filing Receipt	MPEP 211.02(a)(I)
Attachments: supplemental ADS if correcting inventorship information	
- markup copy of original Filing Receipt showing corrections	
PTO response: corrected Filing Receipt acceptance of request for corrected inventorship, if necessary (Rule 48)	

Reading:

How to Read a USPTO Filing Receipt
https://www.cadcrowd.com/patent-an-idea/read-filing-receipt

Errors in USPTO Patent Application Filing Receipts
https://blog.oppedahl.com/?p=1789

Notice of Publication	35 USC 122(b)
- 18 months after filing; unless NPR in place	37 CFR 1.215
- entire application file wrapper (application history) made available on Patent Center	MPEP 1120-21, 1127
Applicant Response: none required; however, the specification should be reviewed for errors	

Reading:

Your Patent Application Published: What Does That Mean?
https://kolitchromano.com/provisional-rights/

What Is a Publication of Patent Application?
https://www.upcounsel.com/publication-of-patent-application

Publication, Nonpublication, and Early Publication of Patent Application—The Strategy
https://www.avvo.com/legal-guides/ugc/publication-nonpublication-and-early-publication-of-patent-application-the-strategy

Petition for Correction of Patent Application Publication Under 37 CFR 1.221(b)

- file within two months of publication
- identify material error of PTO per 37 CFR 1.221(b)

2. Office-Initiated Actions

Notices to Correct Defects in Application Papers	
Informational Notice to Applicant	37 CFR 1.53(f)
Requests applicant to correct deficiencies in application (e.g., missing oath/declaration)	MPEP 506(I)(C)
Applicant Response: Provide requested documents	Apx D-21
- filing oath/declaration may be postponed until application is otherwise in condition for allowance	
(P) **Notice to File Missing Parts of a Provisional Application**	37 CFR 1.53(c) MPEP 506(II), 601.01(b)
Filing date granted, but oath/declaration, fee or translation missing	
Applicant Response: Required per Notice instructions	Apx D-22
- up to 12 months to respond	
Notice to File Missing Parts of a Nonprovisional Application [Filing Date Granted]	37 CFR 1.53(b) MPEP 506(I)(C), 601.01(a)
Filing date granted, but oath/declaration, fee or translation missing	
Applicant Response: Required per Notice instructions	Apx D-23
- up to 12 months to respond	

Reading:

What Is a Notice to File Missing Parts?
https://ocpatentlawyer.com/what-is-a-notice-to-file-missing-parts/

Missing Parts Strategy
https://modal-law.com/missing-parts-strategy/

Notice of Incomplete Reply (Nonprovisional)	MPEP 704.12(b-c); *see also* MPEP 714.03
Notice to correct deficient response to Notice to File Missing Parts	
Applicant Response: Required per Notice instructions	Apx D-24

Notice of Omitted Item(s) in a Nonprovisional Application	MPEP 601.01(d), 601.01(g)
Application filed without all pages of spec or drawing figures	
Applicant Response: Required per Notice instructions	Apx D-25
Notice of Incomplete Application	35 USC 111(a)
Filing date not granted; missing spec or written description	37 CFR 1.53
Applicant Response: Required per Notice instructions	MPEP 506(I)(C), 601.01(g)
Notice to File Corrected Application Papers	37 CFR 1.121
Granted filing date if informalities in spec, drawings	MPEP 608.01, 608.02(a), 714.01(e)
Applicant Response: Required per Notice instructions	Apx D-26
- correct deficiencies with preliminary amendment Attachments: copy of Notice	

Reading:
Notice to Correct Application Papers
https://www.businesspatentlaw.com/notice-to-correct-application-papers/

3. Applicant-Initiated Actions as Needed

File Assignment (if necessary) (via EPAS)	PTO-1595
- Assignment Recordation Cover Sheet	MPEP 302.07
- cover sheet for written assignment	
Attachments: Executed Assignment Agreement	35 USC 261
Joint Ownership Agreement	35 USC 116(a), 262
Establishes shared legal interest or ownership of each of several co-inventors or joint inventors in invention/patent application	37 CFR 1.45 MPEP 602.09, 706.02(I)(2)

Reading:
Sample Joint IP Ownership Clauses
https://www.ipwatchdog.com/wp-content/uploads/2016/02/Sample_Joint_IP_Ownership_Clauses.pdf

Petition to Obtain or Correct Filing Date	37 CFR 1.53(e) MPEP 506.02
Any review of the refusal to grant a filing date as of the date of deposit of the application would be by way of petition, accompanied by the petition fee (37 CFR 1.17(f)). Petitioner should provide any arguments that he or she has that the items noted were not missing or that a filing date should be assigned in the absence of such items if they are believed to be unnecessary. If petitioner alleges that no defect exists, a request for refund of the petition fee may be included in the petition.	
Attachments: petition fee	AIA/17p 37 CFR 1.17(f)
Fee Worksheet	SB/06
- submit as needed	
Substitute: PTO-875	

Extension of Time

Reading:

Extensions of Time, How to Petition for an Extension, and Examples of Petitions
https://patentablydefined.com/2010/07/26/extensions-of-time-how-to-petition-for-an-extension-and-examples-of-petitions/

Patent Extension of Time: Everything You Need to Know
https://www.upcounsel.com/patent-extension-of-time

Authorization to Incorporate Extension of Time With Reply	Apx D-16 37 CFR 1.136(a)(3)
Avoids potential loss of patent rights for applicants who inadvertently omit petition for extension of time	MPEP 710.02(e)
Petition for Extension of Time Under 37 CFR 1.136(a)	AIA/22 37 CFR 1.136(a)
Request to extend period for reply beyond that specified by PTO for submitting response	MPEP 710.02(e)
- when applicant is required to reply within a nonstatutory or shortened statutory time period	
Attachments: petition fee 37 CFR 1.17(a)	
Substitute: Draft petition	Apx D-27

Reading:
No Need for Extension of Time Petitions
https://blog.oppedahl.com/?p=1113

Petition for Extension of Time Under 37 CFR 1.136(b)	SB/23 37 CFR 1.136(b)
When a reply cannot be filed within the time period set for such reply and the provisions of paragraph (a) of this section are not available	MPEP 710.02(e)
Attachments: petition fee	AIA/17p 37 CFR 1.17(g)

Correcting Inventorship	37 CFR 1.48 MPEP 602.01(c)

Reading:
Fixing Inventorship Problems in U.S. Patent Applications and U.S. Patents
https://www.ratnerprestia.com/2014/02/16/fixing-inventorship-problems-in-u-s-patent-applications-and-u-s-patents/

Inventorship: Navigating the Muddy Waters of Inventorship Determination and Correction
https://www.kilpatricktownsend.com/-/media/2019/IP-Desk-Reference-2015/Navigating-the-Muddy-Waters-of-Inventorship

Correct Inventorship Prevents Patent Application Headaches
https://assets.fenwick.com/legacy/FenwickDocuments/Correct_Inventorship.pdf

Correcting Inventorship in the USPTO
https://thelimitedmonopoly.com/inventorship/correcting-inventorship-in-the-uspto/

Request to Correct or Update the Name of the Applicant Under 37 CFR 1.46(c)(1), or Change the Applicant Under 37 CFR 1.46(c)(2)	AIA/41 37 CFR 1.46(c)
Request to update or change applicant(s)	
Attachments: updated ADS	37 CFR 1.76, 3.71, 3.73
Substitute: Draft request in lieu of AIA/41	Apx D-28

Request for Correction in a Patent Application Relating to Inventorship or an Inventor Name, or Order of Names, Other Than in a Reissue Application (37 CFR 1.48)	AIA/40 35 USC 116 37 CFR 1.324, 1.48(a)
Correct/change inventorship in non-provisional application	MPEP 602.01(c)(1)
Attachments: corrected ADS, PAD (or substitute statement per 37 CFR 1.64), if necessary	
- petition processing fee	37 CFR 1.17(i)
Substitute: Draft request may be filed as alternative to AIA/40	Apx D-29
(P) - inventorship correction in PPA under 37 CFR 1.48	37 CFR 1.48(d)
Attachments: processing fee	AIA/17i 37 CFR 1.17(i) 37 CFR 1.17(q)
Substitute: Draft request may be filed as alternative to AIA/40	Apx D-30
- inventorship correction under 37 CFR 1.48(f)	37 CFR 1.48(f)
- request to correct/update name of inventor or joint inventor, or the order of names of joint inventors	MPEP 602.01(c)(2)
Attachments: updated ADS	
Substitute: Draft request may be filed as alternative to AIA/40	Apx D-31
Attachments: processing fee	AIA/17i
PTO Response: Acceptance/Denial	

(P) **Amendment in PPA** 37 CFR 1.121(k)

- seldom filed, but any amendment must only correct informalities or non-substantive deficiencies and comply with 37 CFR 1.121
- amendments are made part of the application record but are not formally entered

Reading:

Can a Provisional Patent Application Be Amended?
https://patentrebel.com/can-a-provisional-patent-application-be-amended-answered/

Can I Amend a Provisional Patent Application?
https://www.clfip.com/ip/blog/can-i-amend-a-provisional-patent-application/

Priority Claim and Document

Reading:

Understanding Priority Claims for U.S. Patent Applications: Part 1
https://www.mintz.com/insights-center/viewpoints/2231/2018-07-22-understanding-priority-claims-us-patent-applications

Understanding Priority Claims for U.S. Patent Applications: Part 2
https://www.mintz.com/insights-center/viewpoints/2018-11-27-understanding-priority-claims-us-patent-applications-part-2

Proving Unintentional Delay
https://patentlyo.com/patent/2020/03/proving-unintentional-delay.html

When Must Foreign Priority Document Be Filed in a US Utility Patent Application?
https://www.patenttrademarkblog.com/when-must-foreign-priority-document-be-filed-in-a-us-utility-patent-application/

Claiming Foreign Priority in U.S. Patent Applications
https://www.jchoilaw.com/news/2015/claiming-foreign-priority-in-u-s-patent-applications

D *Filing of Certified Copies of Priority Documents: No Change for Design Patent Applicants*
http://www.protectingdesigns.com/99-filing-of-certified-copies-of-priority-documents-no-change-for-design-patent-applicants (Des. Appl)

Claim for Priority Under 35 USC 119 and Transmittal of Priority Document	Apx D-14 35 USC 119(a)&(b)
- if claiming priority to foreign application	37 CFR 1.55 MPEP 213.06; 215
Attachments: Certified Copy of Foreign Priority Document(s)	
- file with RPA/Des	
PTO Response: acknowledgment of receipt of priority document	
Request to Retrieve Electronic Priority Application(s)	SB/38
Request that PTO retrieve electronic copies of foreign applications from which priority has been claimed	35 USC 119(a)&(b) 37 CFR 1.55(i) MPEP 213.06, 215.01
- for countries with reciprocal document exchange agreement with U.S.	

Petition to Accept Unintentionally Delayed Priority Document Under 37 CFR 1.55(g)	Apx D-32 37 CFR 1.55(e)&(g)
- use when priority claim/document under 37 CFR 119(a) not made in compliance with MPEP 155(g)	MPEP 214.02
Attachments: petition fee	SB/17p
- certified copy of foreign application, 37 CFR 1.17(g) if necessary; statement averring that the belated claim was unintentional	
PTO Response: Decision on petition	
Certification and Request to Suspend the Requirement in 37 CFR 1.55(f) and (g) for Submission of the Certified Copy Due to the COVID-19 Outbreak	SB/453 MPEP 1.55(f)&(g) *see also* MPEP 1.55(j)
- timeliness requirement suspended	
Petition to Accept Unintentionally Delayed Priority Claim to a Domestic Application Under 37 CFR 1.78(c)	SB/445 37 CFR 1.78(a)&(c) 35 USC 119(e), 120
Request to consider delayed claim of priority to PPA	MPEP 211.01(a), 214.02
Substitute: draft petition	Apx D-33
Attachments: - petition fee - statement averring that the belated claim was unintentional	37 CFR 1.17(m)
PTO Response: Decision on petition	
Petition to Withdraw Abandonment Based on Failure to Receive an Office Action	MPEP 711.03(c)(I)(A)
- issued Office Action was never received by applicant/practitioner	
Attachments: per MPEP 711.03(c)(I)(A)	
- include evidence demonstrating failure to receive Office Action	
PTO Response: Grant or Deny	
Petition to Withdraw Abandonment Based on Evidence That a Reply Was Timely Filed or Mailed	MPEP 711.03(c)(I)(B)
- response to issued Office Action was submitted within specified time period, but Notice of Abandonment inadvertently issued	
Attachments: per MPEP 711.03(c)(I)(B)	
- include averment that timely response submitted and evidence demonstrating same	
PTO Response: Grant or Deny	

Petition to Accept Unintentionally Delayed Priority Claim to a Domestic Application Under 37 CFR 1.78(c)	Apx D-33 SB/445 35 USC 119(e), 120
Request to consider delayed claim of priority to PPA	37 CFR 1.78(a)&(c) MPEP 211.01(a), 214.02
Substitute: draft petition	
PTO Response: Decision on petition	
Derivation Hearing in PTO	35 CFR 135
To contest priority; may be commenced against issued patent with earlier filing date within one year of publication of challenged claim in earlier filed application	37 CFR 42.400 *et seq.* MPEP 2310
- file petition per 35 USC 135(a), 37 CFR 42.405	

Reading:

A Sighting of AIA Derivation
https://www.finnegan.com/en/insights/articles/a-sighting-of-aia-derivation.html

Derivation Proceedings
https://www.ajpark.com/insights/derivation-proceedings/

Why No One Is Talking About Derivation Proceedings at PTAB
https://www.natlawreview.com/article/why-no-one-talking-about-derivation-proceedings-ptab

Derivation Proceedings
https://maicrandmaier.com/practice-areas/post-grant-practice/derivation-proceedings/

How to Contest Inventorship of Patented Subject Matter Through Derivation Proceedings
https://www.mondaq.com/unitedstates/patent/1258604/how-to-contest-inventorship-of-patentedsubject-matter-through-derivation-proceedings

(P) **PPA Conversion to Nonprovisional (RPA) Application**	Apx D-34 37 CFR 1.53(c)(3)
- a pending PPA can be converted to an RPA at any time prior to its expiration (one year from filing)	MPEP 201.04(III), 601.01(c)(II)
- this is rarely done since PPAs are typically converted by filing a corresponding RPA	

Attachments: petition fee	AIA/17i 37 CFR 1.17(i)
- include amendment containing at least one claim if no claims included in PPA	

Reading:

Provisional Patent Application Conversion
https://patentrebel.com/provisional-patent-conversion-everything-you-need-to-know/

Why Would Anyone Convert a US Provisional Application to a Non-Provisional?
https://blog.oppedahl.com/?p=3445

Rescind Non-Publication Request	SB/36
File within 45 days of foreign filing	35 USC 122{b)(2)(B)(ii) 37 CFR 1.213(b) MPEP 1123
PTO Response: Acknowledgment	
U **File RPA Within Pendency of Design Application**	35 USC 119(e), 120
- if using design application as priority document	37 CFR 1.78 MPEP 211

Reading:

Practice Tip: Claiming Priority between Design and Utility Patent Applications
https://www.carterdeluca.com/news/practice-tip-claiming-priority-design-utility-patent-applications/

Change of Entity Status	Apx D-35
Report of change/correction of entity status of applicant, with commensurate fees, if necessary	37 CFR 1.27 MPEP 509.03(b)
- can be filed via Private PAIR	
PTO Response: Acknowledgment of change	

Reading:

How The Wrong Applicant Entity Status Can Doom Your Patent
https://harrityllp.com/how-the-wrong-applicant-entity-status-can-doom-your-patent/

509.03(b) Change or Correction of Status
https://www.clfip.com/ip/blog/mpep/s509-5/

Getting a Refund From the Patent Office If You Are Now a Small Entity
https://www.legalteamusa.net/getting-a-refund-from-the-patent-office-if-you-are-now-a-small-entity/

Now You Can Update Entity Size Yourself
https://blog.oppedahl.com/?p=787

Request for Refund	
Request refund for overpayment or unnecessary payment	PTO-2326 35 USC 42(d) 37 CFR 1.26; 2.209 MPEP 607.02
PTO Response: decision on request	
Request for Refund 37 CFR 1.26/1.28 and Assertion of Small Entity Status	Apx D-36 37 CFR 1.26, 1.28
- refund due to reduction of entity status	MPEP 607.02(IV)
Request to Withdraw as Attorney or Agent and Change of Correspondence Address	AIA/83 37 CFR 1.36(b), 11.116
Notice of withdrawal from representing applicant in subject application	MPEP 402.06, 2804.01
Substitute: may be filed as e-Petition	
PTO Response: Request approved or denied	

Reading:

Attorney Withdrawal: The Ins-and-Outs of Getting Out
https://www.jamisongroup.com/img/~www.jamisongroup.com/forms/risk%20management_attorn ey_withdrawal.pdf

Revocation of POA	37 CFR 1.36(a)
- file as petition if revocation only	MPEP 402.05(a)
Attachments: petition fee	AIA/17p 37 CFR 1.17(f)
- if revoking existing POA and filing new POA, use form	AIA/18A
Authorization to Act in Representative Capacity	SB/84 37 CFR 1.34
Authorization to conduct interviews, file correspondence only	

Express Abandonment

Reading:

Why Aren't There More Express Abandonments?
https://blog.oppedahl.com/?p=1917

How to Abandon a Patent
https://smallbusiness.chron.com/abandon-patent-45100.html

Patent Application/Patent Abandonment
https://ipatentattorney.com/articles/invention-help/patent-application-patent-abandonment/

Express or Formal Abandonment Under 37 CFR 1.138	AIA/24 37 CFR 1.138
File before date of issue or publication	MPEP 711.01
Petition for Express Abandonment to Avoid Publication Under 37 CFR 1.138(c)	AIA/24A
37 CFR 1.138(c) File Express Abandonment to prevent publication	MPEP 711.01; 1125
Attachments: petition fee	AIA/17p 37 CFR 1.17(h)
Petition for Express Abandonment to Obtain a Refund (Under 37 CFR 1.138(d))	AIA/24B 37 CFR 1.138(d)
File Express Abandonment to obtain refund of search fee and excess claims fee	MPEP 711.01

Request Interview With Examiner	PTOL-413A
- Examiner may grant before first OA to advance prosecution	37 CFR 1.133 MPEP 713, 713.02
Substitute: Automated Interview Request Form	

Reading:

Tips From a Former Examiner on How to Conduct Interviews at the USPTO
https://ipwatchdog.com/2022/05/19/tips-former-examiner-conduct-interviews-uspto/id=149124/

5 Tips to Having a Good Patent Examiner Interview
https://iptoolworks.com/patent-examiner-interview/

Examiner Interviews
http://www.leonardpatel.com/examiner-interviews.html

Patent Examiner Interviews
https://patentassociate.com/2023/01/17/patent-examiner-interviews/

USPTO Interview Practice From an Examiner's Perspective
http://www.foundpersuasive.com/USPTO_interview_practice.aspx

Effectiveness of Examiner Interviews
https://www.americanbar.org/groups/intellectual_property_law/publications/landslide/2021-22/december-january/effectiveness-examiner-interviews/

Examiners Who Love (and Hate) to Interview (2021)
https://blog.juristat.com/examiner-interview-2021

Best Practices for Conducting Examiner Interviews
https://www.nutter.com/ip-law-bulletin/best-practices-for-conducting-examiner-interviews

Why Conduct a Patent Examiner Interview?
https://www.patenttrademarkblog.com/patent-examiner-interview/

Examining the Examiner
https://www.americanbar.org/groups/intellectual_property_law/publications/landslide/2019-20/may-june/examining-examiner/

Interviews With Patent Examiners
https://www.goodmanallen.com/blog/interviews-with-patent-examiners

It's Official: Patent Examiner Interviews Are Da Bomb
https://garson-law.com/its-official-patent-examiner-interviews-are-da-bomb/

Patent Examiner Interviews
https://www.merchantgould.com/News-Room/Articles/146504/Practical-Guidance-at-Lexis-Practice-Advisor

Patent Examiner Interviews: Getting the Examiner on Your Side
https://freship.com/patent-examiner-interviews-getting-the-examiner-on-your-side/

Do Examiner Interviews Live Up to the Hype?
https://bigpatentdata.com/2018/06/do-examiner-interviews-live-up-to-the-hype/

Why Patent Examiner Interviews Are a Must
https://smithhopen.com/2021/06/16/why-patent-examiner-interviews-are-a-must/

Three Steps for Effective Examiner Interviews
https://condoroccia.com/three-steps-to-effective-examiner-interviews/

Examiner Interviews: How to Improve Patent Quality While Compressing Prosecution and Reducing Costs
https://www.natlawreview.com/article/examiner-interviews-improving-patent-quality-while-compressing-prosecution-and

Change of Correspondence Address — AIA/122; 37 CFR 1.33

Update applicant mailing address — MPEP 601.03(a)

Substitute: Update address via Private PAIR

[NOTE: This point in the procedure sequence generally marks the effective end of PPA application activity. The PPA will be made public when a corresponding RPA is published on Patent Center.]

(P) **Petition to Expunge Information or Copy of Papers in Application File Under 37 CFR 1.59(b)** — Apx D-37; 37 CFR 1.59(b); MPEP 724.05

Request to have trade secret or proprietary information removed from the public record

Attachments: — AIA/17p

- petition fee — 37 CFR 1.17(g)
- statement averring confidential information was unintentionally submitted and failure to return would cause irreparable harm

Note: see MPEP 724.02 for procedure for preventing submitted confidential or proprietary information from appearing in the public file record

PTO Response: grant or deny petition

Reading:

How Do I Expunge Information From My Submitted Patent Application?
https://www.allgaierpatentsolutions.com/2019/04/how-do-i-expunge-information-from-my-submitted-patent-application/

Petition for Suspension of Rules — 37 CFR 1.183

- in an "extraordinary situation, when justice requires," any requirement of the regulations in this part which is not a requirement of the statutes may be suspended or waived

Attachments: petition fee — 37 CFR 1.17(f)

Reading:

Suspending the Rules: A Year's Worth of USPTO Petitions
https://www.ptablaw.com/2021/08/17/suspending-the-rules-a-years-worth-of-uspto-petitions/#:~:text=In%20some%20circumstances%2C%20patent%20applicants%20may%20petition%20the,of%20situations%20where%20this%20requirement%20would%20be%20met

Optional Application Additions [PPA/RPA]	
Supplemental IDS	Apx D-38
Transmittal of material in addition to initial IDS	37 CFR 1.97 *et seq.*
- newly discovered relevant art must be disclosed	MPEP 609,04(b)
- unreported prior art from searches by foreign patent offices for corresponding applications must be declared via IDS	Apx D-39 37 CFR 1.97(e)(1)
Correction of IDS	Apx D-40
- request to correct clerical errors in IDS	
Preliminary Amendment	37 CFR 1.115
- revise disclosure before examination	*see also* 37 CFR 1.121
- often filed to avoid possible adverse action in U.S. application suggested by prior PCT patentability opinion	MPEP 714.01(e)
- may be filed at any time before first Office Action	
- should be submitted within three months of application filing date to avoid possible disapproval	
- no new matter permitted per 37 CFR 1.121(f) if filed after initial application submittal	
U **Utility**	Apx D-11
D **Design**	Apx D-12
Amendment Under 37 CFR 1.71(g)	37 CFR 1.71(g)
- amendment to disclose the names of the parties to a joint research agreement as defined in 37 CFR 1.9(e)	
Attachments: processing fee may apply if not AIA/17i timely filed (see 37 CFR 1.71(g)(2))	
Notice of Noncompliant (Non-Responsive) Amendment	PTOL-324 37 CFR 1.121
- issued when amendment submitted fails to comply with 37 CFR 1.121	MPEP 714(II)(F)
Applicant Response: submit corrections per Notice	Apx D-13

4. Optional Applicant-Initiated Actions

Foreign Filing	35 USC 184
- initiate foreign filing if desired, using U.S. application as priority	37 CFR 5.11 MPEP 140
- must file foreign counterpart utility applications within one year of U.S. filing date to preserve priority	
D - must file foreign design applications within six months of U.S. filing date to preserve priority	35 USC 172

Foreign Filing License

- Foreign Filing License (FFL) required before foreign filing or lapse of at least six months from filing U.S. application	35 USC 184-85 37 CFR 5.11
- notify PTO within 45 days of foreign filing if NPR in effect	MPEP 1124

Reading:

Foreign Filing Requirements in the United States
https://www.sternekessler.com/news-insights/publications/foreign-filing-requirements-united-states

When to Obtain Foreign Filing and Export Licenses
https://www.sternekessler.com/news-insights/publications/when-obtain-foreign-filing-and-export-licenses

Requesting a Foreign Filing License
https://www.mmviplaw.com/requesting-foreign-filing-license/

Foreign Patent Filing Restrictions in the U.S. – Part 1
https://www.natlawreview.com/article/foreign-patent-filing-restrictions-and-licenses-us-part-1

What Are the Various Options for Filing a Petition for Expedited Foreign Filing License?
https://uspto.report/resources/patent-faq/what-are-the-various-options-for-filing-a-petition-for-expedited-foreign-filing-license/

Navigating Foreign Filing Requirements for Cross-Border Patent Inventions (Part I)
https://ipwatchdog.com/2022/04/26/navigating-foreign-filing-requirements-cross-border-patent-inventions-part/id=148647/

Foreign Filing Licenses – An Overlooked Pitfall of Last Minute Patent Filings
https://www.jdsupra.com/legalnews/foreign-filing-licenses-an-overlooked-1954863/

How to Ensure Your Retroactive Foreign Filing License Petition Isn't Dismissed
https://ipwatchdog.com/2022/11/21/ensure-retroactive-foreign-filing-license-petition-isnt-dismissed/id=153347/

The Good, the Bad and the Missing: Findings From a Review of the Data on Granted Retroactive Foreign Filing Licenses
https://ipwatchdog.com/2021/01/26/good-bad-missing-findings-review-data-granted-retroactive-foreign-filing-licenses/id=129348/

	Petition for Expedited Foreign Filing License	37 CFR 5.12
	- file when FFL not granted automatically with U.S. application	MPEP 140
	- with corresponding pending U.S. application, see 37 CFR 5.14	
	- without corresponding U.S. application, see 37 CFR 5.13	
	Attachments: petition fee	37 CFR 1.17(g)
	Petition for Retroactive Foreign Filing License	37 CFR 5.25
	- if, through error, a foreign application was filed without a FFL in effect, applicant may petition for a retroactive FFL	MPEP 140
	Attachments: per 37 CFR 5.25	
	- petition fee	37 CFR 1.17(g)
	PTO Response: Grant or Deny	
D	**File Design Application Using Pending RPA Application as Priority Document**	35 USC 120 MPEP 1504.20
	- file design application during RPA application pendency	
	- design application cannot claim priority to any earlier PPA claimed by RPA	35 USC 172
U	**File Utility RPA Using Pending Design Application as Priority Document**	35 USC 120
	- file RPA application during design application pendency	
P	**File Additional PPAs**	37 CFR 1.53(c)
	- additional PPAs may be filed on any new matter or improvements to the disclosure in the original PPA; a corresponding RPA filed before the initial PPA expires can claim priority to the first and all subsequent PPAs	35 USC 111(b) MPEP 201.04; 601.01(b)
U	**File RPA Using Prior PPA as Priority Document**	35 USC 119(e); 120
	- file within one year of PPA filing	37 CFR 1.78 MPEP 210; 211
	Request for Deferral of Examination 37 CFR 1.103(d)	SB/37
	- applicant can strategically delay examination for up to 36 months from the priority date	37 CFR 1.103(d) MPEP 709
	- file before first OA	
	Attachments: processing fee	AIA/17i 37 CFR 1.17(i)

Reading:

Deferred Examination of Patent Applications
http://www.yarbroughlaw.com/Publications/pubs_patent10_deferred_examination.htm

Inside Views: Deferred Examination: A Solution Whose Time Has Come
https://www.ip-watch.org/2009/03/12/inside-views-deferred-examination-a-solution-whose-time-has-come/

Post-GSK: Where Do We Go From Here?—Deferred Examination
https://www.patentdocs.org/2007/11/post-gsk-wher-5.html

Petition for Suspension of Action	37 CFR 1.103(a)
- abeyance of application processing by the PTO MPEP 709 for up to 6 months	
- will be granted only if applicant response to OA is not outstanding	
Attachments: petition fee	37 CFR 1.17(g)
- demonstration of good and sufficient cause for suspension	
Application Status Inquiry	Apx D-41
Request status of disposition of application (e.g., when office action might be expected)	
- current application history also available via the PAIR system or Patent Center	
Authorization for Internet Communication or Request to Withdraw Internet Communication	SB/439
Authorizes applicant and examiner to communicate via email	MPEP 502.03
U **Request for Early Publication**	Apx D-42
- Request that application be published earlier than conventional 18 months after filing	37 CFR 1.219 MPEP 1129
Substitute: enter information on ADS?	
PTO Response: acknowledgment	

Reading:

All You Want to Know About "Early Publication of a Patent Application" A Conversation with Dr. Mohan Dewan
https://www.lexology.com/library/detail.aspx?g=878f3236-acd2-44b2-bef7-6f800ed4171f

Early Publication: Is It Right for You?
https://www.boudwinlaw.com/blog/2019/12/early-publication-is-it-right-for-you/

Patent Application Publication
https://www.neustel.com/patents/patent-applications/patent-application-publication/

What Is an Early Publication of a Patent Application?
https://arcticinvent.com/what-is-an-early-publication-of-a-patent-application/

Rescission of Previous Nonpublication Request (35 U.S.C. 122(b)(2)(B)(ii)) and, if Applicable, Notice of Foreign Filing (35 U.S.C. 122(b)(2)(B)(iii))	SB/36 37 CFR 1.213(b) 35 USC 122(b)(2)(B)(ii)
- File within 45 days of foreign filing	MPEP 1123
Attachments: Notice of Foreign Filing (if applicable)	35 USC 122(b)(2)(B)(iii)
PTO Response: Acknowledgment	

Reading:

Warning to Inventors: Failure to Follow Obscure USPTO Rules Can Kill Your Patent Application
http://www.parkerkeough.com/blog/2016/11/18/warning-to-inventors-failure-to-follow-obscure-uspto-rules-can-kill-your-patent-application

U

Petition to Convert to Provisional Application	Apx D-43
- File petition before abandonment, payment of issue fee or lapse of 12 months after filing date, whichever event is earlier	37 CFR 1.53(c)(2) MPEP 201.04(III), 606.01(c)(I)
Reasons: 1. Obtain more time to determine commercial viability 2. Obtain more time to generate data supporting patentability (some industries are aware of the need for data) 3. Defer substantive prosecution costs for an additional year (more and more common in this economy) 4. Avoid non-provisional publication (as you suggested) 5. Obtain more time to address potential issues with the application before filing abroad.	
Attachments: petition fee	37 CFR 1.17(q)
PTO Response: decision on petition	

Reading:

Converting to a Provisional Application
https://galvanilegal.com/converting-to-a-provisional-application/

Petition Relating to Matters Not Specifically Provided For	37 CFR 1.182
- a petition may be filed for any matter not specifically provided for under Title 37	
Attachments: petition fee	AIA/17p
- a detailed statement explaining the matter for which applicant seeks relief, per 37 CFR 1.182	37 CFR 1.17(f)

B. Post-Exam (Prosecution)

In its narrow sense, patent prosecution commences with the examination of the application by the assigned examiner. This action initiates a period of interaction between the applicant, or applicant's representative, and the examiner, during which applicant advocates in favor of the broadest allowance of the stated claims, while the examiner commonly alleges anticipating prior art and/or other deficiencies, which must be overcome in order for patent to issue. Prosecution can continue until both sides are satisfied as to the patentability of the standing claims and the examiner issues a Notice of Allowance. If the applicant cannot overcome the examiner's objections, the applicant may file a continuing application, usually with amended claims, and proceed with another round of examination. Otherwise, the application eventually becomes abandoned. The applicant can continue prosecution even after patent issuance if he/she believes that the issued patent does not provide protection rights as strong as they could be.

Reading:

Patent Prosecution: Everything You Need to Know
https://www.upcounsel.com/patent-prosecution

Understanding U.S. Patent Prosecution
https://www.ipwatchdog.com/2018/06/30/understanding-u-s-patent-prosecution/id=98955/

How to Slow Down Patent Prosecution With the USPTO
https://henry.law/blog/slow-down-patent-prosecution/

How to Speed Up Patent Prosecution at the USPTO
https://henry.law/blog/speed-up-patent-prosecution/#blog-content-anchor

Check Your Examiner's Allowance Rate
https://www.patentbots.com/stats/

Pre-Grant Prosecution

Extension of Time

Reading:
How Does a Patent Extension of Time Work?
https://www.patenttrademarkblog.com/patent-extension-of-time/

Patent Extension of Time: Everything You Need to Know
https://www.upcounsel.com/patent-extension-of-time

Petition for Extension of Time Under 37 CFR 1.136(a)	AIA/22 37 CFR 1.136(a)
Request to extend period for reply beyond that specified by PTO for submitting response	MPEP 710.02(e)
- when applicant is required to reply within a nonstatutory or shortened statutory time period	
Substitute: Draft petition	Apx D-27

Reading:
No Need for Extension of Time Petitions
https://blog.oppedahl.com/?p=1113

Petition for Extension of Time Under 37 CFR 1.136(b)	SB/23 37 CFR 1.136(b)
When a reply cannot be filed within the time period set for such reply and the provisions of paragraph (a) of this section are not available	MPEP 710.02(e)
Attachments: Petition Fee	AIA/17p 37 CFR 1.17(f)

PTO-Initiated Actions

Patent Office Actions

Reading:
Non-Final Office Action and Final Office Action
https://www.menteso.com/ip-docketing-advanced/non-final-office-action/

How to Respond to an Office Action?
https://ocpatentlawyer.com/respond-office-action/

"Final" versus "Non-Final" Office Action
https://btlj.org/2016/03/final-versus-non-final-office-action/

Response to Office Action: Everything You Need to Know
https://www.upcounsel.com/response-to-office-action

Office Action Received in Applications for Patent
https://www.cioncaip.com/PatentInformation/PatentOfficeActionRes

1. Non-Substantive Examination

Restriction/Election Requirement Issued (if necessary) [MPEP Chap. 800]

Response to Restriction/Election Requirement	Apx D-44
Election of one of the inventions/species specified in the Restriction/Election Requirement for prosecution	37 CFR 1.142 *et seq.* 35 USC 121
- and/or traverse	MPEP 802, 803, 818, 1504.05 des
- file on unelected subject matter before patent issues if desired	

Reading:

What Is a Restriction Requirement?
https://www.patenttrademarkblog.com/what-is-a-restriction-requirement/

"Restriction Requirements" Series, Part 1: Considering Restrictions When Developing a Claim Filing Strategy
https://www.mintz.com/insights-center/viewpoints/2015-05-19-restriction-requirements-series-part-1-considering

Election-Restriction Requirement
https://www.yospinlaw.com/2017/05/16/election-restriction-requirement

Restriction Requirements
https://www.obwbip.com/04D540/assets/files/News/Jeff-Bergmann_20180227.pdf

D *Practice Note: Avoid Multiple Embodiments in Design Patent Applications*
https://www.bakerdonelson.com/webfiles/Bios/Practice%20Note%20Chaloner.pdf

Traverse and Reconsideration of Restriction Requirement	37 CFR 1.143 MPEP 818.01(b-c)
- to contest restriction requirement, applicant must traverse requirement, declare a provisional election, and request reconsideration	
- include reasons why the requirement is in error	
PTO Response: Reconsider or make final	
Petition and Review of Restriction Requirement	37 CFR 1.144
- if the Examiner makes a traversed requirement final, applicant may petition the Commissioner to review the requirement	MPEP 818.01(c)
- file Petition not later than an appeal on the merits of final rejection	
Supplemental Amendment and Response to Restriction Requirement	Apx D-45 37 CFR 1.111
Correction of previous amendment	MPEP 714.03(a)
PTO Response:	
Notice of Allowance issued—GO TO **Post-Allowance** at p. 94	
or	
Notification That Amendment Not Fully Responsive (Notice of Incomplete Response)	MPEP 714.02-03
- issued when amendment omits information required per Office Action	
Applicant Response: depends on nature of deficiency (*see* MPEP 714.03)	Apx D-46
or	
Notice of Noncompliant (Non-Responsive) Amendment	PTOL-324 37 CFR 1.121
- issued when amendment submitted fails to comply with 37 CFR 1.121	MPEP 714(II)(F)
Applicant Response: submit corrections per Notice	Apx D-13
or	
Application Examined on the Merits	

Optional Application Additions

Supplemental IDS

- report of prior art in addition to original IDS	Apx D-38
- newly discovered relevant art must be disclosed	37 CFR 1.97 *et seq.*
- unreported prior art from searches by foreign patent offices for corresponding applications must be declared via IDS	Apx D-39 37 CFR 1.97(e)(1)

2. After Substantive Examination

If Notice of Allowance issued—GO TO Post-Allowance at p. 94

- "First Action Allowance" (FFA): application issued Allowance upon initial exam

Reading:

A Closer Look at First-Action Allowance for Patents
http://www.evergreeneditions.com/article/A_Closer_Look_At_First-Action_Allowance_For_Patents/1689287/205754/article.html

A Patent Bigfoot? The Mythical First Action Allowances DO Exist!
https://www.ipwatchdog.com/2012/03/07/a-patent-bigfoot-the-mythical-first-action-allowances-do-exist/id=22628/

If No Allowance—Substantive Examination Action—Non-Final Office Action Issued

Reading:

How Do I Read an Office Action?
https://www.bpmlegal.com/content/howtooa

a.) After Non-Final Office Action

Applicant Response Options to Non-Final OA

- Amendment/Reconsideration
- Traverse
- Interview examiner
- Abandonment

(1.) Failure to Respond to Non-Final

Notice of Abandonment issued (PTOL-1432)	35 USC 133
- if no applicant response to Non-Final OA within six months	37 CFR 1.135, 2.65
- issued by PTO for reason(s) indicated	MPEP 711.02, 711.03(c)(II)(A)(4)
Applicant Response: Revive (optional)	

Reading:

How to Respond to a Notice of Abandonment—Failure to Respond Timely to Office Action
https://www.gerbenlaw.com/blog/how-to-respond-to-a-notice-of-abandonment-failure-to-respond-timely-to-office-action/

Petition to Withdraw Abandonment Based on Failure to Receive an Office Action	MPEP 711.03(c)(I)(A)
- issued Office Action was never received by applicant/practitioner	
Attachments: per MPEP 711.03(c)(I)(A)	
- include evidence demonstrating failure to receive Office Action	
PTO Response: Grant or Deny	
Petition to Withdraw Abandonment Based on Evidence That a Reply Was Timely Filed or Mailed	MPEP 711.03(c)(I)(B)
- response to issued Office Action was submitted within specified time period, but Notice of Abandonment inadvertently issued	
Attachments: per MPEP 711.03(c)(I)(B)	
- include averment that timely response submitted and evidence demonstrating same	
PTO Response: Grant or Deny	

Applicant-Initiated Actions

Reviving Abandoned Applications

Reading:

USPTO Clarifies Practice for Reviving Unintentionally Abandoned Patent Applications and Patents
https://www.ipupdate.com/2020/03/uspto-clarifies-practice-for-reviving-unintentionally-abandoned-patent-applications-and-patents/

How to Revive Abandoned Patent Application
https://www.patenttrademarkblog.com/abandoned-patent-application/

Petition to Revive Abandoned Patent Application
https://www.upcounsel.com/petition-to-revive-abandoned-patent-application

Reviving an Abandoned Application
https://freship.com/reviving-an-abandoned-application/

Reviving Abandoned Patents
https://patentassociate.com/2016/09/21/reviving-abandoned-patents/

New U.S. Application and Patent Revival Standards
https://www.faegredrinker.com/en/insights/publications/2014/4/new-us-application-and-patent-revival-standards

USPTO Increasing Burden on Petitioners in Connection with Petitions to Excuse Delay
https://www.csglaw.com/newsroom/uspto-increasing-burden-on-petitioners-in-connection-with-petitions-to-excuse-delay/

Petition for Revival of Application for Patent Abandoned Unintentionally (37 CFR 1.137(a))	SB/64 37 CFR 1.137(a-b)
- Notice of Abandonment issued due to MPEP 711.03(c) belated response	
Substitute: ePetition (only between 1st OA and Notice of Allowance)	
Attachments: petition fee	37 CFR 1.17(m)
- reply required by the outstanding Office Action or Notice, if necessary	
- statement averring the belated reply was unintentional	
PTO Response: Grant or deny	
Petition for Revival of Application for Patent Abandoned Unintentionally (37 CFR 1.137(a))	SB/64 37 CFR 1.137(a) MPEP 711.03(c)
Substitute: ePetition (to accept dilatory payment of Issue Fee)	
Petition for Revival of Application for Patent Abandoned Unavoidably (37 CFR 1.137(b))	SB/61 37 CFR 1.137(b) MPEP 711.03(c)

Petition for Revival of Application for Patent Abandoned for Failure to Notify Office of Foreign or International Filing (37 CFR 1.137(f))	SB /64a 37 CFR 1.137(f) MPEP 711.03(c)(II)(A)(5)
Substitute: e-Petition	
Attachments: petition fee	37 CFR 1.17(m)
- statement averring the belated reply was unintentional	
PTO Response: Grant or deny	
Petition to Revive If Delay Avoidable but Unintentional	SB/64 37 CFR 1.137(b) MPEP 711.03(c)(II)C)
Substitute: ePetition (to accept late payment of issue Fee)	

Substitute Application (Refile)	MPEP 201.09
- file duplicate application on abandoned original application	
- use when applicant desires to pursue patent after abandonment and original application cannot be revived	
- does not retain filing date of original application	
- new matter can be added	
Request to Change Applicant Under 37 CFR 1.46(c)	AIA/40
Change or correction of inventorship after examination on merits	37 CFR 1.46(c)
	35 USC 116
	MPEP 605.01(II)
Attachments: updated ADS	37 CFR 1.76, 3.71, 3.73
Substitute: Draft request in lieu of AIA/41	Apx D-28

(2.) Respond to Non-Final Office Action

Amendment and Response Under 37 CFR 1.111 [Amendment and Response (NF)]	Apx D-47 37 CFR 1.111(a)(1), 1.112
- request for reconsideration with or without amendment	
- response/amend to first OA on the merits (rejections based on 112, 101, 102, 103)	MPEP 714

- no new matter (35 USC 132; Rule 121(f))
  - amended claims: avoid amending claims during prosecution
  - Doctrine of Equivalents cannot be used to broaden claim that was amended during prosecution to overcome prior art, or when reason for amending unclear (*see Festo v. Shoketsu*, 535 U.S. 722)

Rejection vs. Objection — MPEP 706

- Objection: nonclaim defect (formalities or technicalities related to form)
- Rejection: substantive claim deficiency (based on relation to prior art)

a.) Non-Prior Art Rejections [MPEP 706.03]

(i.) Subject matter — 35 USC 101

- inventions patentable; subject matter eligibility — MPEP 2105
- application of *Alice/Mayo* test

Reading:

Applying Step One of the Alice/Mayo Test
https://www.bitlaw.com/guidance/patent/applying-step-one-of-Alice-Mayo-test.html

(ii.) Lack of Utility — 35 USC 101, MPEP 2700

(iii.) 112—form and content of spec/claims — 35 USC 112, MPEP 2164

Enablement

- three distinct requirements: the enablement requirement, the written description requirement, and the best mode requirement.
- 112(a) 1st paragraph: enabling disclosure — MPEP 2161-63
  - written description; specification
  - enablement (how to make/practice invention) (*see also*, MPEP 608.01(p))
- 112(b) 2nd paragraph: one or more claims must be definite, precise, unambiguous — MPEP 2171-73

Reading:
Patent Amendment Format: Everything You Need to Know
https://www.upcounsel.com/patent-amendment-format

Supplemental After Non-Final Response	37 CFR 1.111(a)(2)
- correct previously filed amendment	MPEP 714.03(a)
- may be entered only for limited reasons after examination	
Utility	Apx D-48
Design	Apx D-49
Declaration Under 37 CFR 1.130(a)	Apx D-50
When any claim of an application is rejected, applicant may submit affidavit to disqualify a disclosure as prior art by establishing that the disclosure was made by the applicant	37 CFR 1.130(a) MPEP 717.01; 2155

Reading:
Three Things You Need to Know About Rule 130 Declarations
https://www.foley.com/en/insights/publications/2018/01/three-things-to-know-about-rule-130-declarations

Invoking an AIA Exception to Prior Art, 1.130 Declarations
https://www.sternekessler.com/news-insights/publications/invoking-aia-exception-prior-art-1130-declarations

"Why, I Declare" … Proper Use of Evidentiary Declarations Under New (Post-AIA) Rule 37 C.F.R. 1.130
https://www.jdsupra.com/legalnews/why-i-declare-proper-use-of-evident-46357/

717.01 Affidavit or Declaration Under 37 CFR 1.130
https://www.clfip.com/ip/blog/mpep/s717-1/

Declaration Under 37 CFR 1.132	Apx D-51
Evidence submitted to traverse objection or rejection of a claim	37 CFR 1.132 MPEP 716

Reading:
Patent Prosecution Tool Kit: 1.132 Declarations for Traversing Rejections
https://www.jdsupra.com/legalnews/patent-prosecution-tool-kit-1-132-89653/

1.132 Declarations for Traversing Rejections
https://www.sternekessler.com/sites/default/files/2020-06/tab_10_1.132_declarations_for_traversing_rejections_final.pdf

Use of Rule 132 Declarations
https://www.napp.org/assets/2016AMC/2-%20patent%20prosecution%20bp-%20culpepper.pdf

37 CFR § 1.132 Practice
https://www.aipla.org/docs/default-source/committee-documents/bcp-files/jwitz_132d.pdf?sfvrsn=a3bd0c05_2

IP: These Claims Are Not Obvious, Just Ask My Expert!
https://www.marshallip.com/content/uploads/2014/10/These-claims-are-not-obvious-just-ask-my-expert_EB.pdf

b.) Prior Art Rejections [MPEP 706.02, 2120 *et seq.*]

Reading:
How to Avoid Your Own Patents and Applications as Prior Art Under the America Invents Act (AIA)
https://henry.law/blog/prior-art-under-aia/

(i.) 102—Conditions for patentability; novelty, anticipation	MPEP 2120-31
- claimed invention must not have been known to the public prior to application	
(ii.) 103—Nonobviousness	
- subject to 35 USC 103, differences between claimed invention and relevant prior art must be nonobvious	MPEP 2141-44

1. Graham Factors Analysis (*Graham v. John Deere*, 383 U.S. 1, 148 (1966); USPO 459); MPEP 2141
    a. scope/content of prior art
    b. novelty of invention
    c. skill level of artisans in the art
    d. determine obviousness of invention on basis of #1–3
2. consider secondary/objective factors
    a. General Arguments
        - unexpected/new/surprising results (must be more than marginal); commercial success; long-felt need; failure of others; etc.

- arguing secondary factors: submit Declaration under Rule 132 (by inventor or expert) with evidence of commercial success (MPEP 1504.03), or to challenge technical issues raised in OA (Rule 132, 37 CFR 1.132)

b. Combinatorial Factors: when combination of references cited (motivation to combine references; references teach away from combination; etc.)

- verify references cited by PTO (valid prior art?)
- confirm that references are properly interpreted and applied by examiner

Non-statutory (obvious-type) Double Patenting MPEP 804

- results in improper time extension through the patenting of subject matter not patently distinct from a parent application
- 103 rejection for obvious-type double patenting on earlier patent/application by same inventor/ owner and it is not early enough to be prior art
- file Terminal Disclaimer (SB/26; to prevent double patenting) response/amend after second(final) OA
- pay fee; post-issue fee (37 CFR 1.20(d))
- receive Terminal Disclaimer review decision

Reading:

Responding to Nonstatutory Double Patenting Rejections: A Practitioner's Perspective
https://www.americanbar.org/groups/intellectual_property_law/publications/landslide/2018-19/march-april/responding-nonstatutory-double-patenting-rejections/

Obviousness-Type Double Patenting
https://www.sternekessler.com/news-insights/publications/obviousness-type-double-patenting

Navigating Through the Obvious-Type Double Patenting Minefield
http://www.mcneillbaur.com/docs/Navigating_Through_the_OTDP_Minefield.pdf

Why Terminal Disclaimers Are Easy to Overlook but Lethal If Ignored?
https://www.greyb.com/terminal-disclaimer/

Non-Statutory Double Patenting Rejections and Terminal Disclaimers
https://www.wnlaw.com/blog/non-statutory-double-patenting-rejections-terminal-disclaimers/

Terminal Disclaimer Double Patenting: Everything You Need to Know
https://www.upcounsel.com/terminal-disclaimer-double-patenting

Terminal Disclaimer to Obviate a Double Patenting Rejection Over a "Prior" Patent	SB/26 37 CFR 1.321(b)
Disclaimer of terminal part of the normal term of any patent granted from current application extending beyond the term of a prior patent	35 USC 253 MPEP 804; 1490
- can be filed alone or concurrently with response to OA	
Substitute: Draft request; eTerminal Disclaimer	Apx D-52
Attachments: Statement Under 37 CFR 3.73(b) (if Terminal Disclaimer signed by assignee)	
PTO Response: Decision on request (Approve or Disapprove)	

Reading:
USPTO Proposes to Close Gap in Terminal Disclaimer Practice
https://www.foley.com/en/insights/publications/2021/01/uspto-proposes-close-gap-terminal-disclaimer

Patent Office Proposal Seeks to Expand Applicability of Terminal Disclaimers in Joint Research Agreement Patent Filings
https://www.vorys.com/publications-2843.html

After AIA Only Applicant Can File Terminal Disclaimer
https://www.finnegan.com/en/at-the-ptab-blog/after-aia-only-applicant-can-file-terminal-disclaimer.html

Terminal Disclaimer to Obviate a Provisional Double Patenting Rejection Over a Pending "Reference" Application	SB/25 37 CFR 1.321(c) 35 USC 253
Disclaimer of terminal part of the normal term of any patent granted from current application extending beyond the term of another pending application	MPEP 804; 1490
Attachments: submit terminal disclaimer with fee and Declaration stating that the patent reference is owned by applicant and has same inventor (Rule 131; 37 CFR 131)	
PTO Response: Decision on request (Approve or Disapprove)	

Reading:
What Is the Impact of Submitting a Terminal Disclaimer on an Application If the Prior Application Is Not Allowed?
https://patents.stackexchange.com/questions/19421/what-is-the-impact-of-submitting-a-terminal-disclaimer-on-an-application-if-the

c.) Applicant-Initiated Actions

Supplemental IDS after Non-final OA, but before Final OA	Apx D-09
- report of prior art in addition to original IDS	37 CFR 1.97 et seq.
- newly discovered relevant art must be disclosed	
- unreported prior art from searches by foreign patent offices for corresponding applications must be declared via IDS	Apx D-39 37 CFR 1.97(e)(1)
- file after three months from filing date or after first OA on the merits, whichever is later, but prior to the close of application prosecution, i.e., before mailing of final OA, a Notice of Allowance, or an *Ex Parte Quayle* action, whichever is earlier.	
- 37 CFR 1.97(e) statement or fee required	
Attachments: Cover Letter	
- Copies of foreign patents and non-patent literature (NPL) (use SB/08(b)) (per 37 CFR 1.98(a)(2))	
- may require statement under CFR 1.97(e) and fee, depending on when filed	
- may be filed online via e-IDS	MPEP 609.07
- PTO response: Notice of Noncompliant IDS issued if irregularities exist if requested, copy of SB/08, initialed by examiner as considered (per MPEP 609)	
Request for Copies of Missing References	MPEP 707.05(a)
- request copies of non-US prior art references cited if PTO fails to provide	
Rescission of Prior Disclaimer/Request to Revisit Art	Apx D-17
Regarding any characterizations of claims or referenced art that could be construed as a disclaimer of any subject matter supported by present disclosure, such disclaimers are retracted	

Reading:
Rescinding Estoppel: The Most Overlooked Means to a Broader Claim Construction
https://www.lexology.com/library/detail.aspx?g=e61a2cba-73a7-489b-884f-47d6268d846b

Request for Clarification of Office Action	
- request clarification from examiner if any part of OA not understandable	
Request Interview With Examiner	PTOL-413A
- advisable in the interest of clarifying and resolving issues to advance prosecution	37 CFR 1.133 MPEP 713 et seq.
- Proposed Interview Agenda	Apx D-53
Substitute: Automated Interview Request Form	

Reading:
Why You Should Use the USPTO's Automated Interview Request (AIR) Form
https://www.mintz.com/insights-center/viewpoints/2017-03-30-why-you-should-use-usptos-automated-interview-request-air

Examiner Interview Summary Record	PTOL-413
Applicant Summary of Interview with Examiner	Apx D-54 37 CFR 1.133(b) MPEP 713.04

Reading:
Best Practices for Conducting Examiner Interviews
https://www.nutter.com/ip-law-bulletin/best-practices-for-conducting-examiner-interviews

Why Conduct a Patent Examiner Interview?
https://www.patenttrademarkblog.com/patent-examiner-interview/

Examining the Examiner
https://www.americanbar.org/groups/intellectual_property_law/publications/landslide/2019-20/may-june/examining-examiner/

Interviews With Patent Examiners
https://www.goodmanallen.com/blog/interviews-with-patent-examiners

It's Official: Patent Examiner Interviews Are da Bomb
https://garson-law.com/its-official-patent-examiner-interviews-are-da-bomb/

Patent Examiner Interviews
https://www.merchantgould.com/News-Room/Articles/146504/Practical-Guidance-at-Lexis-Practice-Advisor

Patent Examiner Interviews: Getting the Examiner on Your Side
https://freship.com/patent-examiner-interviews-getting-the-examiner-on-your-side/

Do Examiner Interviews Live Up to the Hype?
https://bigpatentdata.com/2018/06/do-examiner-interviews-live-up-to-the-hype/

Why Patent Examiner Interviews Are a Must
https://smithhopen.com/2021/06/16/why-patent-examiner-interviews-are-a-must/

Three Steps for Effective Examiner Interviews
https://condoroccia.com/three-steps-to-effective-examiner-interviews/

PTO Response to Amendment/Reconsideration:

Notice of Allowance issued—GO TO **Post-Allowance** at p. 94 or	
Notification That Amendment Not Fully Responsive	MPEP 714.02-03
(Notice of Incomplete Response)	
- issued when amendment omits information required per Office Action	
Applicant Response: depends on nature of deficiency (see MPEP 714.03)	Apx D-24
or	
Notice of Noncompliant (Non-Responsive) Amendment	PTOL-324 37 CFR 1.121
- issued when amendment submitted fails to comply with 37 CFR 1.121	MPEP 714(II)(F)
Applicant Response: submit corrections per Notice	Apx D-13

Reading:
Notice of Non-Compliant Response in a Patent Application
https://galvanilegal.com/notice-of-non-compliant-response-in-a-patent-application/?cn-reloaded=1

or

If No Allowance—Final OA (Final Rejection) issued (Note: PTO may issue another Non-Final OA after Applicant's response to Non-Final)

b.) After Final Office Action — 37 CFR 1.113 MPEP 706.07, 2271

Reading:

Is a Final Office Action Really "Final"?
https://www.patenttrademarkblog.com/final-office-action/#:~:text=A%20Final%20Office%20Action%20issued,i.e.%2C%20in%20an%20Advisory%20Action

Final Rejection: Not the End
https://www.yospinlaw.com/2019/08/12/final-rejection

Avoiding a First-Action Final Office Action
https://www.napp.org/index.php?option=com_dailyplanetblog&view=entry&category=uncategorized&id=2:title-avoiding-a-first-action-final-office-action-may-14-2018

"Final" Doesn't Mean It's Over—Options for Applicants After a Final Office Action
https://www.ipnewswire.blog/blog/2018/5/8/final-doesnt-mean-its-over-options-for-applicants-after-a-final-office-action

Improper Final Rejections and Suggestions for Avoiding Them
https://www.hg.org/legal-articles/improper-final-rejections-and-suggestions-for-avoiding-them-19062

Tactical Approach to Deal With Final Rejection From the USPTO
https://www.invntree.com/blogs/tactical-approach-to-deal-with-final-rejection-from-the-uspto

Is Final Really Final? Alternative Patent Prosecution Routes After a Final Office Action
https://www.wintechblog.com/2016/08/is-final-really-final-alternative-patent-prosecution-routes-after-a-final-office-action/

Decisions, Decisions—Options for Responding to a USPTO Final Office Action
http://plusfirm.com/responding-to-final-office-actions/

Patent Final Rejection: Everything You Need to Know
https://www.upcounsel.com/patent-final-rejection

Overview on After Final Practice at the USPTO
https://www.wnlaw.com/blog/overview-final-practice-uspto/

Applicant Response — 37 CFR 1.113; MPEP 714.12-13

Applicant Response Options after Final OA

- amendment
- After Final Consideration Pilot Program
- file continuing application
- Notice of Appeal
- Request for Continued Examination (RCE)
- petition requesting withdrawal of final OA
- allow application to become abandoned from failure to respond

(1.) Failure to Respond to Final Office Action

Notice of Abandonment issued

- if no applicant response to Non-Final OA
- issued by PTO for reason(s) specified

Applicant Response: Revive (optional)

- *see* Reviving Abandoned Applications at p. 71

Petition for Revival of Application for Patent Abandoned Unintentionally (37 CFR 1.137(a)) — SB/64; 37 CFR 1.137(a-b)

- Notice of Abandonment issued due to MPEP 711.03(c) untimely response

Substitute: ePetition (only between 1st OA and Notice of Allowance)

Attachments: petition fee — 37 CFR 1.17(m)

- reply required by the outstanding Office Action or Notice, if necessary
- statement averring that the belated reply was unintentional

PTO Response: Grant or deny

(2.) Respond to Final Office Action

Petition to Withdraw Finality of Office Action Under 37 CFR 1.181 — Apx D-55; MPEP 706.07

- alleges that Final OA was improper or inappropriate

PTO Response: decision on petition

Reading:

Requesting Withdrawal of the Finality of an Office Action
https://patentablydefined.com/2009/01/25/requesting-withdrawal-of-the-finality-of-an-office-action/

Evaluating When USPTO Actions Should Be Made Final
https://www.nutter.com/ip-law-bulletin/evaluating-when-uspto-actions-should-be-made-final

Improper Final Rejections and Suggestions for Avoiding Them
https://www.hg.org/legal-articles/improper-final-rejections-and-suggestions-for-avoiding-them-19062

Successful After Final Petitions Can Help Advance Prosecution
https://www.ipwatchdog.com/2021/01/19/successful-final-petitions-can-help-advance-prosecution-part-v/id=129066/

Amendment and Response Under 37 CFR 1.116	Apx D-56 37 CFR 1.116(a)
After Final OA amendment	MPEP 714.13

- submit ASAP after Final OA; request amendment be entered
- amendments, affidavits, and other evidence after final action and prior to appeal
- file Supplementary Declaration if necessary

Reading:

Can I Appeal a Final Office Action From the U.S. Patent and Trademark Office?
https://www.nolo.com/legal-encyclopedia/responding-final-office-action.html

After-Final Practice: Navigating Expanding USPTO Options for Compact Patent Prosecution
https://bannerwitcoff.com/wp-content/uploads/2017/07/After-Final-Practice.Navigating-Expanding-USPTO-Options-for-Compact-Patent-Prosecution.pdf

PTO Response to After Final Response:

Notice of Allowance issued—GO TO **Post-Allowance** at p. 94

or

Notification That Amendment Not Fully Responsive (Notice of Incomplete Response)	MPEP 714.02-03
- issued when amendment omits information required per Office Action	
Applicant Response: depends on nature of deficiency (see MPEP 714.03)	Apx D-24
or	
Notice of Noncompliant (Non-Responsive) Amendment	PTOL-324 37 CFR 1.121
- issued when amendment submitted fails to comply with 37 CFR 1.121	MPEP 714(II)(F)
Applicant Response: submit corrections per Notice	Apx D-13
or	
No Allowance	
Advisory Action	PTOL-303
Issued by PTO if amendment does not place application in condition for allowance, and RCE or appeal not filed	MPEP 706.07(f), 714.13(III)
Applicant Response (optional): file RCE if further amendments to claims desired	
- file appeal if no further claim amendments or other evidence (e.g., declarations, affidavits, etc.) entered	
- allow application to become abandoned	

Reading:

Expediting Patent Prosecution After an Advisory Action
https://www.mintz.com/insights-center/viewpoints/2231/2021-01-28-expediting-patent-prosecution-after-advisory-action

What Is an Advisory Action (AA)?
https://www.patenttrademarkblog.com/what-is-advisory-action/

Applicant-Initiated Actions	
Certification and Request for Consideration Under the After Final Consideration Pilot Program (2.0)	SB/434 37 CFR 1.116(a)
Include amendment of at least one independent claim; request interview with examiner if desired	MPEP 714.12-13
- use when it is believed that the amendment will result in allowance without extensive consideration/searching from examiner	
PTO Response: After Final Consideration Program Decision	

Reading:

Opportunity to Get Your Application Allowed After Final Rejection—Introducing the After Final Consideration Pilot
https://www.finnegan.com/en/insights/articles/opportunity-to-get-your-application-allowed-after-final.html

What Is the After Final Consideration Pilot (AFCP Request)?
https://www.patenttrademarkblog.com/after-final-consideration-pilot-afcp-request/

After Final Consideration Pilot Program 2.0—Still Going Strong
https://www.sternekessler.com/news-insights/publications/after-final-consideration-pilot-program-20-still-going-strong

Final Rejections: So You're Telling Me There's a Chance (AFCP 2.0)
https://krdglaw.com/so-youre-telling-me-theres-a-chance-afcp-2/

Request Interview With Examiner	PTOL-413A
- may be granted if examiner believes it will resolve issues before appeal	37 CFR 1.133 MPEP 713.09
- Proposed Interview Agenda	Apx D-53
Examiner Interview Summary Record	PTOL-413
Applicant Summary of Interview with Examiner	Apx D-54
- can be filed alone or included in response to OA	
Petition to Withdraw Application from Issue Before Issue Fee Payment	37 CFR 1.313 MPEP 1308
Attachments: petition fee	AIA/17p
- averment of legitimate reasons for 37 CFR 1.17(h) withdrawal	
PTO Response: Grant or Deny	
Supplemental IDS after Final OA, but before issue fee paid	Apx D-10
- report of prior art in addition to original IDS	
- newly discovered relevant art must be disclosed	
- unreported prior art from searches by foreign patent offices for corresponding 37 CFR 1.97(e)(1) applications must be declared via IDS	Apx D-39

- 37 CFR 1.97(e) statement and fee required	37 CFR 1.97 *et seq.*
- without statement, RCE required for IDS to be considered	
Attachments: Cover Letter	
- Copies of foreign patents and non-patent literature (NPL)(use SB/08(b)) (per 37 CFR 1.98(a)(2))	
- may require statement under CFR 1.97(e) and fee, depending on when filed (e.g., after Allowance)	
- may be filed online via e-IDS	MPEP 609.07
PTO response: Notice of Noncompliant IDS issued if irregularities exist	
- if requested, copy of SB/08, initialed	
- by examiner as considered (per MPEP 609)	
Request for Continued Examination (RCE) Transmittal	SB/30EFS 37 CFR 1.114
- continue prosecution of same or modified claims on same invention	35 USC 132(b) MPEP 706.07(h)
- simpler and cheaper than filing continuation	
- may be filed with Request to Suspend Action on the RCE for up to 3 months (specify on form; Box 2a)	37 CFR 1.103(c) MPEP 709
- processing fee required	AIA/17i 37 CFR 1.17(i)

Reading:

What Is a Request for Continued Examination (RCE) and When Do You Need It?
https://www.patenttrademarkblog.com/request-for-continued-examination-rce/

Request for Continued Examination: Everything You Need to Know
https://www.upcounsel.com/request-for-continued-examination

Request for Continued Examination vs. Appeal
https://www.lexisnexisip.com/knowledge-center/request-for-continued-examination-vs-appeal/

National Stage Applications in Flux as USPTO Shifts Course on Rules Governing RCE Practice
https://www.nixonpeabody.com/en/ideas/articles/2021/02/11/uspto-procedure-changes-for-national-stage-applications

Better to Use an RCE or a Continuation?
https://blog.oppedahl.com/?p=4998

Four Reasons to File an RCE with a Request to Suspend Processing
https://www.mintz.com/insights-center/viewpoints/2016-03-29-four-reasons-file-rce-request-suspend-processing

Amendment and Response to Final Office Action and Request for Continued Examination (RCE) Under 37 CFR 1.114 (RCE)	Apx D-57 37 CFR 1.114, 1.116(a) MPEP 706.07(h),
- RCE may be filed in conjunction with response to final OAMPEP 714.13	
- file before three-month period to respond to FOA expires	
- file amendment to place application in better condition for later appeal	
Attachments: Request for RCE Transmittal (SB/30EFS)	
- submit with Request for Prioritized Examination under 37 CFR 1.102(e)(2) for expedited processing	SB/424
Supplemental Amendment and Response to Final OA With RCE	Apx D-58 37 CFR 1.114, 1.116(a)
- file to correct or augment previous amendment if necessary	MPEP 706.07(h), MPEP 714.13
Amendment and Response to Final OA After Advisory Action	Apx D-59 37 CFR 1.116(a)
- file after Advisory Action	MPEP 714.13
- may be entered only for limited reasons,	
- filed typically to correct previous erroneous amendment	
Attachments: may be filed with RCE if desired	
Supplemental Amendment and Response to Final OA After Advisory Action	Apx D-60 37 CFR 1.116(a)
- correct previous amendment	MPEP 714.13

Continuing Applications

Reading:
Continuation, Continuation-in-Part, and Divisional Applications for Patent
https://www.cioncaip.com/PatentInformation/DivisionalPatent

A Brief Guide to Subsequent Patent Applications in the United States: Part I—The Foundation
https://www.ipwatchdog.com/2020/10/08/brief-guide-subsequent-patent-applications-united-states-part-foundation/id=125949/

Using Continuation Applications Strategically
https://www.cooleygo.com/using-continuation-applications-strategically/

Continuation Patent Applications
https://www.yospinlaw.com/2019/09/23/continuation-patent-application

Continuation Patent Applications: 10 Reasons You Should Consider Filing
https://www.nutter.com/ip-law-bulletin/continuation-patent-applications-10-reasons-you-should-file

Does Your Patent Need a CIP?
https://www.venjuris.com/2017/11/15/does-your-patent-need-a-cip/

Why File a Continuation?
https://founderslegal.com/why-file-a-continuation/

Why File a Continuation Before Your Patent Is Granted?
https://www.patenttrademarkblog.com/why-file-continuation-before-patent-granted/

Divisional Application — 35 USC 121; MPEP 201.06

- filed on non-elected matter in response to restriction while parent application still pending
  - filed like new application (Rule 53(b))
  - file PCT within one year of filing

Reading:
What Is a Utility Divisional Application?
https://www.patenttrademarkblog.com/divisional-application/

Divisional Patent Applications: What Are They and Why Should You Use Them?
https://www.jamesandwells.com/wp-content/uploads/divisional-patent-applications-what-are-they-and-why-should-you-use-them.pdf

Filing a Divisional Patent Application: Everything You Need to Know
https://www.upcounsel.com/filing-a-divisional-patent-application

What Is a Divisional Patent Application?
https://www.waltmire.com/2017/03/26/divisional-patent-application/

Continuation Application (DIV)	SB/05; AIA/15
- second application for the same or similar invention claimed in prior RPA application and filed before it becomes abandoned or granted; rewritten claims	37 CFR 1.53(d), 1.78 35 U.S.C. 120, 121, 365 (c), or 386 (c) MPEP 201.06, 201.07
- typically filed after Notice of Allowance (must file before original patent issues) to pursue another patent with different claims	
- can also be filed after Final Rejection (within three-month response period) to try existing or different claims (RCE normally filed in this case)	
- filed like RPA (35 USC 120; Rule 53(b))	
Continuation-in-Part Application (CIP)	
- repeats all or portion of parent application, and adds new matter (improvement)	SB/05; AIA/15 MPEP 201.08
- new claims given priority date of CIP, not parent application	
- file before parent application issues	
- file Supplemental Declaration if necessary	
- if issued, parent allowed to go abandoned	

Reading:
Beware of the CIP—Parent Applications Can Be Prior Art
https://www.perkinscoie.com/en/news-insights/beware-of-the-cip-parent-applications-can-be-prior-art.html

Pros and Cons of Filing a Continuation-in-Part Application
https://ocpatentlawyer.com/pros-cons-filing-continuation-in-part-application/

Never File a Continuation-in-Part
https://www.napp.org/index.php?option=com_dailyplanetblog&view=entry&category=uncategorized&id=5:title-never-file-a-continuation-in-part

Continuation Patent Application vs. Continuation-in-Part—Which Is Better and Why?
https://sagaciousresearch.com/blog/continuation-patent-application-vs-continuation-in-part/

Patent Continuation in Part: Everything You Need to Know
https://www.upcounsel.com/patent-continuation-in-part

Continuation in Part Patent Term
https://www.upcounsel.com/continuation-in-part-patent-term

Continuation-in-Part (CIP) Patent Applications—Benefits and Detriments
https://www.neustel.com/patents/patent-applications/continuation-part-cip-patent-applications-benefits-detriments/

Difference Between Continuation and Continuation-in-Part (CIP) Patent Application
https://www.copperpodip.com/post/filing-continuation-and-continuation-in-part-cip-patent-applications

Abandonment of Application	35 USC 133
- Application automatically becomes abandoned six months after expiration of the time period for response to Final Office Action	37 CFR 1.135 MPEP 711.04(a), 711.02
- application can be revived under certain circumstances (*see* Reviving Abandoned Applications at p. 71)	
PTO Response: notification of applicant re. abandonment status (Notice of Abandonment)	MPEP 711.04(c)
Independent Application	
- application on improvement to original invention	
- filed after original application abandoned or patent expired	
- does not retain filing date of original application	

Appeal Actions (request PTAB review examiner's rejections and issue allowance)

Pre-Appeal Brief Request for Review and Conference Pilot Program	AIA/33 37 CFR 41.31
- filed before formal Appeal Brief	MPEP 1204.02
Attachments: Notice of Appeal from the Examiner to the Patent Trial and Appeal Board	AIA/31 MPEP 1204.02
- must be accompanied by Pre-Appeal	
Brief setting forth arguments for review	Apx D-61
PTO Response: Notice of Panel Decision from	
Pre-Appeal Brief Review	
- if pre-appeal unsuccessful, appeal brief must be filed within 60 days	

Reading:

Pre-Appeal Brief Review Request—Is It Worth It?
https://www.fredlaw.com/news media/2018/07/16/1936/pre-appeal_brief_review_request_is_it_worth_it/

A Pre-Appeal Brief Conference Is a Winning Strategy, Even If It Probably Won't Lead to Allowance
https://www.ipwatchdog.com/2017/01/12/pre-appeal-brief-conference-winning-strategy/id=76897

55% of PTAB Decisions After a Pre-Appeal Conference Have This Outcome
https://bigpatentdata.com/2018/09/55-ptab-decisions-after-pre-appeal-conferences-have-this-outcome/

5 Strategies for Winning on Pre-Appeal at the USPTO
https://www.sternekessler.com/sites/default/files/2018-01/5_Strategies_For_Winning_On_Pre-Appeal_At_The_USPTO_0.pdf

Appealing the Rejection of a Patent Application
https://www.jdsupra.com/legalnews/appealing-the-rejection-of-a-patent-85748/

Patent Appeals: An Attractive Option
https://kolitchromano.com/patent-appeals-an-attractive-option/

The Appeals Process
https://www.cioncaip.com/BlogComments?BlogId=222

Notice of Appeal from the Decision of the Examiner to the Patent Trial and Appeal Board (PTAB)	AIA/31 37 CFR 41.31(a)(1) 35 USC 134
- applicant may appeal adverse final action of examiner to PTAB	MPEP 1204
- applicant may request oral hearing	MPEP 1209 37 CFR 41.47
Attachments: Amendment and Argument	37 CFR 41.33, 41.37
After Notice of Appeal	MPEP 1205
- Appeal Brief Under 37 CFR 41.37	Apx D-62
PTO Response: Examiner's answer to Appeal Brief	
Appellant's Response: Appellant's Reply Brief	
- Certification and Transmittal of Appeal Forwarding Fee	AIA/34
PTO Response: Decision on Appeal	

Reading:

Understanding the "Twice Rejected" Rule for Initiating an Appeal With the Patent Trial and Appeal Board
https://www.iptechblog.com/2018/03/understanding-the-twice-rejected-rule-for-initiating-an-appeal-with-the-patent-trial-and-appeal-board/

Considerations When Appealing a Patent Application at the USPTO
https://www.sternekessler.com/news-insights/publications/considerations-when-appealing-patent-application-uspto

Patent Appeal Brief Example: Everything You Need to Know
https://www.upcounsel.com/patent-appeal-brief-example

Patent Appeal: What Is the Cost and Process for Appealing a Final Rejection?
https://www.patenttrademarkblog.com/patent-appeal-cost-process-final-rejection/

Ex Parte *Appeals During Examination*
https://www.jdsupra.com/legalnews/ex-parte-appeals-during-examination-2957557/

Petition Fast-Track Appeals Pilot Program	SB/451
- expedited appeal process	

Reading:
USPTO Launches New Fast-Track Appeals Pilot Program
https://www.wlf.org/2020/09/10/publishing/uspto-launches-new-fast-track-appeals-pilot-program/

Petition Fast-Track for COVID-19-Related Appeals Pilot Program	SB/454
- prioritized appeal for rejected COVID-related claims	

USPTO Announces COVID Fast-Track Appeals Pilot Program
https://www.ipwatchdog.com/press/uspto-announces-covid-fast-track-appeals-pilot-program/

USPTO Establishes COVID-19 Prioritized Appeal Pilot Program
https://www.natlawreview.com/article/uspto-establishes-covid-19-prioritized-appeal-pilot-program

Notification of Noncompliant Appeal Brief (37 CFR 41.37)	37 CFR 41.37(c-d) MPEP 1205.03
- defective appeal brief	
Appellant's Response: submit corrected Appeal Brief	

Reading:
Checklist for Appeal Brief Filed Under 37 CFR 41.37
https://patentlyo.com/media/docs/2010/01/ex_parte_appeal_chklst_122009.pdf

c.) Post-Allowance

1.) Office-Initiated Actions

Notice of Allowance	35 USC 151
Receive "Notice of Allowability" if Amendment After Final is acceptable	37 CFR 1.311 MPEP 1302.03, 1303
- receive formal "Notice of Allowance" with form specifying Issue Fee Due (PTOL-85(B), Notice of Allowance and Fees Due)	

Reading:
What Is a Notice of Allowance Patent?
https://smallbusiness.chron.com/notice-allowance-patent-61515.html

What to Do When Your Patent Application Is Allowed
https://www.patenttrademarkblog.com/patent-application-allowed/

Notice of Allowance: Everything You Need to Know
https://www.upcounsel.com/notice-of-allowance

Best Practices for a Comprehensive Post-Allowance Review
https://www.maxval.com/blog/best-practices-for-a-comprehensive-post-allowance-review/

Notice of Allowance/Notice of Allowability
https://www.menteso.com/blog/notice-of-allowance/

D	**Design Post-Allowance** (term of patent—15 years from issue date)	35 USC 173
U	**Utility Post-Allowance** (term of patent—20 years from filing date)	35 USC 154(a)(2)
	Applicant Responses to Notice of Allowance	
	1. Submit Issue Fee form (PTOL-85(B) and payment	Apx D-63
	- can be submitted via EFS-Web)	
	- Issue Fee Transmittal Letter	
	2. Comments on examiner's reasons for allowance	Apx D-64
	- applicant may submit a response for the record on examiner's reasoning for advancing the application to grant status if such reasoning appears on Notice of Allowance	37 CFR 1.104(e) MPEP 1302.14
	- may be submitted alone or with issue fee	

Reading:
Examiner's Statement of Reasons for Allowance—Why We Care?
https://blog.oppedahl.com/?p=4042

Reasons for Allowance Do Matter
https://patentlyo.com/patent/2007/07/reasons-for-all.html

Reasons for Allowance Are Not Required by U.S. Patent Examiners
https://www.chandlerip.com/?p=1685

No Estoppel From Unrebutted Reasons for Allowance
https://ip-updates.blogspot.com/2005/07/no-estoppel-from-unrebutted-reasons.html

3. Amendment Under 37 CFR 1.312 After Notice of Allowance	Apx D-65
- amend spec/drawings if necessary	37 CFR 1.312
- file Supplemental Declaration if material changes to claims MPEP 1303.01, made (e.g., claims broadened)	
- entered only upon recommendation of primary examiner	MPEP 714.16,
- must be filed before or with issue fee	
4. Response to Examiner's Amendment After Allowance	Apx D-66
- Examiner has authority to enter amendment after allowance to correct informalities, with applicant's approval	MPEP 1302.04

Reading:

What Is a Patent Examiner's Amendment?
https://www.patenttrademarkblog.com/examiners-amendment/

5. Respond to Notice to File Corrected Application Papers	Apx D-67
- correction limited to informalities to spec and/or drawings only	37 CFR 1.312 MPEP 714.16,
- file Amendment After Allowance under 37 CFR 1.312	*see also* 1302.05

Reading:

Amending a Patent Application After Allowance
https://www.legalteamusa.net/amending-a-patent-application-after-allowance/

Amend Now or (Almost) Forever Hold Your Peace
https://www.bomcip.com/blog/amend-now-almost-forever-hold-peace/

Can You File an Amendment After Allowance?
https://www.patenttrademarkblog.com/amendment-filed-after-notice-of-allowance/

Filing an Amendment After Notice of Allowance
https://www.uspto.gov/sites/default/files/ebc/portal/efs/dct_amendment_after_noa_tutorial.pdf

***Ex Parte Quayle* Action (Office Action Summary)**	MPEP 714.14
Issued when all pending claims allowed, application is in condition for allowance, except for minor formal matters in disclosure, and prosecution on the merits is closed file amendment after allowance to correct informalities	
Applicant Response: Response to *Ex Parte Quayle* Action	
- Amendment Under 37 CFR 1.111	Apx D-68
- corrected disclosure papers as required	

Reading:

What Is an Ex Parte Quayle *Action?*
https://www.patenttrademarkblog.com/ex-parte-quayle-action/

Dispensing With the Formalities: Ex Parte Quayle *Actions*
https://www.industrialsip.com/2020/05/dispensing-with-formalities-ex-parte.html

What Is an Ex Parte Quayle *Action?*
https://galvanilegal.com/what-is-an-ex-parte-quayle-action/

What Is an Ex Parte Quayle Action?
https://ocpatentlawyer.com/what-is-an-ex-parte-quayle-office-action/

2.) Applicant-Initiated Actions

Petition for Deferment of Issuance of Patent	37 CFR 1.314
- file prior to Issue Fee payment	MPEP 1306.01
Attachments: petition fee	AIA/17p
- statement of legitimate reasons for deferment	37 CFR 1.17(h)
Petition for Revival of Application for Patent Abandoned Unintentionally (37 CFR 1.137(a)) (Petition to Accept Late Payment of Issue Fee)	SB/64 37 CFR 1.137(a-b) MPEP 711.03(c)
- Unintentional untimely payment	
Substitute: ePetition (to accept untimely payment of Issue Fee)	
Attachments: petition fee	37 CFR 1.17(m)
- statement averring the belated reply was unintentional	
PTO Response: Grant or deny	

Supplemental IDS after issue fee paid	37 CFR 1.97 *et seq.*
- file after payment of Issue Fee and up to the time thepatent application can be effectively withdrawn from issue under 37 CFR 1.313(c)	
- after payment of issue fee, IDS will not be considered	
Attachments: Cover Letter	
- Copies of foreign patents and non-patent literature (NPL) (use SB/08(b)) (per 37 CFR 1.98(a)(2))	
- may require statement under CFR 1.97(e) and fee, depending on when filed (e.g., after Allowance)	
- may be filed online via e-IDS	MPEP 609.07
PTO response: Notice of Noncompliant IDS issued if irregularities exist	
if requested, copy of SB/08, initialed by examiner as considered (per MPEP 609)	
Certification and Request for Consideration of an Information Disclosure Statement filed After Payment of the Issue Fee Under the QPIDS Program (Quick Path)	SB/09 37 CFR 1.97 MPEP 609.04(b)
- submittal of IDS after Issue Fee but before grant	
Attachments: IDS, timeliness statement Under 37 CFR 1.97(e)	
Substitute: available through the ePetition to Withdraw from Issue after Payment of Issue Fee	

Reading:

Quick Path Information Disclosure Statement (QPIDS) Pilot Program
http://www.staasandhalsey.com/files/ip/IP_News_2_New%20IDS.pdf

Improving QPIDS
https://blog.oppedahl.com/?p=1271

Petition to Correct Assignee After Payment of Issue Fee (37 CFR 3.81(b))	37 CFR 3.81(b) MPEP 1481.01
Attachments: Request for Certificate of Correction	
Substitute: ePetition	

Petition Under 37 CFR 1.313(c)(2) to Withdraw Application From Issue After Payment of Issue Fee	SB/140 37 CFR 1.313(c)(2) 37 CFR 1.313(c)(1, 3)
- to withdraw application from issue	MPEP 1308
- RCE must be pending	
Substitute: ePetition	
Attachments: petition fee	AIA/17p 37 CFR 1.17(h)
PTO Response: Decision on Petition	

Reading:

Patent Examiner, Will You Please Ignore My Recent Issue Fee Payment Until After You've Considered This New Reference?
https://www.uspatent.com/2010/06/patent-examiner-ignore-issue-fee-payment-youve-considered-reference/

Petition for Express Abandonment After Issue Fee Payment	37 CFR 1.138 MPEP 711.01(I)
Attachments: petition fee	AIA/17p
- statement of Express Abandonment	
- petition to withdraw from issue	37 CFR 1.313(c)
- petition fee	SB/17p 37 CFR 1.17(h)
File Continuation Prosecution Applications (CPA)	
- file Continuation-in-Part (CIP; MPEP 201.08)	
- repeats all or portion of parent application, and adds new matter (improvement)	
- new claims given priority date of CIP, not parent application	
- file Supplemental Declaration if necessary	
- if issued, parent allowed to go abandoned	
- may be filed with Request to Suspend Action on the CPA for up to 3 months	37 CFR 1.103(b) MPEP 709
- specify period of suspension	
- processing fee required	AIA/17i 37 CFR 1.17(i)

Continued Prosecution Application (CPA) Request for Design Applications Only: Continued Prosecution Application (CPA) Request Transmittal	SB/29
- may be filed with Request to Suspend Action on the CPA for up to 3 months (Box 11)	37 CFR 1.103(b) MPEP 709
- specify period of suspension	
- processing fee required	AIA/17i 37 CFR 1.17(i)
For Design Applications Only: Receipt for Facsimile Transmitted CPA	SB/29a
Petition to Accept Late Payment of Issue Fee	37 CFR 1.137(a)
- Unintentional late payment	
Continuation Application	MPEP 201.07
- second application for the same or similar invention claimed in prior RPA application and filed before it becomes abandoned or issues	
- typically filed after Notice of Allowance (must file before original patent issues) to pursue another patent with different claims	
- can also be filed after Final Rejection (within three-month response period) to try existing or different claims (RCE normally filed in this case)	
- filed like RPA (35 USC 120; Rule 53(b))	

Reading:

Continuation Patent Applications: 10 Reasons You Should Consider Filing
https://www.nutter.com/ip-law-bulletin/continuation-patent-applications-10-reasons-you-should-file

The What, Why, and How of Continuation Patent Applications
https://www.patentco.com/continuation-patent-applications/

Continuation Patent Applications
https://neustel.com/patents/patent-applications/continuation-patent-applications-reasons-file/

Using Continuation Applications Strategically
https://www.cooleygo.com/using-continuation-applications-strategically/

Why You Should Consider Filing a Patent Continuation
https://www.dbllawyers.com/filing-a-patent-continuation/

Patent Continuation: Everything You Need to Know 111
https://www.upcounsel.com/patent-continuation

Continuation Applications
http://valuablepatents.com/patent-prosecution/continuation-applications/

Continuation Patent Applications
https://www.yospinlaw.com/2019/09/23/continuation-patent-application

Building a Technological Moat: Strategic Use of Continuing Patent Applications
https://www.foley.com/en/insights/publications/2022/08/technological-moat-continuing-patent-applications

When to File a Continuation Application: When Is the Continuation Deadline?
https://www.patenttrademarkblog.com/when-continuation/

Patent Continuation Practice
https://www.maioranapc.com/blog/2017-01-Continuation-Patent-Practice.htm

Why File a Continuation?
https://founderslegal.com/why-file-a-continuation/

A Brief Guide to Subsequent Patent Applications in the United States: Part 1 - The Foundation
https://ipwatchdog.com/2020/10/08/brief-guide-subsequent-patent-applications-united-states-part-foundation/id=125949/

A Guide to Continuation Patent Applications
https://alloypatentlaw.com/alloy-patent-law-ip-legal-blog/a-guide-to-continuation-patent-applications/

What Is a Continuation Patent Application?
https://quisenberrylaw.com/ip-discovery-blog/what-is-a-continuation-patent-application

What Is a "Continuation" Patent Application?
https://blog.shp.law/index.php/2021/09/14/what-is-a-continuation-patent-application/

Should You File a Continuation Patent Application at the US Patent and Trademark Office (USPTO) Prior to Your Patent Issuing?
https://menloparkpatents.com/2022/03/15/should-you-file-a-continuation-patent-application-at-the-us-patent-and-trademark-office-uspto-prior-to-your-patent-issuing/

Petition Requesting Reconsideration of Patent Term Adjustment Before Issuance of the Patent	37 CFR 1.705(c) MPEP Ch. 2700
Attachments: petition fee	37 CFR 1.18
- demonstration that applicant was unable to reply to the rejection, objection, argument, or other request within three months of the date of mailing of the Office communication notifying the applicant of the rejection, objection, argument, or other request	
Request for Recalculation of Patent Term Adjustment in View of Safe Harbor Statement Under 37 CFR 1.704(d)	SB/133 & 134 37 CFR 1.704(d) MPEP 2732
- submitting an IDS alone during examination can be considered delay of prosecution by the PTO, causing the patent term to be adjusted downward	
- applicant can request recalculation of patent term under certain conditions	

Reading:

Patent Prosecution Tool Kit: Information Disclosure: Avoiding Common Pitfalls
https://www.jdsupra.com/legalnews/patent-prosecution-tool-kit-information-76786/

Update & Reminder: Patent Term Adjustment Related to IDS Safe Harbor
https://www.mondaq.com/unitedstates/patent/823990/update-reminder-patent-term-adjustment-related-to-ids-safe-harbor

VI. Post-Grant (Post-Issue)

Following grant, activities shift from application prosecution to maintaining the issued patent in force. These actions include correcting any residual errors in the Patent Deed, periodic payment of maintenance fees, and also preserving the validity of the patent. Issued patents are presumed valid until determined otherwise; however, the validity of a patent can be challenged by any interested party, including the patentee. Upon request, a patent can be subjected to further examination, resulting in either an invalidated patent or a patent further strengthened.

A. Routine Office Communications

Issue Notification	
- mailed approximately three weeks prior to issue	
Patent Deed (Letters Patent)	MPEP 1309 37 CFR 1.315
- official document issued by PTO to patentee certifying a patent application as an issued patent	
Applicant Response: review Patent Deed for errors and request Certificate of Correction if necessary	

Note: Starting 18 April 2023, statutory patent deeds will issue in electronic format ("eGrant") on Patent Center. Traditional paper patent deeds will be available upon request for a fee. *See* https://www.uspto.gov/patents/apply/patent-center/egrants

B. Patentee-Initiated Actions

Request for Certificate of Correction	Apx D-69
Correction of minor clerical errors in issued letters patent	SB/44 (PTO-1050) 37 CFR 1.322; 1.323
Office Error	37 CFR 1.322 35 USC 254 MPEP 1480
Applicant Error	37 CFR 1.323 35 USC 255 MPEP 1481
Attachments: Certificate of Correction (SB/44)	
PTO Response: Certificate of Correction	37 CFR 1.322/1.323

Reading:

Post-Issuance Patent Office Modification of U.S. Patents
https://www.tms.org/pubs/journals/JOM/matters/matters-9107.html

Certificates of Correction
https://patentlyo.com/patent/2016/06/certificates-of-correction-2.html

Certificate of Correction
https://postgrantproceedings.com/patent_modification/certificate-of-correction/#

Expediting the Issuance of a Certificate of Correction for a United States Patent
https://www.neifeld.com/pubs/exped_cert_corr_030630.htm

Make Proofreading Patents a Priority
https://www.photonics.com/Articles/Make_proofreading_patents_a_priority/a35537

Oh No, I Just Found A Mistake in My Issued Patent! How You Can Fix It.
https://garcia-zamor.com/2014/09/26/oh-no-i-just-found-a-mistake-in-my-issued-patent-how-you-can-fix-it/

Statement Under 37 CFR 3.73(c)	
Establishes assignee's ownership rights in patent application	AIA/96 37 CFR 3.73(c)
- used by legal/obligatory assignee to establish ownership of invention/application	MPEP 325
Attachments: executed assignment if not yet recorded	
Petition Under 37 CFR 1.324(a) for Correction of Inventorship	Apx D-70 37 CFR 1.324(a), 1.48(h)
- erroneous inventorship on issued patent	35 USC 256
- draft petition as under 37 CFR 1.48	MPEP 1481.02
Attachments: petition fee Certificate of Correction (SB/44); statements from all relevant parties agreeing to the change in inventorship per 37 CFR 1.324(b), and any supporting documents	SB/17i
PTO Response: issues Certificate of Correction if approved	

Reading:

Correcting Inventorship in Issued Patents
https://www.invention-protection.com/correcting-inventorship-in-issued-patents/

Fixing Inventorship Problems in U.S. Patent Applications and U.S. Patents
https://www.ratnerprestia.com/2014/02/16/fixing-inventorship-problems-in-u-s-patent-applications-and-u-s-patents/

Oops, You've Got the Wrong Guy . . . Correcting Inventorship in the USPTO
https://thelimitedmonopoly.com/wp-content/uploads/2015/05/201502 Limited-Monopoly-CorrectingInventorship.pdf

Payment of Maintenance Fees (utility only)	
- Maintenance Fee Transmittal Form	SB/45; mail/fax only 37 CFR 1.362 MPEP Chap. 2500

Payment Schedule:

a. yr. 3.0–3.5 (or 3.5–4.0 with late charge)
b. yr. 7.0–7.5 (or 7.5–8.0 with late charge)
c. yr. 11.0–11.5 (or 11.5–12.0 with late charge)

- nonpayment results in premature expiration of patent

Reading:

Patent Maintenance Fees: Everything You Need to Know
https://www.upcounsel.com/patent-maintenance-fees

Everything You Need to Know About Patent Maintenance Fees
https://www.jdsupra.com/legalnews/everything-you-need-to-know-about-22627/

A Guide to Paying Patent Maintenance Fees
https://www.traskbritt.com/a-guide-to-paying-patent-maintenance-fees/

Patent Maintenance Fees: Everything You Need to Know
https://boldip.com/patent-maintenance-fees/

Reducing Costs: Patent Maintenance Fees
https://www.hdp.com/blog/2020/06/02/reducing-costs-patent-maintenance-fees/

What Occurs When You Don't Pay a Patent Maintenance Fee?
https://www.globalpatentsolutions.com/blog/2020/01/what-occurs-when-you-dont-pay-a-patent-maintenance-fee/

Maintenance Fee Address Change	SB/47-EFS
- submit "Fee Address Indication Form" to establish address for maintenance fee correspondence	37 CFR 1.363 MPEP 2540
Petition to Accept Unintentionally Delayed Payment of Maintenance Fee in Expired Patent (37 CFR 1.378(b))	SB/66 37 CFR 1.378(b) MPEP 2590

Attachments: per 37 CFR 1.378(b)

Substitute: ePetition

PTO Response: Decision on petition

Reading:
Reviving a Patent That Was Abandoned for Failure to Pay Maintenance Fee
https://www.legalteamusa.net/reviving-a-patent-that-was-abandoned-for-failure-to-pay-maintenance-fees/

USPTO Tightens Unintentional Delay Standards for Certain Petitions to Revive, Acceptances of Delayed Maintenance Fee Payments, and Delayed Priority or Benefit Claims
https://www.jdsupra.com/legalnews/uspto-tightens-unintentional-delay-60286/

USPTO Issues Clarification Regarding Petitions Based on Unintentional Delay
https://www.patentdocs.org/2020/03/uspto-issues-clarification-regarding-petitions-based-on-unintentional-delay.html

Forgot to Pay the Patent Maintenance Fee: Options to Revive a Patent
https://www.waltmire.com/2017/04/18/forgot-pay-patent-maintenance-fee-revive/

Petition for Acceptance of Maintenance Fee Payments Based on a Refusal to Accept and Record Maintenance Fee Payment Filed Prior to Expiration of the Patent	37 CFR 1.377(a)
- file within two months of disputed action	
Attachments: petition fee	AIA/17p 37 CFR 1.17(g)

C. Post-Grant Prosecution

The patentability of one or more claims of an issued patent can be challenged by an interested party. These proceedings are executed by the PTO and are often implemented in conjunction with infringement actions as an alternative to civil litigation.

Reading:
Challenging Patents Through Post-Grant Proceedings: What Are Your Options?
https://www.fr.com/challenging-patents-through-post-grant-proceedings-what-are-your-options/#:~:text=Post-grant%20proceedings%20are%20often%20cheaper%2C%20faster

Post-Grant Review: Everything You Need To Know
https://www.upcounsel.com/post-grant-review

Patent Challenges: Ex-Parte *Reexamination and Inter-Partes Review*
https://www.keyip.law/key-ip-primers/patent-challenges-ex-parte-reexamination-inter-partes-review/

Chart Summarizing Different Post Grant Proceedings
https://postgrantproceedings.com/aia-uspto-links/pgr-chart/#

Challenging Patents Through Post-Grant Proceedings: What Are Your Options?
https://www.jdsupra.com/legalnews/challenging-patents-through-post-grant-91213/

Request *Ex-Parte* Reexamination	SB/57
- can be filed by anyone upon substantial new question of patentability, based on prior art	37 CFR 1.501 et seq. 35 USC 302
- proceeding involves only patentee and PTO	MPEP 2209 et seq.
Attachments: per 37 CFR 1.510(b)	
PTO Response: determination of request	

Reading:

Ex Parte *Reexamination*
https://fishpostgrant.com/ex-parte-reexamination/

Ex Parte *Reexamination*
https://postgrantproceedings.com/patent_modification/ex-parte-reexamination/#

Ex Parte *Re-Exams: Don't You Forget About Me*
https://www.finnegan.com/en/insights/articles/ex-parte-re-exams-dont-you-forget-about-me.html

What Is a Patent Reexamination?
https://www.patenttrademarkblog.com/patent-reexamination/

Ex Parte *Reexamination*
https://patentassociate.com/2019/10/02/ex-parte-reexamination/

Ex Parte *Reexamination: Everything You Need to Know*
https://www.upcounsel.com/ex-parte-reexamination

Request for Supplemental Examination	SB/59
- asks PTO to consider issues relevant to the patent	37 CFR 1.601 *et seq.*
- file PCT within one year of filing	35 USC 257(a) MPEP Chap. 2800

Reading:

What Is Supplemental Examination?
https://www.patenttrademarkblog.com/what-is-supplemental-examination/

AIA Supplemental Examination Nuts and Bolts: Get It in Your Toolbox and Don't Leave Home Without It
https://www.finnegan.com/en/insights/blogs/at-the-ptab-blog/aia-supplemental-examination-nuts-and-bolts-get-it-in-your-toolbox-and-dont-leave-home-without-it.html

Supplemental Examination Update
https://www.natlawreview.com/article/supplemental-examination-update

Graphical Snapshot of Supplemental Examination
https://www.sternekessler.com/news-insights/publications/graphical-snapshot-supplemental-examination

Supplemental Examination: Potential Benefits vs. Guaranteed Risks
https://www.jdsupra.com/legalnews/supplemental-examination-potential-46289/

Reissue Application

- correct defects in issued patent rendering it wholly or partly unenforceable	AIA/50; AIA/53 37 CFR 1.171
- revises (broaden/narrow) claims of original patent or corrects significant errors in spec; for valid reason; replaces original patent grant	35 USC 251-52 MPEP 201.05 Chap. 1400
- replaces unexpired patent that is defective as result of error made without deceptive intent	
- reissue application to broaden claims must be filed within two years of patent issue date	
Attachments: Reissue Application: Consent of Assignee; Statement of Non-Assignment	AIA/53
- Reissue Application Fee Transmittal	SB/56

Reading:

Broadening Your Issued Patent—A Chance to Fix the Past
https://www.wnlaw.com/blog/broadening-issued-patent-chance-fix-past/

Patent Reissue—Uses and Strategy (Part III)
https://bciptf.org/2015/05/patent-reissue-uses-and-strategy-part-iii/

Reissue Applications
https://postgrantproceedings.com/patent_modification/reissue-applications/#

Reissue Overview
https://www.aipla.org/docs/default-source/committee-documents/bcp-files/lpinchus_ro.pdf?sfvrsn=e4def362_2

Understanding Reissued Patents
https://www.copperpodip.com/post/understanding-reissued-patents

Patent Mistakes Happen. A Patent Reissue Application Can Fix Them.
https://www.patentco.com/patent-mistakes-happen-a-patent-reissue-application-can-fix-them/

A Powerful Weapon for Hardening a Patent Portfolio
https://news.bloomberglaw.com/ip-law/a-powerful-weapon-for-hardening-a-patent-portfolio

What Is a Reissue Patent?
https://www.attorneyatlaw.com/definition/reissue-patent

Reissue
https://www.jdsupra.com/legalnews/reissue-1630252/

'Recapture' Pitfalls to Avoid During Patent Reissues
https://www.sternekessler.com/news-insights/publications/recapture-pitfalls-avoid-during-patentreissues

Correcting Error in Issued Patents - Reissue Request
https://www.lventre.com/reissue/

Correcting an Incorrect or Ineffective Patent
https://www.sandbergphoenix.com/perspectives/blogs/intellectual-property-blog/correcting-an-incorrect-or-ineffective-patent/

6 Charts on Reissue Applications
https://bigpatentdata.com/2018/08/6-charts-on-reissue-applications/

Broadening Your Issued Patent - A Chance to Fix the Past
https://www.wnlaw.com/blog/broadening-issued-patent-chance-fix-past/

Post-Grant Review (PGR)	35 USC 321-329
- administrative review of patent validity conducted by PTAB can be commenced within nine months of issue	37 CFR 42.200 et seq. MPEP 2686.05
- can be petitioned by anyone other than the patentee	

Reading:

Which Invalidity Avenue to Take: Inter Partes Review vs. Post-Grant Review
https://www.ipwatchdog.com/2018/07/31/which-invalidity-avenue-ipr-verses-post-grant-review/id=99460/

Post-Grant Review
https://www.perkinscoie.com/en/practices/intellectual-property-law/post-grant-proceedings/post-grant-review.html

What Is a Post Grant Review (PGR)?, IPR vs. PGR
https://www.legaladvantage.net/blog/what-is-a-post-grant-review-pgr-ipr-pgr/

Post Grant Review: Everything You Need to Know
https://www.upcounsel.com/post-grant-review

Post-Grant Review (PGR)
https://www.morganlewis.com/pubs/2021/04/post-grant-review-pgr-2020

***Inter Partes* Review (IPR)**	35 USC 311-319
- administrative review of patent validity conducted by PTAB can be commenced only after nine months of issue	37 CFR 1.902 *et seq.* 42.100 *et seq.* MPEP 2686.05
- can be petitioned by anyone other than the patentee	

Reading:

You Don't Need to Build an IPR Off-Ramp—It Already Exists
https://www.patentprogress.org/2017/12/04/ipr-offramps-already-exist/

Inter Partes Review (IPR)
https://maierandmaier.com/practice-areas/post-grant-practice/inter-partes-review-ipr/

Inter Partes Review: Everything You Need to Know
https://www.upcounsel.com/inter-partes-review

IPR>>IRL—A Brief Guide to the Essentials of Inter Partes Reviews in Real Life. Post-Grant Patent Law Practice
https://www.jdsupra.com/legalnews/ipr-irl-a-brief-guide-to-the-essentials-7286213/

To Do List: Filing an IPR
https://www.finnegan.com/en/at-the-ptab-blog/to-do-list-filing-an-ipr.html

D. Other Post-Grant Proceedings

Patent Term Extension Proceedings (PTE)	35 USC 156;
- filing a terminal disclaimer may become necessary or desirable during patent term extension proceedings	37 CFR 1.710 et seq.; MPEP 804.05, 2750 et seq.
- enables the owners of patents on human drug products, medical devices, food additives, or color additives, and animal drug products to obtain patent term extension for delays at the regulatory agency	

Reading:

Introduction to Patent Term Extensions (PTE)
https://www.fr.com/intro-patent-term-extension/#:~:text=The%20patent%20owner%20or%20its%20agent%2C%20their%20attorneys,%C2%A7156%20%28a%29%20and%2037%20C.F.R.

Pharmaceutical Patent Term Extension: An Overview
https://www.alacrita.com/whitepapers/pharmaceutical-patent-term-extension-an-overview

Patent Term Extension: Learn How Your Medical Device Inventions Can Benefit
https://arapackelaw.com/patents/medical-device/patent-term-extension-learn-how-your-medical-device-inventions-can-benefit/

Terminal Disclaimer in a Patent	35 USC 253
- patentee/owner disclaims any terminal part of the existing term of one or more claims of granted patent to preclude double patenting with later-filed application	37 CFR 1.321(a) MPEP 1490
Terminal Disclaimer in a Patent or Proceeding in View of an Application	SB/25a
Terminal Disclaimer in a Patent or Proceeding in View of Another Patent	SB/26a

Patent Term Adjustment Proceedings (PTA)	37 CFR 1.705(b)
PTO adds additional time to patent term due to certain delays of PTO in issuing patent	35 USC 154(b), 156 MPEP 2730 et seq.
Patentee Response: petition for term adjustment	Apx D-71
- if patentee unsatisfied with the PTA, petition for reconsideration no later than two months from the date the patent was issued	
- include petition fee	37 CFR 1.18(e)
PTO Response to Petition: Granted or Denied	

Reading:

Patent Term Adjustment: Everything You Need to Know
https://www.upcounsel.com/patent-term-adjustment

Patent Term Adjustment
https://www.sternekessler.com/news-insights/publications/patent-term-adjustment

Petition Requesting Reconsideration of Patent Term Adjustment After Issuance of Patent	37 CFR 1.705(b) MPEP 2734
- response when patentee disagrees with PTA	
Attachments: petition fee	37 CFR 1.18
- statement of facts per 37 CFR 1.705(b)	
PTO Response: Grant or Deny	

PART TWO

Foreign Application Practice

"A country without a patent office and good patent laws was just a crab, and couldn't travel any way but sideways or backwards."

—Mark Twain, A Connecticut Yankee in King Arthur's Court

I. Introduction: Patent World

International patent application can be a daunting undertaking. Several prominent multilateral IP accords have, however, simplified the process somewhat. Under the Paris Convention (the "Convention") an initial application in one of the member nations establishes a priority date for any later national filings in other Convention members. The European Patent Convention (EPC) makes it potentially possible to obtain regional patent protection in all 39 current contracting nations with a single application and prosecution phase, although a granted patent must still be "validated" by each designated country.

The Patent Cooperation Treaty (PCT) application acts, in some respects, like an international provisional application, providing a priority date for subsequent applications in member countries, but never maturing into patent itself. Finally, under the Hague Agreement, industrial design registration (comparable to U.S. design patent) can be secured simultaneously in all participating nations with a single application.

Each sovereign nation ultimately has the right to recognize what it holds patentable within its borders. Thus, under any of the aforementioned agreements, an application deposited with a regional or centralized patent office must eventually pass muster with each national IP authority elected by the applicant.

There is an effort in Europe, however, to establish a true multinational patent. When enacted, the so-called Unitary Patent will make it possible to submit a single application in a designated central office, which would extend patent rights to all participating EU-member states without further examination at the national level. Thus far, 17 EU nations have ratified the Unitary Patent, which was launched June 1, 2023.

Practitioners should be mindful that foreign patenting rules often differ from those in the United States. Notably, any public disclosure before filing anywhere can act as a bar to patent in many foreign jurisdictions. Foreign patent offices can also vary in what they consider patentable subject matter.

Reading:

The Dawn of the Unitary Patent Era in Europe
https://www.crowell.com/NewsEvents/AlertsNewsletters/all/The-Dawn-of-the-Unitary-Patent-Era-in-Europe

What Is Unitary Patent?
https://www.fillun.com/what-is-unitary-patent#:~:text=Unitary%20Patent%20is%20a%20single%20European%20patent%20with,of%20unitary%20patents%20are%20only%20relevant%20after%20grant.%29

Patent Foreign Filing Guide
https://www.matterlightip.com/patent-foreign-filing/

International Patent Protection
https://www.justia.com/intellectual-property/patents/international-patent-protection/

Foreign Patent Filing
https://smithhopen.com/services/patents-protect-inventions/foreign-patent-filing/

II. Sources of International Patent Law and Regulations

Applying for and securing patent protection in multiple foreign jurisdictions is an intricate process, requiring the practitioner to engage a complex of diverse laws and rules of procedure. Many jurisdictions, typically non-English speaking, require a U.S.-domiciled applicant to liaise with an in-country legal representative who is competent in the local patent practice. Nevertheless, U.S. practitioners may wish to consult the following resources for encoded statutes and rules for the international IP organizations addressed in this manual.

A. Patent Cooperation Treaty

(PCT) Patent Cooperation Treaty
Regulations under the Patent Cooperation Treaty Administrative
Instructions under the Patent Cooperation Treaty
Guidelines for Search and Examination at the EPO as PCT Authority
PCT Receiving Office Guidelines

B. European Patent Convention (EPC)

European Patent Convention, 17th ed., November 2020
Implementing Regulations to the Grant of European Patents, last amended 15 Dec. 2020
Guidelines for Examination in the European Patent Office, March 2022 ed.
European Patent Guide—How to get a European Patent, 21st ed.; updated to Oct. 2021
Guidelines for Search and Examination at the EPO as PCT Authority

C. Paris Convention

Paris Convention for the Protection of Industrial Property (as amended Sept. 1979)

D. The Hague Agreement

Hague Agreement Concerning the International Registration of Industrial Designs Acts of the Agreement Currently in Force:
- Geneva Act (1999)
- Hague Act (1960)

Common Regulations under the 1999 Act and the 1960 Act of the Hague Agreement (as in force on February 1, 2021)
Administrative Instructions for the Application of the Hague Agreement (as in force on January 1, 2019)

III. Principal International IP Accords

The most frequently used multinational IP organizations for foreign filing by U.S. applicants are the Paris Convention, PCT, EPC, and the Hague Agreement.

There are a number of other patent agreements (e.g., Trade-Related Aspects of Intellectual Property Rights (TRIPS), African Intellectual Property Organization (OAPI), Eurasian Patent Organization (EAPO)), but they are relatively little-used, at least by U.S. filers, and will not be addressed in this manual.

A. Patent Cooperation Treaty (PCT) [35 USC Part IV; 37 CFR 1.401 *et seq.*; MPEP Appendix T (treaty text); Ch. 1800]

The Patent Cooperation Treaty (PTC) is an international IP organization administered by WIPO, and currently includes 157 member nations, encompassing most industrial countries. Filing an "International Application" under the PTC is comparable to filing a provisional application simultaneously in all elected PCT jurisdictions. Like a U.S. provisional application, the PCT establishes a priority filing date for subsequent national applications in selected contracting members, although it does not, itself, proceed to patent grant.

Applicants may file a PCT application through EFS-Web, or the WIPO website (via ePCT).

Notable Provisions

- an original U.S. application establishes priority for a PTC application filed before the one-year anniversary of the U.S. filing
- single formalities review by International Bureau (IB) after filing
- U.S. resident/national applicant can choose to file PCT in either USPTO or IB as Receiving Office (RO); but may select among several International Search Authorities (ISA) to conduct prior art search and written opinion on patentability (WO); some ISAs may be more amenable to specific subject matter, or offer lower fees, higher quality or faster search, etc.
- allows applicants to shop for most desirable RO/ISA
- right to file PCT in a certain RO determined by residence/nationality of at least one applicant; competent ISA determined by selected RO
- an ISA of applicant's choosing conducts prior art search and produces rapid patentability opinion
- applicant has option of requesting preliminary examination or a formal examination by ISA before national applications must be prosecuted

- permits later application (can be deferred for additional 18 months after filing PCT, providing for up to a 30-month (31 months in certain countries) grace period before filing nonprovisional national applications with priority in elected nations during the "National Stage" under control of national or regional IP offices. This allows applicant to defer most expenses of foreign filing. A PCT application also allows one to defer certain foreign filing decisions, which often results in decision-making that is more informed.

Reading:
PCT Process: Everything You Need to Know
https://www.upcounsel.com/pct-process

Which RO and ISA Should You Select When Filing a PCT Application?
https://www.neifeld.com/pubs/WhichROAndISAShouldYouSelectWhenFilingPCT.pdf

Patent Cooperation Treaty: Evaluating the Benefits and Risks, Obtaining International Patent Protection
http://media.straffordpub.com/products/patent-cooperation-treaty-evaluating-the-benefits-and-risks-obtaining-international-patent-protection-2017-09-14/presentation.pdf

When to Use the Patent Cooperation Treaty—And Why It's So Popular
https://www.ipwatchdog.com/2021/02/14/use-pct-popular/id=129994/

PCT Design Patent: Everything You Need To Know
https://www.upcounsel.com/pct-design-patent

Which Countries Do Not Belong to the International Patent System?
https://inventa.com/en/news/article/491/which-countries-do-not-belong-to-the-international-patent-system

What Is a PCT Application (Patent Cooperation Treaty)?
https://ocpatentlawyer.com/what-is-a-patent-cooperation-treaty-pct-application-2/

What Is a PCT Application?
https://www.patenttrademarkblog.com/international-pct-application/

B. European Patent Convention (EPC) [17th ed. Nov. 2020, text available on EPO website]

The European Patent Office (EPO) administers the European Patent Convention (EPC), a regional patent agreement for obtaining patents through a single application that can be extended ("nationalized") and enforced in up to 44 separate European jurisdictions, comprising all 27 current members of the European Union. American applicants may file an EPC application online via the EPO website, or file on paper in the EPO in Munich.

Notable Provisions

- one-year grace period to apply in EPO after filing initial U.S. application
- application subjected to single substantive examination and prosecution in EPO
- EPO issues "Europatent" enforceable in most European nations, pending "validation" in each elected jurisdiction; Note: Unitary Patent will eliminate national validation in separate jurisdictions; pre-grant procedures will remain unchanged
- patent subjected to public opposition period after grant

Reading:
European Patent: Protection in 44 Countries With a Single Application
https://abg-ip.com/european-patent-application-system/

European Patent Cost: Everything You Need to Know
https://www.upcounsel.com/european-patent-cost

C. Paris Convention for the Protection of Industrial Property ("The Convention") [Convention text can be found at MPEP Appendix P]

The Paris Convention is an international treaty administered by the World Intellectual Property Organization (WIPO), headquartered in Geneva, Switzerland. It currently encompasses 177 member states, including the majority of industrial nations. An original application in any Convention member establishes a priority date with a one-year grace period for future filings. However, subsequent applications must be filed and prosecuted in each desired contracting nation according to its respective national patent regulations.

Notable Provisions

National treatment [Articles 2, 3]: Each member country must extend the same protections it gives its own nationals for covered IP to nationals of other member countries.

Right of priority [Article 4]: An applicant for patent, industrial design (design patent in the US) or utility model (where protected) protection in one member country may use that application, within a certain grace period, as the basis for filing successive applications for that IP in other member jurisdictions (including EPO and PCT). Any following application is considered filed on the same date as the first application if filed within:

- six months of the earlier application, for industrial designs; or
- 12 months of the earlier application, for patents and utility models.
- subsequent applications must be accompanied by a certified copy of the original filing, along with a translation into the language of the foreign country.

Common rules: The Convention sets forth a few common rules that all Contracting States must follow. The most significant are:

- patents granted in different Contracting States for the same invention are independent of each other: the granting of a patent in one Contracting State does not obligate other Contracting States to grant a patent; a patent cannot be refused, annulled, or terminated in any Contracting State on the ground that it has been refused or annulled or has terminated in any other Contracting State
- the inventor has the right to be named as such in the patent.
- the grant of a patent may not be refused, and a patent may not be invalidated, on the ground that the sale of the patented product, or of a product obtained by means of the patented process, is subject to restrictions or limitations resulting from the domestic law.

Reading:
The Paris Convention
https://www.iatp.org/sites/default/files/THE_PARIS_CONVENTION.htm

Paris Convention Filing
https://www.globalpatentfiling.com/services/paris-convention-filings

Validly Claiming Priority Rights Under the Paris Convention
https://www.schleeip.com/patents-2/priority-rights-paris-convention/

Ten Facts You Didn't Know About the Paris Convention
https://www.morningtrans.com/ten-facts-you-didnt-know-about-the-paris-convention/

D. Hague Agreement (Concerning the Int'l Registration of Industrial Designs) [35 USC Part V; 37 CFR 1.1001 *et seq.*; MPEP Ch. 2900]

The Hague Agreement became effective in the United States in May 2015. With a single international application, the Hague Agreement permits simultaneous registration of up to 100 industrial designs (equivalent to a U.S. design patent) in 75 contracting parties comprising 92 countries. The Agreement is administered by WIPO, but U.S. applicants may apply via EFS-Web, or the WIPO website using eHague. The international application may claim the priority of an earlier national or regional filing made in any state that is party to the Paris Convention, provided that you file within six months of the date of filing of the original application.

Notable Provisions

- permits application for and managing industrial designs in multiple jurisdictions with a single application in the USPTO
- applicants can claim priority to or from an international design patent application
- it is possible to include up to 100 different designs in one application (provided they all belong to one class in the International (Locarno) Classification of Industry Designs), and you are also free to designate any number of Contracting countries or international organizations
- able to choose the level of generality at which patent or design is classified. There are limits however: if the level is too general, your design may not be considered valid, and if it is too specific, it may need to be protected against designs that are similar.
- level of protection on design is dependent on the interpretation of the registration, and specifically on the images included
- although the Hague Agreement permits up to 100 designs per application, those designating the U.S. must still be directed to a single invention. The USPTO may issue a restriction requirement if "distinct inventions" are submitted, requiring divisional applications to protect those inventions.
- with favorable examination, designs are registered in all elected nations, but a country may file a "refusal" with WIPO

- increased filing efficiencies and cost savings for applicants, who may file through the USPTO or directly with the International Bureau of the World Intellectual Property Organization (WIPO). However, only persons who are nationals of the U.S. or who have a domicile, a habitual residence, or a real and effective industrial or commercial establishment in the territory of the U.S. may file international design applications through the USPTO as the direct office of filing the design patent application must be judged through existing patent laws, unless otherwise noted by the Hague Design Treaty
- extends the design patent terms to 15 years
- provisional rights are expanded to include the ability to obtain royalties that occur before the patent is issued
- renewal or maintenance fees paid only to central administration, extendable in five-year increments up to maximum 15 years

Reading:
US Design Patents and the Hague Agreement Concerning Industrial Designs
https://bannerwitcoff.com/wp-content/uploads/2016/05/Practical-Law.US-Design-Patents-and-the-Hague-Agreement-Concerning-Industrial-Designs.pdf

What Is the Hague Convention for Design Patents?
http://www.legendslaw.com/what-is-the-hague-convention-for-design-patents/

The U.S. Enters the International Design Frontier: The Ins and Outs of the Hague Agreement on Industrial Design
https://www.mcciplaw.com/the-ins-and-outs-of-the-hague-agreement-on-industrial-design/

Hague Agreement on Industrial Designs
https://www.upcounsel.com/hague-agreement-on-industrial-designs

Industrial Designs and the Hague Agreement: An Introduction
https://www.wipo.int/edocs/pubdocs/en/designs/429/wipo_pub_429.pdf

What You Need to Know About the Hague Agreement: Benefits and Potential Pitfalls
https://www.hrfmtoday.com/2015/06/what-you-need-to-know-about-the-hague-agreement-benefi ts-and-potential-pitfalls.html

IV. Pre-Application Activities and Considerations

Prior to filing overseas, applicants should carefully weigh the advantages and disadvantages of foreign patenting, especially anticipated revenue from sales and licensing, as opposed to cost of patenting. Prospective applicants should also be aware that, although an invention may be nominally patentable in the United States, the same may not hold true in many foreign jurisdictions. Inclusion in certain classes of subject matter, as well as public disclosure before filing in many foreign countries, can render an invention ineligible for patent.

A. Pros/Cons of Foreign Application

Extending the monopoly on an invention or product to overseas markets can be lucrative; however, foreign filing is expensive for U.S. applicants. Application, translation, and maintenance fees can be substantial, and U.S. applicants may be required to engage local legal counsel or agents to prosecute their applications in some foreign jurisdictions, as required by law. Applicants should consider costs and risks of application, such as potential market, product distribution, and sales in foreign countries, as well as expenditures to maintain and enforce patents abroad, in order to determine whether the expense of patenting is economically worthwhile. Applicants should also be mindful that many nations impose a "working requirement" on patents they grant, requiring that the patented invention be practiced (i.e., manufactured or imported) within the country that issued the patent, subject to penalties.

Reading:
Paris Convention vs. Patent Cooperation Treaty: Pros and Cons
https://www.intepat.com/blog/patent/paris-convention-vs-patent-cooperation-treaty-pros-and-cons/

Considerations for Follow-on and Foreign Filing
https://www.bpmlegal.com/content/howforfile

Paris Convention Filing
https://www.globalpatentfiling.com/services/paris-convention-filings

We'll Always Have Paris: PCT Applications and the International Patent
https://kolitchromano.com/pct-applications/

PCT

Reading:

Strategic Use of the PCT: A US User's Perspective
https://www.wipo.int/export/sites/www/pct/en/pct_strategies/strategic_use_users_perspective.pdf#:~:text=Via%20the%20PCT%3A%20Pros%3A%20Search%20report%20and%20

Pros and Cons of Securing Worldwide Patent Protection and Their Steps
https://ocpatentlawyer.com/pros-cons-securing-worldwide-patent-protection-steps/

Pros

- a single application can be filed in the applicant's home country, in the local language, to gain protection in more than 150 PCT signatories simultaneously
- receive valuable information about the patentability of your invention from the international written opinion and search report
- the PCT International Search Report (ISR) often can help applicants determine how likely it is that the application will proceed to grant in individual countries after national phase entry
- search report and written patentability opinion available within nine months of filing PCT (within 16 months of priority document)
- other patent offices can largely rely on the international search report and written opinion, thus, streamlining the processing phase
- if invention is not patentable, you will have saved the costs of seeking direct protection in foreign nations
- provides an additional period of 18 months to consider seeking patent protection in specific nations, prepare the necessary translations, and pay required fees
- delays cost (useful in seeking funding)
- additional time to make final "filing" decisions and get information, licensees, capital, partners, etc.
- hold geographic "filing" options open for a longer time
- in contracting states with PCT-Patent Prosecution Highway agreements, you may be able to fast-track the examination phase
- opportunity to amend your application, argue your case with the examiner, and make adjustments during the international preliminary examination phase
- invention receives international public notice and can be highlighted on PATENTSCOPE, allowing you to advertise to potential licensees

- provides global publicity for invention via PCT publication even accounting for the additional cost of the PCT application, slightly lower costs for national phase entry as compared with direct filings means the PCT route for more than a couple of countries can actually be cheaper overall

Cons

- requires filing of separate applications in each elected country and hiring local legal representatives to prosecute application
- it takes a longer duration to obtain patents through PCT
- not all countries are PCT members, notably Taiwan, Argentina, Chile, and Hong Kong
- cannot enter French national application from PCT; only through EPO application
- cannot enter Hong Kong directly from PCT, only through China
- PCT is difficult because the formal requirements of its member states are complex
- costs more overall; high charges for filing fees
  - cost: $3,500–$4,500 for U.S. applicant
  - notably higher initial and overall costs and a longer processing time than individual foreign patent applications.
  - costs more overall (vs. Paris Convention)
- if interest in only a limited number of countries, direct filing may be more economical than PCT (especially if no translations necessary)
- patent term in all PCT states begins on the date of first (PCT) filing via a U.S. provisional application

Reading:
Which Countries Are Not PCT Members?
https://www.patenttrademarkblog.com/non-pct-countries/

Countries Which Are Not in the PCT
https://www.bpmlegal.com/content/notpct

EPC

Pros

- one application in EPO can mature into patent in all European countries elected
- European patent more economical than Paris Convention if desiring protection in three or more non-English-speaking countries (jurisdictions)

- more economical than PCT if filing in more than two non-English-speaking EPC countries
- the European patent application has several advantages: (1) spreading of examination costs over a larger number of countries (compared to pursuing applications in several countries simultaneously); (2) an examination conducted in English involving a single foreign patent law firm; and (3) a rigorous examination that theoretically produces a stronger patent

Reading:
European Union: Pros and Cons of Using the European Patent Application System Rather Than Separate National Patent Applications?
https://www.mondaq.com/uk/patent/1037580/pros-and-cons-of-using-the-european-patent-application-system-rather-than-separate-national-patent-applications

Cons

- no public disclosure permitted before filing
- must pay substantial annual annuity fee to EPO for each year application pending until issue
- can be filed by U.S.-based agent or non-practitioner, but post-filing prosecution only by European-based legal agent registered with EPO (*see* Article 134(1) EPC, Article 134(8) EPC), except for paying fees
- protection in all those countries comes at a cost, due to the need to validate (register and translate the Europatent in each registered nation) the European patent in individual countries once granted and the high official fees at the EPO [Note: the Unitary Patent will eliminate validation in each elected jurisdiction]
- cost depends on the number of countries in Europe where patent protection is needed and, to some extent, which countries they are. The European application system is beneficial in that the single European patent application can be prosecuted in only one language (i.e., English, German, or French) and by only one representative for the whole of Europe. In contrast, the official fees are lower at national patent offices in Europe, but many countries will require a local representative to be appointed for that country, as well as a translation into the national language
- there is a break-even point, after which national patent applications become less cost-effective than a single European patent application

- the European patent application system via the EPO remains the default choice where it is necessary to preserve the option of obtaining protection in three or more European countries. However, national patent applications still hold a place for the cost-conscious applicant, particularly where only one or two European countries are of key strategic value

Paris Convention

Pros

- the Paris Convention gives the broadest rights of patent, utility model, and industrial design to individuals and firms
- the 12-month Convention cycle helps the applicant to seek funding, perform market research, and turn the concept into a commercial product. The Convention enables one to achieve all these with a single filing without causing a loss of rights in other countries.
- advantages only direct filing can offer:
- vs. PCT: if fast grant desirable, may lead to quicker grant; direct filings can often lead to quicker grant than PCT route
- there are a few notable countries excluded from PTC (viz., Taiwan, Argentina, Hong Kong, Chile); coverage in these nations requires Paris Convention filing; for Taiwan, an equivalent bilateral agreement with the applicant's country, if one exists
- with PTC, applicants must file a single spec that accommodates the different legal requirements of all countries; but, there may be situations where an applicant would prefer content tailored to specific jurisdictions, for example, Europe and U.S.
- the sorts of problems that such tailored content would seek to avoid tend to be industry-specific; for example, different approaches to info technology and pharma patent in certain jurisdictions may make it difficult to provide a "one size fits all" spec that is perfectly suited to all jurisdictions

Cons

- separate application in each country; U.S. filers must hire local legal agent to prosecute application, especially in non-English-speaking countries
- most foreign countries require "absolute novelty" of an invention prior to filing, meaning no public disclosure
- most foreign countries have "opposition" proceedings where anyone can challenge a published application's patentability

- some nations do not patent computer programs, some biotech subject matter, or business methods
- high fees for translation
- may have to tailor claims to individual countries

Hague Agreement
Reading:
4 Key Takeaways: The Hague Agreement & Design Filings—Things You Need to Know & Do
https://www.kilpatricktownsend.com/en/Insights/Alert/2017/10/4-Key-Takeaways-Hague-System

Hague Weighed: Should I Change My Design Filing Strategy?
https://bannerwitcoff.com/wp-content/uploads/2015/07/Hague-Weighed.pdf

US Design Applications Based on Hague Agreement: 80% Failure Rate
http://www.smartpat.us/us-design-patent-hague-agreement/

International Design Patent Applications—Another Tool in the Toolbox
https://www.bomcip.com/blog/international-design-patent-applications-another-tool-toolbox/

The Hague Agreement Concerning the International Registration of Industrial Designs
https://www.inta.org/wp-content/uploads/public-files/advocacy/committee-reports/20210615-Designs-Committee-Report-Hague-Agreement-Designs.pdf

Pros

- cost-effective way to get design protection in many countries
- single application and unified process for registering up to 100 industrial designs in as many as 92 jurisdictions
- minimizes law firm fees, avoids multiple filings; one fee to be paid
- overcomes some shortcomings in national systems due to harmonization
- minimizes administration; bypasses additional six-month inquiry
- broader and quicker initial coverage
- application will publish, but publication can be delayed
- no need for a national agent in many countries since each country sets its own requirements, and countries that treat each application as a registration do not require local counsel for prosecution/examination; many countries simply register designs without thorough examination; agent not required unless country issues office action

- although it is available, there is no need for an earlier national priority filing, since one application provides the same effective date in all countries
- refusal (or invalidation) in one member country based on local substantive examination (or litigation) does not directly affect corresponding registrations/applications in other member countries

Cons

- increased risk that application does not meet requirements or standards of one or more designated countries; quality of drawings are of special concern
- each country has different standards and requirements of which applicants must be aware. Thus, although certain countries may not require a local agent during the "national phase," applicants are encouraged to review the substantive laws of each designated state prior to filing, especially the drawing requirements and rules for claiming and describing the design for which protection is sought
- the ability to file up to 100 designs per application may provide strategic options for addressing and complying with different jurisdictions' distinctive drawing requirements, and not just for seeking to protect different embodiments of similar designs. Drawings not compatible with a particular jurisdiction's requirements can be canceled upon entry thereto, and divisional applications can be used to pursue multiple designs/embodiments in jurisdictions like the U.S. that permit only one "invention" per application/patent
- substantive examination in other jurisdictions may identify items that are material to prosecution of a U.S. design case, triggering the applicant's duty of candor under 37 CFR § 1.56.
- substantial number of countries are not contracting parties to the Hague Agreement; protection in those countries still requires a separate application. Notably absent members include Canada, Mexico, Brazil, Russia, China, India, and Australia. With the U.S. and Japan's accession to the Hague Agreement, however, more countries may soon follow

Filing U.S. National Design Application Instead of Hague Registration (Home Country Registration)

Pros

- single regime for standards of allowance and a mature body of case law for enforcement

Cons

- need to navigate U.S.-specific laws. For example, the U.S. requires "unity of invention," meaning only one inventive design is allowed per application
- applicants could inadvertently forfeit foreign filing rights if they do not plan carefully and make certain that any and all design and precedent utility patents are timely filed. For example, under the Paris Convention rules and U.S. law, any design patent application claiming subject matter disclosed in a provisional application must be filed within six months of the provisional filing date, even though a design patent cannot claim priority to the provisional application and any utility application claiming priority to that provisional can be filed within 12 months. Also, unlike the U.S., at least some jurisdictions do not allow a design patent to make a priority claim to a utility patent (e.g., the EU)

B. Subject Matter Eligibility for Patent

Applicants and practitioners should be mindful that many foreign jurisdictions differ from the United States in what they regard as patent-eligible inventions. Specific areas of subject matter to be aware of include computer software, business methods, and biotechnology. Practitioners should consult the laws of individual national patent offices for current information.

1. PCT

The PCT encompasses the filing of applications for patents for inventions, inventors' certificates, utility certificates, utility models, and various kinds of patents and certificates of addition (*see* Article 2(i)).

An international application thus cannot validly be filed for certain other forms of industrial property rights that fall outside the scope of inventions, such as, for example, purely ornamental designs (*see* Ch. 5.002).

Prospective applicants should check the patent laws of individual countries for specific information on what is patentable, especially if the claimed invention is related to computer software, business methods, and biotechnology, or may otherwise be questionable.

2. EPC

EPC Art. 52(1): patentable and non-patentable subject matter

> (1) European patents shall be granted for any inventions, in all fields of technology, provided that they are new (Art. 54, 55), involve an inventive step (Art. 56) (analogous to nonobviousness in U.S. patent law), and are susceptible of industrial application (Art. 57).

Under the EPC, an invention is patentable only if it is:
- New and previously undisclosed;
- Distinguished by an inventive step not obvious to someone expert in that technology;
- Amenable to industrial application—that is, it is physically possible to make the invention;
- An invention can be, for example, a product, a process or an apparatus.

(2) The following in particular shall not be regarded as inventions within the meaning of paragraph 1:
  (a) discoveries, scientific theories, and mathematical methods;
  (b) aesthetic creations;
  (c) schemes, rules, and methods for performing mental acts, playing games or doing business, and programs for computers;
  (d) presentations of information

Art. 53: exceptions to patentability

European patents shall not be granted in respect of:

inventions the commercial exploitation of which would be contrary to "ordre public" or morality (ethical principles); such exploitation shall not be deemed to be so contrary merely because it is prohibited by law or regulation in some or all of the Contracting States;
  (a) plant or animal varieties or essentially biological processes for the production of plants or animals; this provision shall not apply to microbiological processes or the products thereof;
  (c) methods for treatment of the human or animal body by surgery or therapy and diagnostic methods practiced on the human or animal body; this provision shall not apply to products, in particular substances or compositions, for use in any of these methods.

Specific Subject Matter

Computer software, in and of itself, can be protected by copyright but not by patent in Europe. However, an invention that is implemented on computers by means of software may be patent-eligible. For example, an improved data handling system is patentable in Europe.

Reading:

Software Patents Under the European Patent Convention
https://www.iusmentis.com/patents/software/epc/

Securing Software Patents Through the EPO
https://www.bardehle.com/europeansoftwarepatents/software-patent-epo/
https://www.iam-media.com/securing-software-patents-through-epo

- business methods may be patentable in the United States but not patentable elsewhere.
- business methods or software inventions patentable only if it can be shown that the claimed invention contains at least one novel feature that is "technical" and that solves a "technical problem" in a non-obvious manner
- some countries (e.g., Italy) do not patent drugs
- inventions contrary to ethical principles, such as means of cloning human life or the use of human embryos for commercial and industrial purposes, are not patentable
- biotech inventions are generally patentable, with some exceptions (*see* EPO web page for details)

3. Paris Convention

Article 1(3): Industrial property shall be understood in the broadest sense and shall apply not only to industry and commerce proper, but likewise to agricultural and extractive industries and to all manufactured or natural products, for example, wines, grain, tobacco leaf, fruit, cattle, minerals, mineral waters, beer, flowers, and flour.

Article 1(4): Patents shall include the various kinds of industrial patents recognized by the laws of the countries of the Union, such as patents of importation, patents of improvement, patents and certificates of addition, etc.

The Paris Convention does not require biotechnology to be accorded patent protection. But, at the same time, it does not prohibit it, leaving it for individual countries to decide whether to accord protection to biotechnology

Patentability in Selected PC Countries

Canada
Canadian Intellectual Property Office
https://www.ic.gc.ca/eic/site/cipointernet-internetopic.nsf/eng/home

Prima Facie Requirements for Patentability

1. New—first in the world
2. Useful—functional and operative
3. Inventive—showing ingenuity and not obvious to someone of average skill who works in the field of the invention

The invention must also be:

- a product (example: a door lock)
- a composition (example: a chemical composition used in lubricants for door locks)

- a machine (example: a machine for making door locks)
- a process (example: a method for making door locks)
- an improvement on any of the preceding

For details on what can be patented, see Chapter 17: Statutory Subject-Matter in the Manual of Patent Office Practice (MOPOP), available on Canadian Patent Office website.

Computer code and computer-implemented inventions
Computer code by itself is not something physical and, therefore, not patentable by law.

A computer program may be patentable if it offers a new and inventive solution to a problem by modifying how the computer works.

Certain subject matter that cannot be patented include:

- disembodied ideas, concepts or discoveries
- scientific principles and abstract theorems
- methods of medical treatment or surgery
- higher life forms
- forms of energy
- features of solely intellectual or aesthetic significance
- printed matter

For details on what cannot be patented, see Chapter 17.03: Excluded Subject-Matter in the Manual of Patent Office Practice (MOPOP).

Republic of Korea (South Korea)
Republic of Korea Intellectual Property Office
https://www.kipo.go.kr/en/MainApp?c=1000

Under the Korean Patent Act and Korean Intellectual Property Office's (KIPO) Requirements for Patentability, the following are not patentable in Korea:

- any invention detrimental to public order, morality, or public health
- scientific discoveries
- inventions not based on the law of nature (e.g., laws of economics, mathematical methods, etc.)
- arbitrary arrangements (e.g., rules for playing games)
- mental activities
- aesthetic effects (e.g., paintings, carvings)
- animal and plant varieties
- methods for medical treatment of the human body

For more detailed information, see the Korean Patent Act and KIPO's Requirements for Patentability (available on KIPO website)

Japan
Japan Patent Office
https://www.jpo.go.jp/e/index.html

According to the Japan Patent Act and the JPO's Examination Guidelines for Patents, the following items are not patentable in Japan:

- inventions not using the laws of nature (e.g., economic laws, mathematical methods, etc.) For more information, see the Japan Patent Act and the JPO's Examination Guidelines for Patents
- any invention that is liable to injure public order, morality, or public health
- laws of nature
- scientific discoveries
- inventions not using the laws of nature (e.g., economic laws, mathematical methods etc.)
- inventions contrary to a law of nature
- arbitrary arrangements (e.g., rules for playing a game)
- mental activities
- personal skills
- mere presentation of information
- aesthetic effects (e.g., paintings, carvings)
- methods for medical treatment of the human body

For more information, see the Japan Patent Act and the JPO's Examination Guidelines for Patents and Utility Models (available on JPO website)

Australia
Australian Intellectual Property Office
https://www.ipaustralia.gov.au/patents

Patent protection can be applied to a wide range of inventions. In addition to traditional inventions (such as appliances and mechanical devices), protection can also cover:

- computer-related inventions
- business methods
- biological inventions
- micro-organisms and other biological materials

Non-Patentable Subject Matter includes:

- human beings or the biological process for their generation
- artistic creation
- mathematical models
- plans, schemes, or other purely mental processes

India
India Intellectual Property Office
https://ipindia.gov.in/index.htm

The Patent Act of 1970 defines what is patent-eligible.

Prima Facie Requirements for Patentability:

- Novelty
- Inventive step
- Industrial applicability

Patent eligible subjects are, therefore, products and processes without any limitation of field or technology

Patent-Ineligible Subject Matter

- mathematical algorithms, mathematical methods, business methods, and computer programs
- discovery of living things occurring in nature; discovery of living things or non-living substances or materials in nature
- plants and animals in whole or any part thereof including seeds; varieties, species and mostly the biological processes for production or propagation of the plants and animals
- genetically modified multicellular organisms including plants, human beings, animals and their parts
- human beings and embryonic stem cells
- methods of medical treatment
- the invention is related to any essentially biological processes for the production or propagation of plants and animals
- invention related to any process for the medicinal, curative, surgical, prophylactic, diagnostic or therapeutic or other treatment of human beings or animals to render them free from a disease or to increase their economic value or that of their products
- invention related to specific methods of agriculture or horticulture
- invention includes a traditional knowledge

- inventions against public order or immoral, harmful to the animal, human or plant life, or harmful to the environment
- a mathematical or business method or a computer program *per se*, or algorithms
- traditional knowledge or which is an aggregation or duplication of known properties of traditionally known component or components

Taiwan (Republic of China) [Note: Taiwan is not a signatory to PCT or Paris Convention]
Taiwan Intellectual Property Office
https://www.tipo.gov.tw/en/mp-2.html

Prima Facie Requirements for Patentability:

- the invention must have a "technical character" so that the problem must be solved by technical means in the relevant technical field
- an invention must include the creation of technical ideas using the laws of nature
- the invention must demonstrate industrial applicability

Patent-Ineligible Subject Matter

- mere discovery, scientific theories, presentation of information, and aesthetic creations
- non-physical substances, such as manufacturing method, processing method, chemical substance without concrete shape
- animals, plants, and essential biological processes for the production of animals or plants, except for processes for producing microorganisms
- diagnostic, therapeutic, and surgical methods for the treatment of humans or animals
- an article that is detrimental to public order, morality

Note: Taiwan is not a member of the World Intellectual Property Organization (WIPO) and has not signed on to most WIPO-administered agreements, but Taiwan has bilateral intellectual property related agreements and memorandums of understanding with a number of countries, including the U.S. and EU. Even though Taiwan is not a contracting state to the European Patent Convention (EPC), or the Patent Cooperation Treaty (PCT), a foreign applicant can still claim priority to a first-filed EPC or PCT application in a later-filed Taiwanese application.

Taiwan is not a PCT member; the 30-month timeframe for national phase entry is not applicable with regards to Taiwan. Instead, a Taiwanese national application must be filed within 12 months from the earliest filing date to appropriately claim priority.

4. Hague Agreement

An industrial design is that aspect of a useful article which is ornamental or aesthetic. It may consist of three-dimensional features, such as the shape or surface features of an article, or of two-dimensional features, such as patterns, lines, or color.

The object of protection of an industrial design is to be distinguished from that of a patent, primarily because the former relates to the appearance of an article. An industrial design consists precisely of that aspect of an article which is ornamental or aesthetic and which is not determined by technical or functional necessity.

As a general rule, to be registrable, the design must be "new" or, under some laws, "original." What constitutes "new" or "original" may vary from country to country. The same is true for the registration procedure itself, in particular, whether an examination as to form only or also as to substance, especially to determine novelty or originality, is carried out.

Subject Matter That Cannot Be Registered:

- purely ornamental designs
- designs not reproducible by industrial means (i.e., "works of art")

For further information, see WIPO website.

C. Bars to Filing

An applicant may be precluded from filing by not being compliant with certain statutory requirements. Of principal concern are public disclosure of the invention prior to filing, and possession of a Foreign Filing License (FFL).

1) Public Disclosure Before Filing

- unlike the U.S.'s one-year grace period, many foreign countries bar grant of patent if the invention is publicly disclosed prior to filing an application (i.e., "absolute novelty" requirement)
- see IP5 Offices' *Catalogue of Differing Practices* for comparison of grace periods in several relevant foreign countries (https://www.fiveipoffices.org/home)

- no foreign filing permitted beyond grace period after filing priority application
- if U.S. patent issues in less than one year from filing, foreign application can still be filed until grace period expires
- prospective applicants should consult the patent laws of individual countries for specific information

Reading:
Grace Periods for Disclosure of an Invention Before Applying for a Parent
https://www.mewburn.com/law-practice-library/grace-periods-for-disclosure-of-an-invention-before-applying-for-a-patent

2) Foreign Filing License (FFL) MPEP 140, 706.03(s); 37 CFR 5.11–5.15; 35 USC 184, 185

- foreign filing licenses allow for the disclosure of technology to foreign jurisdictions for the limited purpose of filing patent applications abroad
- pursuant to 37 C.F.R. § 5.11, a foreign filing license is required before filing any application for patent in a foreign country, foreign patent office, foreign patent agency, or any international agency, if the invention was made in the United States, and (1) an application on the invention was filed in the United States less than six months prior to the date on which the foreign application is to be filed; or
- (2) no application on the invention has been filed in the United States.
- prior to filing application for patent in any foreign country or international IP association on any invention made in the US, a foreign filing license must first be issued by USPTO

Options for Obtaining a Foreign Filing License:

(a) filing a patent application with the USPTO (which is considered to include a petition for a foreign filing license) and waiting for a foreign filing license to be issued;
(b) filing an express petition for the issuance of a foreign filing license; or
(c) waiting six months after filing a patent application in the USPTO at which time a license on that subject matter is no longer required as long as no secrecy order has been imposed.

Petition for Expedited Foreign Filing License	37 CFR 5.12
- file when FFL not granted automatically with U.S. application	MPEP 140
- with corresponding pending U.S. application, *see* 37 CFR 5.14	
- without corresponding U.S. application, *see* 37 CFR 5.13	
Attachments: petition fee	37 CFR 1.17(g)
Petition for Retroactive Foreign Filing License	37 CFR 5.25
- if, through error, a foreign application was filed without a FFL in effect, applicant may petition for a retroactive FFL	MPEP 140
Attachments: per 37 CFR 5.25	
- petition fee	37 CFR 1.17(g)
PTO Response: Grant or Deny	

Reading:
Foreign Filing Requirements in the United States
https://www.sternekessler.com/news-insights/publications/foreign-filing-requirements-united-states

Getting a Faxed Foreign Filing License From the USPTO
https://blog.oppedahl.com/?p=2550

What Is a Foreign Filing License?
https://www.drm.com/resources/what-is-a-foreign-filing-license

Beware of Foreign Filing License Requirements
https://www.ipwatchdog.com/2019/06/12/beware-foreign-filing-license-requirements/id=110332/

Global Collaborations and Foreign Filing Licenses
https://www.americanbar.org/groups/intellectual_property_law/publications/landslide/2019-20/march-april/global-collaborations-foreign-filing-licenses/

D. Filing Strategy

Assuming that the decision to file internationally has been, at least tentatively, determined, applicants should next consider their options regarding the sequence of filing; namely, whether to file first in the U.S. or overseas. The order of filing can have tactical benefits. For instance, American applicants ordinarily apply for U.S. patent first, then frequently file a PCT, or perhaps an EPO regional application within a year. Filing a U.S. provisional or nonprovisional application reduces initial filing costs compared to overseas filing, and gives the applicant a year to reconsider foreign filing. Submitting a PCT originally, although initially expensive, affords the applicant up to 30 months before national applications must be filed, thereby delaying national fees outlay and allowing more time to consider international applications. A PCT also provides a rapid prior art search and patentability assessment, and the ability to evaluate claim amendments before U.S. application.

Reading:
First File PCT or US Patent Application?
https://www.patenttrademarkblog.com/first-pct-or-us-patent/

Foreign Patent Filing: 5 Strategies to Develop an International Patent Portfolio
https://triangleip.com/patent-filing-strategies/

International or Foreign Patent Filing Strategies
https://www.ipeg.com/international-or-foreign-patent-filing-strategies/

International or Foreign Patent Filing Strategies
https://ipstrategy.com/2012/09/10/international-or-foreign-patent-filing-strategies/

Strategies for Filing Internationally: Including the PCT and the Hague System for Industrial Designs
https://ncai.nhlbi.nih.gov/ncai/resources/docs/PatentCooperationTreaty(PCT)StrategiesforFilingAbroad.pdf

V. Application/Prosecution

A. PCT Application

PCT Articles 4, 11; Regulations Under the Patent Cooperation Treaty; Administrative Instructions Under the Patent Cooperation Treaty; Guidelines for Search and Examination at the EPO as PCT Authority; 37 CFR 1.401 *et seq.*; MPEP Appendix T (treaty text); Ch. 1800; 35 USC, Chs. 35–37

Summary
The PCT system is the widely favored choice when patent protection in various countries worldwide is desired. The PCT application acts somewhat like a PPA; it establishes a priority filing date for later applications in individual jurisdictions, although it does not, itself, issue as patent.

The PCT process consists of two phases. The International Phase commences by filing a "Request" for an international application, which can be filed online in the PTO, or directly in the International Bureau (IB) of WIPO. During the initial period of this phase (Chapter I), the Receiving Office (RO) conducts a formalities review before transferring the application to an International Search Authority (ISA) of the applicant's choice.

Within 16 months of the priority date, the ISA issues a prior art Search Report and a preliminary patentability assessment for the applicant. If requested within 22 months of the priority date, the applicant can elect Chapter II of the International Phase by filing a "Demand" for a preliminary examination by the IPEA (International Preliminary Examination Authority) of the applicant's choice. Finally, within 30 months of the priority date, the application must enter the National Phase, during which the application is transmitted to national patent offices designated by the applicant for formal substantive examination. Pending successful prosecution at the national level, patent is granted in the designated country.

PCT Applicant's Guide
https://www.wipo.int/export/sites/www/pct/guide/en/gdvol1/pdf/gdvol1.pdf

Note: Full details on PCT application can be found on WIPO website.

Reading:
PCT Patent Filing: All That You Need to Know
https://thepatentfilingcompany.com/pct-patent-filing/

PCT International Patent Application Formalities
https://www.patentek.com/pct-application-formalities/

Filing a New International Application Under the Patent Cooperation Treaty (PCT)
https://www.uspto.gov/sites/default/files/patents/process/file/efs/guidance/indexing-pct-new-appl.pdf

1. **Pre-Application Activities and Considerations**
    - public disclosure before US filing can be bar to patent; consult national patent laws for specific information
    - file U.S. application (PPA/RPA/DES) to establish priority filing date (35 USC 119(e), 120, 365; 37 CFR 1.78(a)&(d))
    - file PCT application within one year of U.S. application to preserve priority; within six months for design application
        - must have foreign filing license or wait at least six months after U.S. filing (*see* MPEP 1832)

- no filing permitted after U.S. patent issues
- hire legal agents in jurisdictions where required to file and/or prosecute applications
- some foreign countries may require U.S. filers to act through an in-country legal representative for application submittal and/or prosecution; consult national patent laws for specific information
- generally, English-speaking countries allow application activities without an in-country agent; Japan allows only initial application filing
- remember to file with sufficient time before deadlines to give foreign agents enough time to prepare documents if necessary

2. Filing

a. Application Prep/Assembly

1) Required Parts (PCT Articles 3 & 11; 37 CFR 1.431; MPEP 1812)

PCT Request	Apx F-01
PCT standard application form	PCT/RO/101 Article 4 Rules 3, 4 37 CFR 1.434 MPEP 1821

[sample completed form on WIPO]
https://www.wipo.int/export/sites/www/pct/en/docs/forms/request/filled_request.pdf

Complete request form as follows:

Box 1. Title of Invention: the title is the main heading of the invention. The preferred word-limit for the title is two to seven words when in English or translated to English. Fill the title in Box I (1) of the request form.

Box 2–3. Applicants and Inventors information: name (surname and then first name) and address details identify an applicant and/or inventor. Where the applicant is a legal entity or a corporation, mark the check-box "applicant only." Provide some contact detail, such as telephone number, email, and/or facsimile number. Information of the applicant and inventor(s) are part of Box II (2) and III (3) respectively.

Box 4. Agent or common representative (37 CFR 1.455; MPEP 1807): add the details of the agent in the Box IV of the request. Otherwise, a separate document "Power of Attorney" signed by the applicant. Include contact and address details of agents, as for applicant and/or inventor.

Box 5. Designation of States (37 CFR 1.432): filing automatically constitutes the designation of all the contracting states. But note, Japan, Republic of Korea, and Germany are not a part of the automatic designation process.

- fees do not increase with designation of more countries; applicants typically designate all countries and later can select which countries to file national applications in

Box 6. Priority Claim and Restoration of the Right of Priority (Article 4; 37 CFR 1.451-452): an applicant can claim priority of an earlier application filed in or for another country in some other convention or for a member of **World Trade Organization (WTO)** that is not a part of PCT. It serves to establish a priority date for the current application.

Box 7. International Searching Authority (ISA) (see Art. 16; Rule 35; 37 CFR 1.413; MPEP 1840): sometimes two or three ISAs are eligible to carry out the international search; in this case, the applicant indicates one ISA chosen by him/her in Box No. VII (7).

- specify an *International Search Authority* (*ISA*), which is the patent office that will perform an initial review of the claims in the PCT application

Box 8. Declarations: the applicant can declare any of the following declarations:

- Regarding the identity of the inventor;
- Applicant's entitlement as at the international filing date, to apply for and for grant of patent;
- Applicant's entitlement as at the international filing date, to claim priority of the earlier application;
- Declaration of Inventorship (only for **USPTO**);
- Regarding non-prejudicial disclosures or exceptions to absence of novelty. Box VIII (8) incorporates the declaration part of the request.

Box 9. Checklist: Box IX (9) comprises the checklist. It allows the receiving office to verify that all the documents constituting the international application are present.

Box 10. Signature of Applicant or Agent: the applicant signs the request form in the BOX No. X (10). An enlisted agent can sign the form if the application generates a separate "Power of Attorney." Also, sign the request form in black ink and print the name next to the signature.

Invention Disclosure [Application Body as Filed]

Description: this part discloses every detail regarding the invention in a clear and complete manner as produced by a person skilled in the art. Starting with the Title as mentioned in Box 1 of the request form. It also comprises the technical field of the invention, Disclosure of Invention, Description of Drawings, and Industrial Applicability. Additionally, the applicant and/or inventor can add biological sequence listing (i.e., nucleotide and/or amino acid) where applicable (eligible for both electronic and paper format filing).

- *See* Article 5; Rule 5; 37 CFR 1.435; MPEP 1823

Claim(s): draft the claims in a clear and concise format. The content of claims must be consistent with the description. Also, write them in two distinct parts: first the statement of the prior art, and second, the differentiating features for which you are seeking protection.

- *See* Article 6; Rule 6; 37 CFR 1.436; MPEP 1824

Abstract: a brief summary of the invention description. It serves to assist scientists, technologists, and others researching the field. Draft in English with length ranging between 50 and 150 words.

- *See* Rule 8; 37 CFR 1.438; MPEP 1826

Drawing(s) (if any): Drawings assist in understanding of the invention. Add different views of the drawings and always present them on different sheets.

- Article 7; Rule 7; 37 CFR 1.437; MPEP 1825

[Note: color drawings not permitted; *see* PCT Rule 11.13]

Reading:
Filing Informal Drawings in a PCT Application
https://blog.oppedahl.com/?p=4437

WIPO Patent Drawing Rules for PCT Applications
https://thepatentdrawingscompany.com/wipo-patent-drawing-rules-pct-applications/

Sequence Listing of the Description (if necessary)

Points to Remember: [If filing on paper, *see* Rule 11]

- number the sheets in Arabic numerals. The date on the right of the priority application is also in the Arabic language, with day, name of month, and year, in that order.
- language of filing depends upon the jurisdiction of the receiving office. Some offices allow choosing between two or more languages.

- the application papers must indicate that it is intended as an international application pursuant to PCT Article 11(1)(iii)(a).
- at least one Contracting State must be designated pursuant to PCT Article [11(1)(iii)(b).
- the application must contain the name of the applicant, a description, and a claim or claims pursuant to PCT Article 11(1)(iii)(c)–(e).

Note: if there are multiple patent applicants belonging to different jurisdictions they can file the application in one of the jurisdictions of the PCT convention countries.

Transmittal Letter to the U.S. RO	PTO-1382
- if using PTO as RO	Apx F-02

Selection of Receiving Office (*see* Art. 10; Rule 19)

The international application must be filed in an authorized Receiving Office. The Receiving Office functions as the filing and formalities review organization for international applications. Patent Offices of the countries that are members to the PCT serve as Receiving Offices. You cannot simply file an international patent application in any Patent Office, but rather must file in the appropriate Receiving Office. Where there are several applicants who are not all nationals and/or residents of the same country, any Receiving Office where at least one of the applicants is a resident or national is authorized to receive an international application filed by those applicants. Alternatively, the international application may be filed with the International Bureau (IB) as the Receiving Office. In the United States, the U.S. Patent and Trademark Office acts as a Receiving Office for United States residents and nationals, but the International Bureau of the World Intellectual Property Organization may also act as a Receiving Office for U.S. residents and nationals.
[Note: filing directly in IB avoids transmittal fee for transmission of Request from PTO to IB]

- for USPTO as Receiving Office, *see* 35 USC 361; 37 CFR 1.412; MPEP 1805
- for fees payable to USPTO, *see* 35 USC 376

Application Data Sheet (ADS)

Inventorship bibliographic, representative, correspondence address, and other application information	AIA/14 37 CFR 1.76 MPEP 601.05(a)
- via EFS, can be prepared before filing (optional) or will be generated automatically upon e-filing	

Assertion of Small Entity (SE) status for discounted fees Asserting SE status	37 CFR 1.27(a) 35 USC 41(h)(1)
- determining Small Entity: individual, small biz (500 employees max), university, or 501(c)(3) nonprofit	MPEP 509.02
Certification of Micro Entity (ME) status for discounted fees	37 CFR 1.29 35 USC 123 MPEP 509.04
Certification of Micro Entity Status	
- determination of Micro Entity: must meet SE Criteria (37 CFR 1.27(a)), and (1) applicant has not been named as inventor on more than four utility, design, or plant patents; (2) applicant (or assignee) had gross income in previous year of less than 3x median household income (ca. 57K; 3x = ca. 170K); (3) majority of applicant's employment income is from institution of higher learning, or applicant has assigned, or is obligated to assign, rights to institution of higher learning	
Micro Entity—Income-based	SB/15A
Asserts eligibility for fee discount based on gross income of inventor(s)	37 CFR 1.29(a) MPEP 509.04
Micro Entity—Employment-based	SB/15B
Asserts eligibility for fee discount based on employment by institution of higher learning, or being independent inventor	37 CFR 1.29(d) MPEP 509.04
Attachments: SB/15A (income)	
SB/15B (higher education employment; independent inventor)	
Fee Calculation Sheet Annex	Apx F-03
- assists in calculation of the total amount of fee payable to the patent office. Attach it right after the Request form, as it is not a part of the request form. Three types of fees are payable within one month of filing: transmittal fee, international filing fee, and search fee (when using EPO as search authority)	

2) *Accompanying Papers as Appropriate*

Appointment of Legal Representative	Rule 90
- if the Receiving Office is the USPTO, then a Power of Attorney is not required, as the appointment of an agent may be indicated in the PCT Request form (see MPEP 1807)	
Power of Attorney	Apx F-04

General POA	Apx F-05
- covers multiple applications	
RO Response: Acknowledgement of receipt	
PCT—List of Docs Filed with IB	Apx F-06
- include with any document submittal RO/198	
Request for Restoration of Right to Priority Under PCT Rule 26bis.3	37 CFR 1.452
- if the international application has an international filing date which is later than the expiration of the priority period (as defined by PCT Rule 2.4) but within two months from the expiration of the priority period, the right of priority in the international application may be restored upon request if the delay in filing the international application within the priority period was unintentional.	Rule 26bis.3; 49ter.2 MPEP 1828.01
Request for Participation in the Global/IP5 Patent Prosecution Highway (PPH) Pilot Program in the USPTO	SB/20GLBL 37 CFR 1.102
Expedited application prosecution for corresponding applications filed in participating IP offices	
Attachments: OEE Work Product/Translation and refs. cited therein	MPEP 708.02(c)
PTO Response: decision to grant or deny request	

Reading:

Timing Considerations for Concurrent Track One and PCT Applications
https://www.nixonpeabody.com/insights/alerts/2021/01/05/timing-considerations-for-concurrent-track-one-and-pct-applications

Patent Prosecution Highway (PPH) – Fast Track Examination of Patent Applications
https://www.copperpodip.com/post/patent-prosecution-highway-pph-fast-track-examination-of-patent-applications

Expedited Patent Examination: Understanding Your Options in the US and Abroad
https://www.foxrothschild.com/publications/expedited-patent-examination-understanding-your-options-in-the-us-and-abroad

Implementation of the Global and IP5 Patent Prosecution Highway (PPH) Pilot Programs With Participating Offices
https://www.uspto.gov/sites/default/files/documents/global-ip5.pdf

Communication where no other document code applicable	
- use to communicate issue for which no other established document code exists	
Assignment Recordation Cover Sheet	PTO-1595
Cover sheet for written assignment	MPEP 302.07
- file via EPAS	
Attachments: Executed Assignment Agreement	Apx F-07
Statement Under 37 CFR 3.73(c)	
Establishes assignee's ownership rights in patent application	AIA/96 37 CFR 3.73(c)
- used by legal/obligatory assignee to establish ownership of invention/application	MPEP 325
Attachments: executed assignment if not yet recorded	
- file if PCT application not covered under assignment recorded for initial U.S. application	

b. *Application Submittal*

1) E-Filing
   - use A4 paper format (Rule 11)
   - reduced application fees may apply for electronic filing

File Indirectly in U.S. via EFS-WEB

When filing via EFS-Web, the request may be filed in one of two different formats:

(1) conventional format, and

(2) PCT-Safe Easy format.

(a) The request may be filed via EFS-Web in conventional format by uploading the pdf format of the Request (Form PCT/RO/101, which includes the last sheet—EFS-Web). Document code category: PCT Form and PCT Application Part Document code description: RO/101 Request form for new IA conventional

(b) Alternatively, the request may be filed via EFS-Web in PCT-Safe Easy format by uploading a zip file containing the request which is created using the PCT-Safe Easy mode software
- e-file on EFS-Web (at least one month before one-year deadline to complete any corrections)

PCT-Easy Validation Log

- e-filing program automatically scans entered data for errors and generates list of any problems detected

File Directly to International Bureau (IB) of WIPO
E-file directly with International Bureau (IB); WIPO software (PCT-Safe; ePTC) automates preparation process (www.wipo.int/pct-safe/en/download/download_client.html)

Reading:
Best Practice for Filing a PCT Application in RO/US
https://blog.oppedahl.com/?p=757

2) Via U.S. Mail
   - complete "Request" form (PCT/RO/101) PCT-Easy
   - prep PPA/RPA in PCT acceptable format (A4 paper); or convert to PCT format (Rule 11)
   - Fee Calculation Sheet
   - Transmittal Letter (PTO-1382)
   - request PTO to prep certified copy of US application and attach to PCT (A4 format)
   - fee payment
   - If using PTO as RO mail to: Mail Stop PCT Commissioner for Patents PO Box 1450 Alexandria, VA 22313-1450
   - If using IB as RO mail to: International Bureau of WIPO PCT Receiving Office Section 34, chemin des Colombettes 1211 Geneva 20 Switzerland

3. Post-Filing

a. Enter International Phase—Chapter I [see PCT Chap. I]

Reading:
What Is the International Phase of the PCT?
https://ocpatentlawyer.com/what-is-the-international-phase-of-the-pct/

Filing a communication with the United States Receiving Office (RO/US) or with the United States International Searching Authority (ISA/US) relating to a previously filed PCT international application

https://www.uspto.gov/sites/default/files/patents/process/file/efs/guidance/indexing-pct-chapter-1.pdf

[NOTE: After initial application submittal, subsequent document submittals to the PTO should be accompanied by a Certificate of Transmission and Transmittal Form or Letter.]

Certificate of Transmission	Apx F-08
Establishes that correspondence has been sent to PTO as of date thereon	*see also* D-18 37 CFR 1.8
- for suggested formats see MPEP 512 MPEP 512	
Substitute: Certificate of Mailing or Transmission Under 37 CFR 1.8	SB/92
Transmittal Form	SB/21
Cover sheet/letter for transmittal of correspondence to PTO after initial filing	
Substitute: Transmittal Letter	
Transmittal Letter	Apx D-19
Cover letter for transmittal of miscellaneous correspondence after initial filing	
Substitute: Transmittal Form	SB/21

l) *Routine Office Communications*

Filing receipt with serial number	
Notification concerning payment of prescribed fees	RO/102
Notification of the international application number and of the international filing date	RO/105 Art. 11
Document made available under the Patent Coop. Treaty (PTC) (Priority Doc)	
Notification of receipt of record copy	IB/301
Notification of receipt of search copy	ISA/202
Notification concerning submission or transmittal of priority doc	IB/304
Notification concerning representation	RO/123
Notification concerning availability of the publication of the international application	IB/311

- International Publication: as soon as possible after the expiration of 18 months from the earliest filing date (i.e., priority date), the content of the international application is disclosed to the world, along with the written opinion and the International search report (ISR). The International Bureau of WIPO carries out this procedure.

First Notice informing the applicant of the communication of the int'l appl (to the designated offices) (which do not apply the 30-month time limit under Art. 22(1) (IB/308, first notice)

Second and Supp. notice informing the applicant of the communication of the int'l appl (to the designated offices) (which apply the 30-month time limit under Art. 22(1) (IB/308, second and supplementary notice)

Notification of transmittal of the international search report and the written opinion of the international searching authority, or the declaration (ISA/220)

2) *Office-Initiated Actions*

Invitation to correct defects in the int'l appl.	RO/106
- receive Invitation to Correct Defects in the Int'l Appl (correct any errors in appl within one month of filing)	Rule 26
Applicant Response: Replacement/substitute sheets	
Correct Request	Apx F-09
Correct Title	Apx F-10
Correct Spec	Apx F-11
Correct Claim	Apx F-12
Correct Drawings	Apx F-13
Correct POA	Apx F-14
Invitation to correct declarations made in the request under PCT Rule 4.17	IB/370
Rule 4.17 Applicant Response: file replacement declaration(s)	Apx F-15
Invitation to Pay Additional Fees and, Where Applicable, Protest Fee	ISA/206 Rule 16bis.1
Notification of Defective Power of Attorney or Defective Revocation of Power of Attorney	RO/124
Applicant Response: submit corrections as per Notice	
Notification Regarding Certain Corrections Made Ex Officio	RO/146 PCT Admin, Instr.
- notification of revisions to informalities in disclosure made by Receiving Office	sec. 327
Applicant Response: notify Office if disagreeing with revision(s)	

Communication in Cases for Which No Other Form Is Applicable	IB/345
- catchall form from Office transmitting communication to applicant	
Applicant Response: per Notice, if necessary	
Notification of transmittal of copies of int'l preliminary report on patentability Chap. I	IB/326
- receive Chap. I 'Search Report' (from PTO or EPO if selected) after several months from filing, including Patentability Opinion	Art. 15 Rule 43bis; 44bis
Applicant Response: comment on report and amend claims if desired	

3) *Applicant-Initiated Actions*

Rescind Non-Publication Request (NPR)	SB/36
- within 45 days of foreign filing if prior U.S. filing	37 CFR 1.213(b) 35 USC 122{b)(2)(B)(ii) MPEP 1123
PTO Response: Acknowledgment	
Rescission of Previous Nonpublication Request (35 U.S.C. 122(b)(2)(B)(ii)) and, if applicable, Notice of Foreign Filing (35 U.S.C. 122(b)(2)(B)(iii))	SB/36 37 CFR 1.213(b)
- file within 45 days of foreign filing	35 USC 122(b)(2)(B)(ii) MPEP 1123
Attachments: Notice of Foreign Filing (if applicable)	35 USC 122(b)(2)(B)(iii)
PTO Response: Acknowledgment	
Request Rectification of Obvious Mistakes	Apx F-16
- correction of inadvertent errors in disclosure	Rule 91.1, 26.4 MPEP 1836
Office Response: Notification of decision concerning request for rectification	
ePTC Action: Rule 92bis Change Request	Rule 92bis
- changes to names, addresses	37 CFR 1.472
Change agent (PCT Rule 90; MPEP 1808)	Apx F-17
Change correspondence address	Apx F-18
Change inventor/applicant name	Apx F-19
Change inventor address	Apx F-20
Office Response: Notification of the Recording of a Change	PCT/IB/306

Amendments to claims	Apx F-21 37 CFR 1.471 Art. 19 MPEP 1853
Office Response: Notification Concerning the Filing of Amendments of the Claims	IB/346 Art. 28; Rule 46
Notice of Withdrawal of Application	PCT/IB/372
- formal withdrawal of application	35 USC 366
- file within 30 months of priority date	MPEP 1859 Rule 90bis
ePCT Cover Letter	Apx F-22
- cover letter for communication to IB via ePCT	

4) *Search and Exam-Related Office Communications*

Information on search strategy	EPO Form PO4A42
- issued by selected ISA	
Documents Related to Search Strategy—Search History	
International Search Report & Written Report on Patentability	ISA/210 Art. 18 PCT Rule 43bis *see also* Art. 17; MPEP 1843

Within 16 months of the priority date, an International Search Authority (ISA) (one of the world's major patent offices) designated by applicant conducts a detailed search of the relevant prior art and produces an International Search Report (ISR) and a nonbinding Preliminary Written Opinion on Patentability (WOISA or WO) containing its evaluation of the potential patentability of the claims as filed. If the WO is adverse, the claims may be amended before nationalization, after nationalization in each individual country, or the PCT application can be allowed to expire without nationalizing it.

Reminder: new prior art recorded from foreign patent office searches must be reported for corresponding U.S. applications via IDS (see 37 CFR 1.97(e)(1)).

- for USPTO as ISA, see 35 USC 362; MPEP 1844-45

Supplementary International Search (optional) (Rule 45bis; MPEP 1856): Upon request within 22 months of the priority date, a second ISA will identify additional prior art that may not have been found by the first ISA which carried out the main search because of the diversity of prior art in different languages and technical fields. Another Preliminary Report on Patentability will be issued. Applicant is given an opportunity to amend the claims beforehand.

Written opinion of the int'l searching authority	ISA/237 Rule 43bis MPEP 1845
Int'l preliminary report on patentability Chap. I	IB/373 Rule 44bis

Documents Related to Published International Application

Declaration: Entitlement to claim priority (Box VIII)	Rule 4.17
Declaration: Entitlement to apply for and be (Box VIII) granted a patent	Rule 4.17
Initial Publication with ISRI (Int'l Appl published under Patent Coop. Treaty (PCT))	Rule 48 Art. 21

- appl., written opinion, ISR by WIPO (IB) within 18 months of priority date

Sequence listing (nucleotide/amino acid sequence)

Initial Publication without ISR (A2 32/2006)
Corrected version of pamphlet (A2 38/2006)

Communication to the Regional Patent Offices:

Submission of the following documents to the respected patent offices:

- International Application
- International Search Report and written opinion
- Supplementary International Search Report (optional)
- International Preliminary Report on Patentability (optional)

Elect International Phase—Chapter II (optional) [see PCT Chap. II]

Filing a communication in the United States International Preliminary Examining Authority (IPEA/US)

https://www.uspto.gov/sites/default/files/patents/process/file/efs/guidance/indexing-pct-chapter-2.pdf

PCT Demand PCT/IPEA/401

Art. 31; Rule 53

- within 22 months (for most countries; 19 months for some) of U.S. filing (or three months from transmittal of Search Report), elect Chap. II — MPEP 1864-65
- file PCT Demand (PCT/IPEA/401); pay demand fee
- receive formal exam and written opinion
- permits prosecution/amendments
- cite any new refs in supp. IDS to PTO

Sample Demand
https://www.wipo.int/export/sites/www/pct/en/docs/forms/demand/filled_demand.pdf

International Preliminary Exam (optional)	Art. 33; Rule 66, 70
- within 22 months of priority date, request IPEA to generate Preliminary Exam Report	37 CFR 1.480-489 MPEP 1860

International Preliminary Examination (optional): Upon applicant's request, an International Preliminary Examination Authority (IPEA) (selected by applicant) conducts an additional patentability analysis (usually on an application amended in light of the Written Opinion) and generates a Preliminary Examination Report. Request must be made within 22 months from the priority date

- for USPTO as IPEA, see 35 USC 362

b. Enter National Phase (37 CFR 1.490-499; MPEP 1893)

National Phase: Before the end of the PCT (international) process, usually at 30 months (31 for some jurisdictions, including Australia, European Patent Office (EPO), India, and South Korea, among others) from the earliest filing date of the priority application, applicant must begin filing national applications for prosecution in each desired jurisdiction. This involves payment of fees, providing translations and appointment of an agent (where required). After entering the national phase, the application is subject to rejection if it fails to meet country-specific patentability requirements. Additionally, each country or region may charge annual taxes ("annuities") for sustaining the application pending.

- within 30 months of U.S. filing (whether or not Chap. II elected), enter "National Phase"
- file application (translated if necessary) in each PCT jurisdiction where patent protection desired

Reading:

US National Stage Entry Based on PCT Application: What to Know
https://www.patenttrademarkblog.com/us-national-stage-pct-application/

US National Stage Patent Application Basics
https://www.watson-ip.com/blog/us-national-stage-patent-application-basics

Requirements for Filing PCT National Phase Patent Application in USPTO
https://www.mondaq.com/unitedstates/patent/958328/requirements-for-filing-pct-national-phasepatent-application-in-uspto

What Is PCT National Phase Application?
https://www.upcounsel.com/pct-national-phase-application

Petition for Revival of an International Application for Patent Designating the U.S. Abandoned Unintentionally Under 37 CFR 1.137(a)	SB/64PCT 37 CFR 1.137(a) MPEP 711.03(c)
- revival of PCT abandoned for missing 30-month deadline for entering national phase in US	
Attachments: per form SB/64PCT	
Transmittal Letter to the U.S. Designated/Elected Office (DO/EO/US) Concerning a Submission under 35 U.S.C. 371 (for PCT filing dates on or after March 16, 2013) (sometimes referred to as "371 Application")	PTO-1390 35 USC 371
- enter national phase in U.S. if PCT filed before U.S. application	
- request certified copy of U.S. appl from PTO	
Notice of Insufficiency	
Deficiency in National Stage application in U.S. of international application	37 CFR 1.492 and/or 1.495
Applicant Response: Required per Notice instructions	Apx F-23

4. Post-Grant

- the patent laws of many countries require opposition proceedings (aka, validity challenges) against issued patents, as well as the periodic payment of annuities (maintenance fees). Consult the laws and regulations of individual countries for information regarding post-grant activities.
- for effect of U.S. patent issued on international application, see 35 USC 375

B. EPC Application

European Patent Convention, 17th ed., November 2020
Guidelines for Examination in the European Patent Office, March 2021 ed.

Overview

An initial filing in the U.S. must be followed by an EPO application within one year of the U.S. filing in order to preserve the original priority date. Under the EPC, a unitary examination of the application is conducted by the European Patent Office in a selected language (which can be English). If examination of the application in the EPO is favorable, a European Patent or "Europatent" is granted and is then subjected to a public opposition period. If claims survive this opposition period, the European Patent can be "nationalized" to provide patent rights in each member country designated in the application, contingent upon a fee payment ("validation") in each country. If requested, the Unitary Patent will eliminate validation and provide uniform patent protection in each elected EU member state participating in the unitary scheme.

- more economical than PCT if filing in more than two non-English-speaking EPC countries

Reading:

European Patent Application Timeline With Expected Costs
https://www.fillun.com/european-patent-application-timeline-with-expected-costs

European Patents—The Basics
https://www.mewburn.com/law-practice-library/european-patents-the-basics

Foreign Filing Patent Applications
https://youngbasile.com/foreign-info/

European Patent Filing
https://pintz.com/european-patent-filing

1. **Pre-Application Activities and Considerations**
   - public disclosure before US filing can be bar to patent; consult national patent laws for specific information
   - no filing permitted after US patent issues
   - file U.S. application (PPA/RPA/DES) to establish priority filing date (35 USC 119(e), 120; 37 CFR 1.78(a)&(d))
   - file PC application within one year of U.S. appl to preserve priority; within six months for design application
     - should file within nine months to give foreign agents enough time to prep docs
     - must have foreign filing license or wait at least six months after U.S. filing

Reading:

Priority Pitfalls in European Patent Applications Based on U.S. Priority Applications
https://www.finnegan.com/en/insights/articles/priority-pitfalls-in-european-patent-applications-based-on-u-s.html

- U.S. applicants can submit requests for a European patent, but must engage a European-based representative, registered with the EPO, to prosecute the application [*see* EPC Article 133(2); Article 134(1,8)]
- if applicant domicile or principal place of business is outside Europe, you must have representation in proceedings before the Office, and are only allowed to file the patent application and pay the fees yourself (European Patent Guide 4.1.023). You can engage a professional representative before the European Patent Office or a legal practitioner who is authorized to represent applicants before the Office. See www.epo.org/representatives [European Patent Guide 4.1]
- retain EPO-approved professional representative or practitioner to prosecute application after submittal

2. Filing

a. Application Preparation and Assembly

1) Required Parts (Art. 78(1); R. 49; R. 50; GL A-VIII, 2.1)

Request for Grant of a European Patent	EPO Form 1001
- for completion of Request, see "Notes on the request for a European patent" and "European Patent Guide—How to get a European patent," 20th ed., April 2020	Apx F-24
- available on EPO website	
- Copy of Priority Doc not required	Art. 88(1)

Notes on the Request for Grant of a European Patent
https://archive.epo.org/oj/issues/1997/06/p263/1997-p263.pdf

Designation of Inventor	EPO Form 1002
- use where applicant is not the inventor or not the sole inventor	
Invention Disclosure	Art. 83, 84
i. Description	
ii. Claim(s)	
iii. Drawings (where necessary)	
iv. Abstract	

Related Forms (*see* https://www.epo.org/applying/forms/forms.html)

1003	Authorization
1004	General Authorization

2) *Accompanying Papers as Appropriate*
- certified copy of priority document (if claiming priority to prior application)
  - must be filed within two months of Request submittal

Related Forms (*see* https://www.epo.org/applying/forms/forms.html)

1005	PACE Request (expedited prosecution)
1009	Request for participation in Patent Prosecution Highway (PPH)
1011	Designation of applicant for purposes of reduced fees

b. Application Submittal

1.) E-Filing
- online filing via EPO website
- must register to use online filing services (see EPO website)
  - fees can be paid online

2.) Via Mail (paper)
- for instructions on applying by mail, see EPO website

3. Post-Filing

Rescind Non-Publication Request (NPR) (if necessary)	SB/36
- within 45 days of foreign filing if prior U.S. filing	37 CFR 1.213(b)
PTO Response: Acknowledgment	35 USC 122{b)(2)(B)(ii) MPEP 1123
- after application submittal, in-country legal representative carries forward with prosecution	

Find a Professional Representative
https://www.epo.org/applying/online-services/representatives.html

[Note: consult EPO website for details on post-filing activities]

4. Post-Grant
- within one month of issue, the patentee has the option of requesting Unitary Patent status; otherwise, the European patent must be validated in each elected jurisdiction
- European patent (Europatent) issued (term—20 years from filing)
- validation (nationalization) procedure
  - patent holder must register in and file translation in each designated country and appoint agent
  - pay validation fees

C. Paris Convention Application (PC)

Paris Convention for the Protection of Industrial Property

Overview

The Paris Convention does not have a centralized patent office for receiving applications; patent applications in any of the member states must be directly filed and prosecuted individually in each country or regional office (e.g., EPO) in accordance with its procedural regulations. An initial application filed in the U.S. or any Convention member establishes a priority date for subsequent filings in other Convention countries within one year of the priority application (six months for design applications).

1. Pre-Application Activities and Considerations

- public disclosure before U.S. filing can be bar to patent; consult national patent laws for specific information
  - no filing permitted after U.S. patent issues
- file U.S. application (PPA/RPA/DES) to establish priority filing date (35 USC 119(e), 120; 37 CFR 1.78(a)&(d))
- file PC application within one year of U.S. appl to preserve priority; within six months for design application
  - should file within nine months to give foreign agents enough time to prep docs
  - must have foreign filing license or wait at least six months after U.S. filing
- hire agents in jurisdictions where required to file and/or prosecute applications
- some foreign countries may require U.S. filers to act through an in-country legal representative for application submittal and/or prosecution; consult national patent laws for specific information
- generally, English-speaking countries allow application activities without an in-country agent; Japan allows only initial application filing

Application Policies in Selected Foreign Countries Regarding Application Filing/ Prosecution

Reading:

Pursuing International IP Protection

https://www.uspto.gov/patents/basics/international-protection/filing-patents-abroad

Canadian Intellectual Property Office
https://www.ic.gc.ca/eic/site/cipointernet-internetopic.nsf/eng/home

UK (applicant filing/prosecution permitted)
http://www.patentoffice.org.uk/

France (filing/prosecution only by agent)

Germany (filing/prosecution only by agent)

Italy (filing/prosecution only by agent)

Japan (applicant can only file initial application, pay fees)
https://www.jpo.go.jp/e/

Republic of Korea (filing/prosecution only by agent)

Australia (applicant can file/prosecute)
https://www.ipaustralia.gov.au/

2. Filing

- consult patent rules of specific countries for application procedures
- if necessary, file certified copy of U.S. application and translation into the approved language of the country, along with application before one year anniversary of U.S. filing
- file within sufficient time for certified U.S. application to be transmitted before deadline
- it can take a month for the USPTO to transmit a certified copy

3. Post-Filing

Rescind Non-Publication Request (NPR) (if necessary)	SB/36
- within 45 days of foreign filing if prior U.S. filing	37 CFR 1.213(b)
PTO Response: Acknowledgment	35 USC 122(b)(2)(B)(ii) MPEP 1123
- in many countries, after application submittal, in-country legal representative or agent carries on with prosecution	

[Note: for post-filing activities, consult the patent office websites of individual jurisdictions]

4. Post-Grant

- the patent laws of many countries mandate opposition proceedings (validity challenges) against issued patents, as well as the periodic payment of annuities (maintenance fees). Consult the laws and regulations of individual countries for information regarding post-grant activities.

Reading:
Foreign Oppositions—Considerations
https://www.sternekessler.com/services/patent-office-litigation/patent-oppositions#:~:text=The%20cost%20of%20an%20opposition%20proceeding%20in%20a,the%20same%20patent%20application%20in%20many%20foreign%20countries

D. Hague International Registration of Industrial Designs

MPEP Ch. 2900; 35 USC Ch. 38; 37 CFR 1.1001 *et seq.*

Overview
The Hague Agreement permits up to 100 industrial designs per application to be registered in multiple jurisdictions by filing a single application either directly in WIPO headquarters in Geneva, Switzerland, or indirectly through a national RO, including the USPTO. The application is subjected to a unitary formalities examination by WIPO, and then given a substantive examination by each elected jurisdiction, reserving the right to refuse registration if finding the subject matter unpatentable. Although, ostensibly, the Hague application permits up to 100 designs per application, applicants should be aware that the USPTO will allow examination of only a single patentably distinct design (*see* 37 CFR 1.1064; MPEP 2920.05(b), 1504.05).

Reading:
US Design Patents and the Hague Agreement Concerning Industrial Designs
https://bannerwitcoff.com/_docs/library/articles/Practical%20Law.US%20Design%20Patents%20and%20the%20Hague%20Agreement%20Concerning%20Industrial%20Designs.pdf

1. Pre-Application Activities and Considerations

To be eligible for international design application, applicant must:

1. Be a national of a contracting party or of a member state of an intergovernmental organization that is a contracting party (e.g., the European Union);
2. Have a domicile or habitual residence in the territory of a contracting party; or
3. Have a real and effective industrial or commercial establishment in the territory of a contracting party.

- for eligibility to file in USPTO, *see* 37 CFR 1.1011; MPEP 2904
- public disclosure before U.S. filing can be bar to patent; consult national patent laws for specific information
- no filing permitted after U.S. patent issues
- file Hague application within six months of any previous U.S. priority filing in order to preserve priority date (*see* 35 USC 172)
- must have foreign filing license or wait at least six months after U.S. filing

2. Filing

a. Application Prep/Assembly

For instructions on completing application form, see

Hague Guide for Users: How to Submit an International Application to the International Bureau—E-filing or DM/1 Form, available on WIPO website;

EFS-Web Quick Start Guide for Filing International Design Applications Through the USPTO as an Office of Indirect Filing, available on PTO website

1) Required Parts (Art. 5; Common Regs. Rule 7; 35 USC 383; 37 CFR 1.1021; MPEP 2909)

Application for International Registration	eHague (e-filing)
- includes Annexes I–V (submit as appropriate)	DM/1 (paper filing) Apx F-25
Disclosure	
i. Reproductions (Drawings) (37 CFR 1.1026; Apx F-26; MPEP 2909.02, 2920.04(b); Admin. Instruction Part 4; Common Regs. Rule 9)	Apx F-26

Reproductions may generally be in the form of drawings and/or photographs of the industrial designs. An international design application may include up to 100 industrial designs in a single Locarno classification. However, all of the designs must belong to the same class of the International (Locarno) Classification. The list of classes of the Locarno Classification together with explanatory notes is available on the WIPO website at: http://www.wipo.int/classifications/locarno/en/.

- For requirements of reproductions, see Rule 9 of Hague Agreement and Part 4 of Admin. Instructions
- Only one independent and distinct design may be claimed in the U.S. examination phase
- Color drawings permitted (no petition required)
- For one International Design (Patent) Application (IDA), the applicant must prepare a single set of reproductions for all of the designated Contracting Parties. Before filing an IDA, the applicant's country selection and drawings should be based on its strategy to maximize its design rights. For example, applicant should consider: the Contracting Party's IP rights regime, such as whether the Contracting Party accepts partial designs or shaded or unshaded figures; the strength of IP enforcement in the Contracting Party; where the product covered by the design is to be sold; the likelihood of copying; design prosecution and examination cost; and the Contracting Party's requirements for the design's reproductions.
- For submittal of drawing via EFS-Web, *see* MPEP 2909.02(a)

ii. **Specification** (Common Regs. Rule 11; 37 CFR 1.1067; — Apx F-27; MPEP 2920.04(a))

(1) Title

- must designate particular article by name generally known by the public
- title and claim must correspond

(2) Description

- reference to the drawing(s) only

iii. **Claim** (Common Regs. Rule 11; 37 CFR 1.1025) — Apx F-28

- specify name of article
- one claim only (for U.S. designation)

Inventor Oath/Declaration	37 CFR 1.1067 MPEP 2909.01, 2920.04.04(c)
- **Annex I: Declaration of Inventorship**	Apx F-29
Substitute: **Patent Application Declaration (PAD)**	
- inventor(s) attest to be true and original inventors of subject matter	AIA/08 37 CFR 1.63, 1.63(e), 1.64
- each joint inventor must have contributed to at least one claim (Rule 45)	35 USC 115
- can be submitted after initial filing	MPEP 602
Use AIA/10 (Supp. Date Sheet for Declaration) if including additional inventors	
- use copy from prior appl.	37 CFR 1.63(d)
Patent Appl. Declaration (PAD; can be filed later) (AIA/08; use AIA/01 if including ADS)(use AIA/10, Supplemental Sheet for Declaration, if including additional inventors)	
- each joint inventor must have contributed to at least one claim (Rule 45)	
Substitute: Substitute Statement in Lieu of an Oath or Declaration for Utility or Design Patent Application (35 U.S.C. 115(d) and 37 CFR 1.64)	AIA/02
Application Data Sheet (ADS)	
Inventorship bibliographic, representative, correspondence address, and other application information	37 CFR 1.76 MPEP 601.05(a) AIA/14
ADS (EFS)	
- can be prepared before filing (optional) or will be automatically generated upon e-filing	

2) *Accompanying Papers as Appropriate*

Appointment of Representative	Apx F-30
- for appointment of representative before the IB	DM/7 Common Regs. Rule 3 37 CFR 1.1041 MPEP 2911
Substitute: **Power of Attorney**	
Authorization of practitioner to represent applicant before the USPTO during application activities	37 CFR 1.32 MPEP 402.02(a)

1. Authorization by assignee who wishes to become applicant (*see* 37 CFR 1.46(c)) to appoint practitioner as representative	AIA/80
Attachments: Statement Under 37 CFR 3.73(c)	
2. Authorization by applicant to appoint practitioner as representative	AIA/82A & B
PTO Response: Notice of Acceptance (or Denial)	PTOL-308
Entity Status Fee Reduction (Annex IV)	
- indicate Small Entity (SE) or Micro Entity (ME) for discounted fees	
Assertion of Small Entity (SE) status for discounted fees	37 CFR 1.27(a)
Asserting SE status	35 USC 41(h)(1)
- determining Small Entity: individual, small biz (500 employees max), university, or 501(c)(3) nonprofit	MPEP 509.02
- also indicate SE status on ADS	
Certification of Micro Entity (ME) status for discounted fees	37 CFR 1.29
- also indicate ME status on ADS	35 USC 123 MPEP 509.04
Certification of Micro Entity Status	
- determination of Micro Entity: must meet SE Criteria (37 CFR 1.27(a)), and (1) applicant has not been named as inventor on more than four utility, design, or plant patents; (2) applicant (or assignee) had gross income in previous year of less than 3x median household income (ca. 57K; 3x = ca. 170K); (3) majority of applicant's employment income is from institution of higher learning, or applicant has assigned, or is obligated to assign, rights to institution of higher learning	
Micro Entity—Income-based	SB/15A
Asserts eligibility for fee discount based on gross income of inventor(s)	37 CFR 1.29(a) MPEP 509.04
Micro Entity—Employment-based	SB/15B
Asserts eligibility for fee discount based on employment by institution of higher learning or being independent inventor	37 CFR 1.29(d) MPEP 509.04
Attachments: SB/15A (income) SB/15B (higher education employment; independent inventor)	

Assignment Recordation Cover Sheet	PTO-1595
Cover sheet for written assignment	MPEP 302.07
- file via EPAS	Common Regs. Rule 21, 22
Attachments: Executed Assignment Agreement if not yet recorded	Apx F-31
Statement Under 37 CFR 3.73(c)	AIA/96
Establishes assignee's ownership rights in patent application	37 CFR 3.73(c)
- used by legal/obligatory assignee to establish ownership of invention/application	
Request for Expedited Examination (Rocket Docket)	SB/27
- only international applications published by WIPO are eligible	37 CFR 1.155 MPEP 1504.30

b. Application Submittal

1.) E-Filing	
(a.) EFS-Web (indirect filing in USPTO)	Common Regs. Rule 13 MPEP 2905.01 35 USC 382 37 CFR 1.1002

For procedure on e-filing via EFS-Web, see EFS-Web Quick Start Guide for Filing International Design Applications Through the USPTO as an Office of Indirect Filing (May 2015)

Payment of application fees	Common Regs. Rule 12, 27-28 MPEP 2910 37 CFR 1.1031
- Transmittal fee: payable to USPTO; should be paid upon filing	
- Other application fees: payable to WIPO; IB will solicit payment after receiving application [Note: filing fees are based in part on number of embodiments, number of figures, and number of words exceeding 100 in the application]	

The International Bureau provides an online tool, the Hague System Fee Calculator, to assist the applicant in calculating the appropriate WIPO application fees. The Fee Calculator is available at http://www.wipo.int/hague/en/fees/calculator.jsp.

(b.) eHague (direct filing in IB) MPEP 2905

- Avoids PTO transmittal fee
- Quicker formalities review
- Ability to correct defects in application via e-filing Portfolio Manager (*see* https://www.wipo.int/edocs/hagdocs/en/2016/hague_2016_5.pdf)
- FFL may be required

2.) Via U.S. Mail (paper filing)

- subject to added fee

Form DM/1 (E)
https://www.wipo.int/hague/en/forms/

THE INTERNATIONAL DESIGN APPLICATION (IDA) must:

- be filed in English, French, or Spanish
- include a reproduction of the industrial design the applicant seeks to protect
  - may include up to 100 different designs if the designs all belong to the same International Classification of Industrial Designs (Locarno Classification)
- identify the Contracting Parties where the applicant seeks protection
- include the payment, in Swiss francs, of: the basic filing fee; the publication fee; and a fee for each designated Contracting Party. The fees are generally payable when the applicant files the IDA, except if the applicant requests deferment of publication (*see* Common Regs. Rule 16). The applicant may then pay the fees later (*see* Common Regs. Rule 12(2)).

3. **Post-Filing**

a. Pre-Exam

NOTE: After initial application submittal, subsequent document submittals to the PTO should be accompanied by a Certificate of Transmission and Transmittal Form or Letter.

Certificate of Transmission	Apx D-18
Establishes that correspondence has been sent to PTO as of date thereon	37 CFR 1.8 MPEP 512
For suggested formats, *see* MPEP 512	
Substitute: Certificate of Mailing or Transmission	
Under 37 CFR 1.8	SB/92

Transmittal Form SB/21

Cover sheet/letter for transmittal of correspondence to PTO after initial filing

Substitute: Transmittal Letter

Transmittal Letter Apx D-19

Cover letter for transmittal of misc. correspondence after initial filing

Substitute: Transmittal Form SB/21

1) *Routine Office Communications*

- EFS Acknowledgment Rcpt (immediate after e-filing submittal)

  RESPONSE: none

Electronic Patent Application Fee Transmittal SB/06

- Fee Worksheet (EFS-generated)
  - immediate after e-filing submittal
- Official Filing Rcpt (within ca. two weeks after filing) RESPONSE: if inaccurate, request Corrected Filing Receipt

Request for Corrected Filing Receipt Apx D-20

Requests correction and replacement of erroneous Official Filing Receipt Attachments: supplemental ADS if correcting inventorship information

- markup copy of original Filing Receipt showing correction
- include markup copy of ADS if necessary

PTO response: corrected Filing Receipt

- acceptance of request for corrected inventorship, if necessary (37 CFR 1.48)

Notification Regarding Receipt and Transmittal of the International Design Application to the International Bureau

- issued if USPTO used as RO
- includes grant of FFL
- notification of transmittal typically occurs about two weeks after application received by PTO

WIPO Routinely Publishes International Application 6 Months After Registration	Common Regs. Rule 17; *see also* Rule 16
- applicant may request immediate publication upon registration	Art. 10, 15
- applicant may request deferment of publication of up to 30 months from priority date	MPEP 2907
- not possible when U.S. is designated	

2) Applicant-Initiated Actions

IDS (use Annex III or SB/08(a) & (b))

- can be filed within three months of application date

Information Disclosure Statement (IDS)	SB/08
Fulfills Duty of Disclosure, Candor and Good Faith per	37 CFR 1.97 et seq. 37 CFR 1.56(a)
(1) can be filed with initial application, through pendency	MPEP 2920.05(f)
- file within three months of appl filing date, or before mailing date of first OA on merits, whichever is later; or before first OA on merits after filing RCE; otherwise statement under 1.97(e) and fee required	Apx D-08
(2) after the period in (1), but prior to the prosecution of the application closes, i.e., before the mailing of a final Office action, a Notice of Allowance, or an *Ex parte Quayle* action, whichever is earlier;	Apx D-09
(3) after the period in (2) but on or before the date the issue fee is paid; and	Apx D-10
(4) after the period in (3) and up to the time the patent application can be effectively withdrawn from issue under 37 CFR 1.313(c).	MPEP 609.04(B) MPEP 609
- e-IDS	MPEP 609.07

Attachments: Copies of foreign patents and non-pat lit. (per 37 CFR 1.98(a)(2))

- may require statement under CFR 1.97(e) and fee, depending on when filed (e.g., after Allowance)

PTO response: notice of noncompliant IDS if irregularities exist

- if requested, copy of SB/08, initialed by examiner as considered (per MPEP 609)

Rescind Non-Publication Request	SB/36
Within 45 days of foreign filing	37 CFR 1.213(b) 35 USC 122(b)(2)(B)(ii) MPEP 1123
PTO Response: Acknowledgement	
Request for Correction in a Patent Application Relating to Inventorship or an Inventor Name, or Order of Names, Other than in a Reissue Application (37 CFR 1.48)	
Correct/change inventorship in non-provisional application	MPEP 602.01(c)(1) AIA/40 37 CFR 1.48(a) 37 CFR 1.324 35 USC 116
Attachments: fee; corrected ADS, PAD, if necessary	
Substitute: Draft request may be filed as alternative to AIA/40	
PTO Response: Acceptance/Denial	
Request to Correct or Update the Name of the Applicant Under 37 CFR 1.46(c)(1), or Change the Applicant Under 37 CFR 1.46(c)(2)	Apx D-28
Request to update or change applicant(s)	MPEP 602.01(c)(2) SB/41
Attachments: fee; updated ADS	37 CFR 1.46
Transmittal of Certified Copy of Priority Document	Apx F-32
- if priority claimed to foreign application	37 CFR 1.55 35 USC 119, 386 MPEP 213.06, 251, 2920.05(d)
Attachments: Certified Copy of Priority Document(s)	

Reading:

When Must Foreign Priority Document Be Filed in a US Utility Patent Application?
https://www.patenttrademarkblog.com/when-must-foreign-priority-document-be-filed-in-a-us-utility-patent-application/

The Confused USPTO Policy on Certified Copies of Patent Applications
https://www.foley.com/en/insights/publications/2014/12/the-confused-uspto-policy-on-certified-copies-of-p

Claiming Foreign Priority In U.S. Patent Applications
https://www.jchoilaw.com/news/2015/claiming-foreign-priority-in-u-s-patent-applications

Filing of Certified Copies of Priority Documents: No Change for Design Patent Applications
http://www.protectingdesigns.com/99-filing-of-certified-copies-of-priority-documents-no-change-for-design-patent-applicants

Request to Retrieve Electronic Priority Application(s)	SB/38
Request that PTO retrieve electronic copies of foreign applications from which priority has been claimed	37 CFR 1.55(i) MPEP 213.06 35 USC 119
Petition to Accept Unintentionally Delayed Priority Document Under 37 CFR 1.55(g)	Apx D-32 37 CFR 1.55(e)&(g) MPEP 214.02
- use when priority claim/document under 37 CFR 119(a) not made in compliance with MPEP 155(g)	
Attachments: petition fee	SB/17p
- certified copy of foreign application, 37 CFR 1.17(g) if necessary; statement averring that the belated claim was unintentional	
PTO Response: Decision on petition	
Petition to Accept Unintentionally Delayed Priority Claim to a Domestic Application Under 37 CFR 1.78(c)	SB/445 35 USC 119(e), 120 37 CFR 1.78(c)
Request to consider delayed claim of priority to PPA	MPEP 214.02
Substitute: draft petition	Apx D-33
Attachments: petition fee	37 CFR 1.17(m)
- statement averring that the belated claim was unintentional	
PTO Response: Decision on petition	
Change of Entity Status	Apx D-35
Report of change/correction of entity status of applicant, with commensurate fees, if necessary	MPEP 509.03(b)
- can be filed via Private PAIR	
PTO Response: Acknowledgment of change	
Change of Correspondence Address	

Update applicant mailing address	AIA/122
Substitute: Update address via Private PAIR	
Authorization to Incorporate Extension of Time with Reply	Apx D-16 37 CFR 1.136(a)(3)
Avoids potential loss of patent rights for applicants who inadvertently omit petition for extension of time	MPEP 710.02(e)
Petition to Convert International Application to U.S. Design Application	37 CFR 1.1052 MPEP 2914
- only international applications filed in USPTO as RO, and designating U.S. are eligible - petition must be filed before WIPO publication of international registration and include petition fee under 37 CFR 1.17(t)	

b. Post-Exam

1) Non-Substantive (Formalities) Exam by WIPO

WIPO reviews application for compliance with applicable requirements (Common Regs. Rules 7 to 9, and Parts 3 and 4 of the Administrative Instructions), including payment of fees

- if application is noncompliant, WIPO will notify applicant of the irregularity, normally requiring correction within three months
- if application is compliant, WIPO will record it in the International Register and issue the International Registration certificate
- WIPO will then publish the International Registration in the International Designs Bulletin
- where required under its own domestic legislation, each contracting party may proceed with substantive examination of the application
- applications are not subjected to further formalities review after the WIPO examination

2) Substantive Exam by Each Designated Jurisdiction

Each designated country has the right to examine the application on substantive grounds and may refuse registration if application fails to meet its national substantive requirements (*see* Common Regs. Rule 20).

For examination in USPTO, *see* 35 USC 389; MPEP 2920.05.

Notification of Refusal—Restriction/Election	Common Regs. Rule 18 Admin. Instr. Part 5 37 CFR 1.1064 35 USC 121 MPEP 2920.05(b)
Notification of Refusal—Non-Final Office Action	Common Regs. Rule 18 Admin. Instr. Part 5 37 CFR 1.1063 MPEP 2920.05(a)
Applicant Response: Response Under 37 CFR 1.111	
Correction in the International Register Under Rule 22	Art. 16 Common Regs.
- announcement of correction of International Register data	Rule 22 37 CFR 1.1065 MPEP 2930
Request Interview With Examiner	PTOL-413A
Applicant Initiated Interview Request Form	37 CFR 1.133 MPEP 713
- Proposed Interview Agenda	Apx D-53
Substitute: Automated Interview Request Form	
Express or Formal Abandonment Under 37 CFR 1.138	AIA/24 35 USC 388
- file before date of issue or publication	37 CFR 1.138 MPEP 711.01
Notice of Abandonment issued	
- if no applicant response to Non-Final OA	
- issued by PTO for reason(s) indicated	
Applicant Response: Revive (optional)	
- see Revival of Abandoned Applications	
Final Office Action	
Applicant Response: Amendment After Final or Under 37 CFR 1.116	
Allowance (Term of Protection—15 years from grant date)	35 USC 173 MPEP 2920.06

Notice of Allowance and Fees Due	PTOL-85
Receive "Notice of Allowability" if Amend After Final is acceptable	
- receive formal "Notice of Allowance" with form specifying Issue Fee Due (PTOL-85(B)), Notice of Allowance and Fees Due	
Applicant Response:	
- submit Issue Fee form (PTOL-85(B)) and payment (can be submitted via EFS-Web)	
- Issue Fee Transmittal Letter	
Notification Under Rule 12(3)(d) of the Common Regulations of the Hague Agreement	Common Regs. Rule 12
- notification that second part (Part B) the individual designation fee for the U.S. has not been paid within applicable period	
- international registration is canceled in U.S.	
- Notice of Abandonment issued	
Petition Under 37 CFR 1.313(c)(2) to Withdraw Application from Issue After	SB/140
Payment of Issue Fee	37 CFR 1.313(c)(2)
- to withdraw application from issue RCE must be pending	MPEP 1308
Substitute: ePetition	37 CFR 1.313(c)(1-3) 35 USC 388
Attachments: petition fee	AIA/17p 37 CFR 1.17(h)
PTO Response: Decision on Petition	
Amendment After Allowance Under 37 CFR 1.312	Apx F-33; *see also* Apx D-65
- correction of formalities to Spec/Drawings if necessary	
***Ex Parte Quayle* Action (Office Action Summary)**	MPEP 714.14
Issued when all pending claims allowed, application is in condition for allowance, except for minor formal matters in disclosure, and prosecution on the merits is closed	
- file amendment after allowance to correct formalities	
Applicant Response: Response to *Ex Parte Quayle* Action	
- Amendment Under 37 CFR 1.111	Apx D-68
- corrected disclosure papers as required	

4. Post-Grant

Issue Notification	
- mailed approx. three weeks prior to issue	
- term of registration—15 years from issue date in U.S.	35 USC 173
Statement of Grant of Protection	Common Regs.
- includes registration number	Rule 18bis 37 CFR 1.1068 MPEP 2940
- valid in U.S. only upon grant of U.S. design patent	37 CFR 1.1071 MPEP 2950
Registration Renewal Through WIPO	Common Regs Rules 23-25
- initial period of registration is five years from issue date	Admin. Instr. Part 7
- renewal periods are for five years each, up to the maximum term in each designated country	
[Note: renewal not necessary for U.S. design patents issued from an International Application]	37 CFR 1.1031

PART THREE

Biotechnology Applications

"I think the biggest innovations of the 21st century will be at the intersection of biology and technology. A new era is beginning."

—Steve Jobs

I. Introduction—Patents for Life

Part Three (this supplement) will consider specialized utility patent applications disclosing nucleotide and/or amino acid sequences, and/or requiring deposit of biological materials in an authorized depository. The disclosed biological materials in these applications have often been genetically modified, rendering them biologically distinct from their naturally occurring counterparts. Biotechnology subject matter has generally been genetically manipulated via non-conventional means, such as cellular and molecular techniques, to create useful products and processes. Examples include viable material such as genetically altered (e.g., recombinant DNA, transgenic) microorganisms, plants, animals, and cell lines that are capable of self-replication. Aside from genetically modified living organisms, biotechnology subject matter also includes nonviable molecular material, such as nucleotide and amino acid sequences that differ in composition and structure from those found in nature.

Utility patent-eligible subject matter also includes novel varieties of plants produced by conventional techniques like pedigree (Mendelian) hybridization, selective breeding, cell/tissue culture, or use of agents to induce genetic mutation. Proprietary new and useful varieties of plants created by such methods can also be protected under the Plant Patent Act of 1930 (PPA; *see* 35 USC 161) (for asexually propagated plants) or the Plant Variety Protection Act of 1970 (PVPA) (for sexually propagated plants); however, these laws provide weaker rights than a utility patent.

Provisions of the PPA and PVPA will not be addressed in this supplement. For details on plant patent applications under the PPA, refer to MPEP Ch. 1600.

Filing biotechnology-related patent applications varies somewhat from other utility applications, notably in requirements for proper disclosure of biosequences and/or the deposit of biological samples. Nonetheless, these elements add an extra layer of complexity to the application that practitioners should be attentive to. After filing, biotech applications are prosecuted in substantially the same manner as other utility applications. Accordingly, it should be noted that Part Three (this annex) will examine matters relevant to biotech applications. The reader should consult Part One for treatment of utility applications generally.

Part Three will address both domestic and international biotech patent application.

Reading:

Preparing Biotech Patent Applications—Ten Strategies for Success
https://www.knobbe.com/news/2017/03/preparing-biotech-patent-applications-ten-strategies-success

Nature and Types of Biotechnology Patents
https://www.upcounsel.com/nature-and-types-of-biotechnology-patents

The Biotechnology Patent Landscape
https://www.biospace.com/article/the-biotechnology-patent-landscape/

Are Biotechnology Patents Dead?
https://www.genengnews.com/insights/are-biotechnology-patents-dead/

Intellectual Property Biotechnology: Everything You Need to Know
https://www.upcounsel.com/intellectual-property-biotechnology

Biotech Patents: Everything You Need to Know
https://www.upcounsel.com/biotech-patents

How to Patent a Natural Product: Everything You Need to Know
https://www.upcounsel.com/how-to-patent-a-natural-product

The U.S. Patent System, Biotechnology, and the Courts
https://www.ncbi.nlm.nih.gov/books/NBK19867/

Unique Issues Involved in Patenting Biotechnology Inventions
https://www.spiersgroup.com/unique-issues-involved-in-patenting-biotechnology-inventions

II. Domestic Biotechnology Patent Applications

Overview

The United States leads the world in number of biotechnology patents awarded, due, at least in part, to a favorable patenting system and legislation promoting biotech R&D. There are, however, some challenges ahead for the prospective biotech applicant, as the law tries to keep pace with the burgeoning technology. Continuing uncertainty surrounding patent-eligibility of biotech subject matter will persist as the courts and patent office deal with the quickening stream of innovation in the biological arts. The Supreme Court's decision in *Myriad* (*Association for Molecular Pathology v. Myriad Genetics, Inc.*, 133 U.S. 2107 (2013)) is likely not the last word on how far a claimed invention needs to depart from naturally occurring material in order to qualify for patent. Associated issues of novelty, utility, nonobviousness, and enablement also await further clarification. The inherent variability and unpredictability of biological material leads to difficulties in drafting enabling disclosures, poor patent quality, and, inevitably, legal challenges to claim validity. Biotech applicants should be aware of the risks involved in patenting, as well as the rewards.

Reading:

Patents and Biotechnology
https://www.uschamberfoundation.org/patents-and-biotechnology

The Biotechnology Patent Landscape
https://www.biospace.com/article/the-biotechnology-patent-landscape/

Why Patents Matter in Biotechnology
https://healthcaremba.gwu.edu/blog/why-patents-matter-in-biotech/

The Patent Landscape of Genetically Modified Organisms
https://sitn.hms.harvard.edu/flash/2015/the-patent-landscape-of-genetically-modified-organisms/

A. Sources of Domestic Biotechnology Patent Law and Rules of Practice

1. **Federal Rules and Regulations**
   a. 37 CFR Part 1—Rules of Practice In Patent Cases (37 CFR 1.1 *et seq.*)
      - Subpart B—National Processing Provisions
        - Language, Paper, Writing, Margins, Compact Disc Specifications
        - 37 CFR 1.52
      - Subpart G—Biotechnology Invention Disclosures Deposit of Biological Material
        - 37 CFR 1.801–.809
      - Application Disclosures Containing Nucleotide and/or Amino Acid Sequences
        - CFR 1.821–.825, 37 CFR 1.831–835

   b. Manual of Patent Examination Procedure (MPEP): Pertinent MPEP Chapters:
      - Ch. 600—Parts, Form, and Content of Applications
        - MPEP 608.05 Sequence Listing, Table, or Computer Program Listing Appendix Submitted in Electronic Form
      - Ch. 2100—Patentability
        - MPEP 2105 Patent Eligible Subject Matter—Living Subject Matter
        - MPEP 2106 Patent Subject Matter Eligibility
      - Ch. 2400—Biotechnology
        - 2402–2411 Deposit of Biological Material
        - 2412–2419, 2420–2431 Nucleotide and/or Amino Acid Disclosures

2. **Case Law**
   - U.S. Supreme Court
   - Federal Courts of Appeal—U.S. Court of Appeals for the Federal Circuit (CAFC)
   - Agency Decisions (USPTO)—Patent Trial and Appeal Board (PTAB)

Biotechnology Patent Law Updates:
Patents4Life—Biotech Patent Law Blog
https://www.patents4life.com/

Case Law Index Biotechnology
https://nationalaglawcenter.org/aglaw-reporter/case-law-index/biotechnology/

Reading:
A Guide to Biotechnology Law
https://readingroom.law.gsu.edu/cgi/viewcontent.cgi?article=1030&context=lib_student

3. International Treaties

- Budapest Treaty [on the International Recognition of the Deposit of Microorganisms for the Purposes of Patent Procedure]
  - administered under WIPO

B. Pre-Filing Activities and Considerations

Prior to filing on biotechnology inventions, the principal concerns include the patent-eligibility, novelty, and enablement of the proposed subject matter. The boundaries of what is patent-eligible in biotechnology subject matter is evolving in the judiciary. Inventions in this area are especially prone to scrutiny under the "judicial exceptions" doctrine. Practitioners should be informed on current patentability policy, particularly when the subject matter involves nucleotide and/or amino acid sequences, and genetically altered biological material.

Additionally, patent regulations require the deposit of samples of any biological materials disclosed when necessary to make and practice the invention. Such deposits are preferably made before filing so that deposit information can be referenced in the disclosure, and also to ensure priority for subsequent international applications.

Reading:
Preparing Biotech Patent Applications—Ten Strategies for Success
https://www.knobbe.com/news/2017/03/preparing-biotech-patent-applications-ten-strategies-success

Patents and Biotechnology
https://www.uschamberfoundation.org/patents-and-biotechnology

The Complications Around Patenting Biotechnology
https://www.labiotech.eu/in-depth/biotechnology-patents-intellectual-property/

1. Patentability Assessment [MPEP 2105–06]

Generally, biotechnology inventions are classified as compositions of matter, manufactures, and processes. They may also be patent-eligible as "new uses" of existing technology. Biotech subject matter must not be classified as a "judicial exception," which would place it outside the bounds of patent-eligible invention. It is only important that the invention under consideration fall under at least one of the qualifying categories. Special attention should be paid to the judicial exception doctrine, as the courts continue to define what is patent-eligible in biotechnology. Once the invention is placed into a statutory class, it must still satisfy the remaining threshold requisites for patentability pursuant to 35 USC 102 and 103.

Reading:
Patentability of Biotech Inventions in the USA—Patentable Subject Matter
https://www.bananaip.com/ip-news-center/patentability-of-biotech-inventions-in-4/

a. Patentable Subject Matter
The subject matter must satisfy the following patentability requirements:

1.) Statutory Class	35 USC 101
- subject matter must fall within a statutory category eligible for patent	MPEP 2106
- what biotech subject matter qualifies as patent-eligible continues to emerge in the courts	

Reading:
Patentable Subject Matter: Everything You Need to Know
https://www.upcounsel.com/patentable-subject-matter#

Complications in Patenting Biotech Inventions: A Peek at US Law
https://www.bananaip.com/ip-news-center/complications-in-patenting-biotech-inventions-a-peek-at-us-law/#:~:text=USPTO%20considers%20gene%20and%20protein%20sequences%20as%20large,proved%20that%20it%20has%20been%20made%20by%20man

Trends in Subject Matter Eligibility for Biotechnology Inventions
https://www.ipwatchdog.com/2015/07/12/trends-in-subject-matter-eligibility-for-biotechnology-inventions/id=59738/

Evaluating the Evaluation: Breaking Down New USPTO Guidance for Patent-Eligible Subject Matter
https://www.pillsburylaw.com/en/news-and-insights/uspto-guidance-patent.html

What Is Patentable Subject Matter?
https://www.fr.com/what-is-patentable-subject-matter/

Summary of Subject Matter Eligibility: Biotech/Pharma Inventions
https://www.sternekessler.com/news-insights/publications/summary-subject-matter-eligibility-biotechpharma-inventions

Patent Subject Matter Eligibility in the Biotechnology Industry
http://www.fordhamiplj.org/2021/12/11/patent-subject-matter-eligibility-in-the-biotechnology-industry/

Patentable Subject Matter for a Utility Patent—Explained
https://thebusinessprofessor.com/en_US/property-law/patentable-subject-matter-for-a-utility-patent

Patentable Subject Matter Under Section 101
https://cardinal-ip.com/patentable-subject-matter-under-section-101/

USPTO Releases New Guidance on Patent Subject Matter Eligibility
https://www.jonesday.com/en/insights/2019/01/uspto-releases-new-guidance-on-patent-subject-matt

2014 Interim Guidance on Patent Subject Matter Eligibility
https://www.bitlaw.com/source/pto/uspto-guidance-section-101.html

Section 101 Index
https://www.bitlaw.com/patent/section-101-index.html#pto

Section 101 Court Cases
https://www.bitlaw.com/patent/section-101-cases.html

Statutory Classes [MPEP 2106.03]

1) Process or Method
    - process, art, or method, and includes a new use of a known process, machine, manufacture, composition of matter, or material
    - inventions that consist of a series of steps or acts to be performed
2) Manufactures
    - articles of manufacture made by hand or machine
    - a tangible article that is given a new form, quality, property, or combination through man-made or artificial means
3) Compositions of Matter
    - combination of two or more substances and includes all composite articles

4) New Uses
   - new/nonobvious processes for using known invention
   - must be claimed as process (35 USC 100(b))
5) Judicial Exceptions — MPEP 2106.04–05
   - laws of nature, natural phenomena, abstract ideas do not, themselves, qualify for patent
   - inventions incorporating exceptions into a practical application may be eligible
   - use two-step Mayo test analysis (*Alice Corp. v. CLS Bank*, 573 U.S. 110 (2014) (citing *Mayo v. Prometheus*, 566 U.S. 66, 101 (2012))
   - Step 1: inquire if invention embodies exception; if yes, proceed to Step 2
   - Step 2: determine if invention integrates exception into practical application (inventive concept; i.e., implementation of the idea must not be generic, conventional, or obvious); if yes, invention may be potentially patentable

Reading:
Applying Step One of the Alice/Mayo Test
https://www.bitlaw.com/guidance/patent/applying-step-one-of-Alice-Mayo-test.html

Applying Step Two of the Alice/Mayo Test
https://www.bitlaw.com/guidance/patent/applying-step-two-of-Alice-Mayo-test.html

2.) Judicial Guidance on Patent-Eligible Biotechnology

a.) Organisms

Under current policy, genetically modified microorganisms, plants, and (non-human) animals are patent-eligible, provided that they are sufficiently different from naturally occurring counterparts.

Diamond v. Chakrabarty, 447 U.S. 303 (1980)
- a living microorganism was recognized as eligible subject matter because it was a genetically engineered bacterium with the new ability to break down crude oil, and the bacterium was produced by human technology rather than occurring in nature, and was, therefore, patent-eligible.
- the invention in this case was a new bacterium with **markedly different characteristics** from any found in nature. Because this

bacterium was not a previously unknown natural phenomenon, but rather a non-naturally occurring manufacture or composition of matter, the Supreme Court found that the invention qualifies as patentable subject matter. The Supreme Court emphasized that here, the invention was not nature's handiwork, but the handiwork of the inventor.

J.E.M. AG Supply, Inc. v. Pioneer Hi-Bred Intern., Inc., 122 S. Ct. 593 (2001)

- the Plant Patent Act and the Plant Variety Protection Act do not preclude novel plant varieties from qualifying for utility patent

b.) Nucleotide/Amino Acid Sequences

Manufactured or synthetic nucleotide and amino acid sequences are patent-eligible if like sequences do not exist naturally. Merely producing an identical copy of a naturally occurring sequence is not sufficient.

Association for Molecular Pathology v. Myriad Genetics, Inc., 133 U.S. 2107 (2013)

- The U.S. Supreme Court famously held that "a naturally occurring DNA segment is a product of nature and not patent eligible merely because it has been isolated"
- However, the Court also held that manipulation of a gene to create something not found in nature—such as a strand of synthetically produced complementary DNA (cDNA)—could still be eligible for patent protection
- cDNA, an edited man-made copy of the gene, was patent-eligible (not naturally occurring)
- "Markedly different characteristics (from naturally occurring counterpart) analysis"—patentable (not a "product of nature" exception [MPEP 2106.04(c)]
- When the sequence has been modified so it is different than that in nature, it is eligible as markedly different
- Product of nature exceptions include both naturally occurring products and non-naturally occurring products that lack markedly different characteristics from any naturally occurring counterpart. *See, e.g., Myriad Genetics, Inc. v. Ambry Genetics Corp*, 774 F.3d 755 (Fed. Cir. 2014), 113 USPQ2d at 1244 ("Contrary to Myriad's argument, it makes no difference that the identified gene sequences are synthetically replicated. As the Supreme Court made clear, neither naturally occurring compositions of matter, nor synthetically created compositions that are structurally identical to the naturally occurring compositions, are patent eligible."). *See also In re BRCA1 – & BRCA2 – Based Hereditary Cancer Test Patent Lit.*, 774 F.3d 755 (Fed. Cir. 2014)

- Naturally occurring nucleotide sequences not patentable (*Roche Molecular Sys., Inc. v. Cepheid*, No. 2017-1690, 2018 U.S. App. LEXIS 28411 (Fed. Cir. Oct. 9, 2018))
- The decision in *Roche* reiterates the previous holdings from *BRCA1* and *Myriad* that naturally occurring nucleotide sequences are not patent-eligible under 35 U.S.C. § 101. As seen in *Roche*, emphasizing the *structural differences* between synthetic nucleotide primers and naturally occurring DNA may not be sufficient to establish patent eligibility, especially when the nucleotide sequences are identical.
- Compare to *Myriad*—cDNAs made from mRNA had exons removed resulting in acceptable structural difference

Section 101 Examples—Example 15 (7): Nucleic Acids
https://www.bitlaw.com/source/pto/examples/15.html

3.) New (novel) — 35 USC 102; MPEP 2131

- subject matter must be unanticipated, original, and unknown in public domain before filing date in terms of novelty, the main challenge is demonstrating that the biotechnology product or process claimed is new, rather than merely a naturally occurring one

Reading:
Inherent Anticipation in the Pharmaceutical and Biotechnology Industries
https://www.ncbi.nlm.nih.gov/pmc/articles/PMC4526724/

4.) Usefulness (utility) — 35 USC 101; MPEP 2107

- functional usefulness; useful purpose
- operability (theoretical; "on paper")
- demonstrable, current use or some social benefit
- usefulness must be specific, substantial, and credible
- by statute, biotech inventions must demonstrate a specific usefulness. In practice, however, the PTO has been permissive in granting patents for subject matter that is immediately useful for only for research purposes. Thus, biotech inventions with only a speculative future utility may be patent-eligible.

Reading:
Understanding the Patent Law Utility Requirement
https://www.ipwatchdog.com/2015/11/07/understanding-the-patent-law-utility-requirement/id=63007/

5.) Obviousness	35 USC 103
- as with novelty, applicants must demonstrate that their invention is new, rather than an obvious improvement on a naturally occurring product or process	MPEP 2112, 2141-42, 2158
- often called "inventive step" in some foreign jurisdictions	

Reading:
Biotechnology Patents and Problem of Non-Obviousness
https://www.lawctopus.com/academike/biotechnology-patents-problem-non-obviousness/

Inherency in the Patenting of Biotechnology and Pharmaceutical Innovation
https://liebertpub.com/doi/full/10.1089/blr.2020.29165.cmh

Inherency in Obviousness – A Worrying Trend?
https://www.finnegan.com/en/insights/articles/inherency-in-obviousnessa-worrying-trend.html

Biopharma Patentees Must Navigate Inherent Obviousness
https://www.sternekessler.com/news-insights/publications/biopharma-patentees-must-navigate-inherent-obviousness

6.) Enablement	35 USC 112(a)
- disclosure must be enabling; i.e., how to make/practice invention	MPEP 2164, 2164.06(b), *see also* MPEP 608.01(p)
- disclosure (written description; specification) must contain detail of sufficient particularity to provide enablement, i.e., allow one skilled in the art to make and practice the invention	
- biological material is inherently variable and can change over time. Practitioners should be mindful that the disclosure describes all possible embodiments, and claims subject matter that is well defined, and reasonably stable and predictable	

Reading:
Enablement Is Key—Especially in Biotech Patents
https://www.theiplawblog.com/2015/04/articles/patent-law/enablement-is-key-especially-in-biotechpatents/

Locke Lord QuickStudy: The Supreme Court Arguments on Enablement in Amgen v. Sanofi
https://www.lockelord.com/newsandevents/publications/2023/03/supreme-court-arguments-amgen-v-sanofi

2. Prior Art Search
[MPEP 904; Rule 56 (37 CFR 1.56): Duty of candor and good faith; duty to disclose]

Biological Sequence Search
Listed next are noncommercial databases for searching published biosequences. A number of commercial databases and search services are also available.

Nucleotide/Amino Acid Databases:
NCBI National Center for Biological Info (GenBank)
https://www.ncbi.nlm.nih.gov/

PatSeq Finder
https://www.lens.org/lens/bio/patseqfinder

PatSeq Data
https://support.lens.org/help-resources/patent-sequence-tools/patseq-data/

EMBL—EBI (European Bioinformatics Institute)
http://www.ebi.ac.uk/patentdata/

USPTO—Publication Site for Issued and Published Sequences (PSIPS)
https://seqdata.uspto.gov/

BLAST—Basic Local Alignment Search Tool (NIH)
https://blast.ncbi.nlm.nih.gov/Blast.cgi

WIPO—Published Nucleotide and/or Amino Acid Sequence Listings Contained in Published PCT Applications
https://patentscope.wipo.int/search/en/sequences.jsf

Protein Databases:
RCSB Protein Data Bank
https://www.rcsb.org/search

Nucleotide Databases:
NCBI—Gene
https://www.ncbi.nlm.nih.gov/gene

NCBI—GenBank
https://www.ncbi.nlm.nih.gov/genbank/

RefSeq: NCBI Reference Sequence Database
https://www.ncbi.nlm.nih.gov/refseq/

DDBI DNA Databank Japan
https://www.ddbj.nig.ac.jp/about/index-e.html

Scientific (Non-Patent) Literature:
NIH—National Center for Biotechnology Information (PubMed)—U.S. National Library of Medicine
https://www.ncbi.nlm.nih.gov/home/literature/

Google Scholar
https://scholar.google.com/

Lens
https://www.lens.org/

3. Statutory Bars to Patent

- an assessment of statutory factors that may preclude application

a. Prior Public Disclosure (35 USC 102; MPEP 2133.03, 2152)
   - biotech applications are often derived from academic and/or industrial research which is typically reported upon in journal papers, presentations at scientific meetings, and elsewhere. Applicants should be careful that disclosure of the invention, either in publications or through casual sharing of information, is not made prior to filing. This is especially critical if foreign filing is contemplated.
   - before application, practitioners should inquire of inventors/applicants whether proprietary material has been disclosed, and, if so, where and when. Forms of public disclosures to consider include scientific papers (submitted, pending (in press), and published), reports, review articles, lectures, presentations, posters, abstracts, manuscripts, books, grant proposals, trade papers, and the like. Any possible internet disclosure should also be considered.

b. Eligibility of Inventor/Applicant (35 USC 116, 118; 37 CFR 1.42; MPEP 605.01, 2109)
   - biotech inventions are commonly products of partnerships or collaborative research among investigators in different laboratories or entities, including academic, industrial, and government, and often separated geographically. Due to this separation, the researchers involved may not be entirely aware of the contributions of their colleagues.
   - the practitioner should take care that all *bona fide* co- and joint-inventors are accounted for in the application, as well as any assignment issues. Practitioners should also be aware of any existing research agreements in effect between and among entities.

4. **Deposit of Biological Material [37 CFR 1.801–.809; MPEP 2401–11]**
   - assuming an application is being contemplated, U.S. and international rules of practice require a deposit of biological material disclosed in the application, if necessary to make and practice the invention, pursuant to 35 USC 112. Failure to comply with deposit rules may result in rejection of the application (*see* MPEP 2411.01). Such deposit can be made on or before the application filing date, or during the pendency of the application (37 CFR 1.804; MPEP 2406). If possible, however, the original deposition should be made prior to the filing date, especially if filing internationally, in order to assure a valid priority date (*see* MPEP 2406.03).

Reading:

Deposit of Biological Materials in Support of a U.S. Patent Application
https://www.ipmall.info/sites/default/files/hosted_resources/IP_handbook/ch10/ipHandbook-Ch%2010%2010%20Harney-McBride%20Biological%20Material%20Deposits.pdf

A Guide to the Deposit of Biological Material for Patent Purposes
https://www.ncimb.com/wp-content/uploads/2021/07/Patent-deposit-guide-June2020.pdf

Biological Deposits: Strategic Considerations
https://jakemp.com/en/briefings/biological-deposits-strategic-considerations/

Biological Deposits for Patenting Purposes Under the Budapest Treaty
https://www.lexology.com/library/detail.aspx?g=7d48befb-99d6-4b32-a109-3a807f2d0a71

Guide to the Deposit of Microorganisms Under the Budapest Treaty
https://www.wipo.int/budapest/en/guide/index.html

Protocol for Biological Deposit
Inventions involving biological material that cannot be described adequately to satisfy enablement under 35 USC 112 are subject to rules requiring deposit of a physical sample made available for examination by interested parties. Rules of deposit are set forth under the terms of the Budapest Treaty and the USPTO rules of practice.

Material Subject to Deposit (37 USC 1.801–.802; MPEP 2402–2404)

- any biological material essential for practicing the invention and whose written description alone cannot satisfy the enablement requirement for patentability under 35 USC 112 (*see* MPEP 2402-03)
- deposit of viable microorganisms or other biological material for preservation for purposes of patent application procedure required:
  - when the invention is or relies on such biological material, and if necessary to make/practice the claimed invention under 35 USC 112 (37 CFR 1.802(a); MPEP 2402–04);
  - where such material is not known ***and*** readily available to the public (MPEP 2403, 2404.01) or cannot be made or isolated without undue experimentation (37 CFR 1.802(b); MPEP 2402.02)
  - single deposit at recognized depositary satisfies requirement in all other Treaty member states where patent protection desired
  - deposit should be made prior to filing date to assure priority for international filing (see MPEP 2406.03)

INTERNATIONAL DEPOSITARY AUTHORITIES (IDAs) UNDER ARTICLE 7 OF THE BUDAPEST TREATY located in US:

[See individual depositary websites for deposit procedures]

American Type Culture Collection (ATCC)
https://www.atcc.org/services/depositing-with-atcc/patent-deposit

Provasoli-Guillard National Center for Marine Algae and Microbiota (NCMA)
https://ncma.bigelow.org/

Agricultural Research Service Culture Collection (NRRL)
https://nrrl.ncaur.usda.gov/

INTERNATIONAL DEPOSITARY AUTHORITIES UNDER ARTICLE 7 OF THE BUDAPEST TREATY (List of all currently recognized depositaries) (*see* 37 CFR 1.803; MPEP 2405) https://www.wipo.int/export/sites/www/treaties/en/registration/budapest/pdf/idalist.pdf

Acceptable Deposits (MPEP 2403)
IDAs have accepted deposits of biological materials that do not fall within a literal interpretation of "microorganism." The Treaty does not define "microorganism."

Acceptable deposits include material capable of self-replication, either directly or indirectly (MPEP 2403.01):

1. Directly (reproduces by itself) (37 CFR 1.801; MPEP 2403.01)
   - Examples (not exhaustive): bacteria, fungi including yeast, algae, protozoa, eukaryotic cells, cell organelles, cell lines, hybridomas, plant tissue cells, plant spores, lichens, and seeds
   - Plant material is generally not subject to deposit for plant patent applications (MPEP 2403.02)
2. Indirectly (only capable of replication when another self-replicating biological material is present; e.g., self-replication after insertion in a host)
   - (37 CFR 1.801; MPEP 2403.01)
   - Examples (not exhaustive): viruses, phages, plasmids, symbionts, and replication defective cells, genetic vectors containing a gene or DNA/RNA fragments, organisms used for expression of a gene (making protein from DNA), cell organelles and other non-living material existing in and reproducible from a living cell may be deposited by deposition of the host cell capable of reproducing the non-living material

Reading:
Deposit of Biological Materials in Support of a U.S. Patent Application
http://www.iphandbook.org/handbook/ch10/p10/

Guide to the Deposit of Microorganisms under the Budapest Treaty
https://www.wipo.int/budapest/en/guide/index.html

Time for Making Deposit (37 CFR 1.804(a); MPEP 2406)

- prior to filing date; or during application pendency, subject to 37 CFR 1.809; *see also* MPEP 2406.02
  - deposition in advance of filing allows deposit to be referenced by accession number in specification/claims (37 CFR 1.804(a); MPEP 2404.03, 2406.01); otherwise, this information must be added by preliminary amendment
  - applicants contemplating international filing should make deposit in advance of filing of priority application to preserve priority date (*see* MPEP 2406.03)
  - deposits made after initial filing require applicant to file a statement to verify such deposit (37 CFR 1.804(b); MPEP 2406.02)

Other Deposit Issues
Replacement/Supplemental deposit (37 CFR 1.805; MPEP 2407)
Term of Deposit (37 CFR 1.806; MPEP 2408)
Furnishing of Samples (37 CFR 1.808; MPEP 2410)

C. Filing

Provisional Patent Application (PPA)

Overview
If possible, sequence listings should be included with the PPA, especially if foreign filing is intended. Biological deposits can be made prior to or during PPA pendency, but may be delayed until a subsequent RPA is filed. For full details on provisional filing, see Part One.

Non-Provisional (Utility) Patent Application (RPA)

[35 USC 111(a); 37 CFR 1.53(b); MPEP 201.01, 601.01(a)]

Overview
This section will cover preparation of a nonprovisional biotechnology application. For full details on nonprovisional application, see Part One.

1. Application Preparation and Assembly

a. Requisite Parts

1) Associated Docs/Elements

Transmittal of New Application

Transmittal Cover Sheet

PPA: specify number of CDs included, if necessary SB/16

RPA: indicate "Nucleotide and/or Amino Acid Sequence Submission" (Application Elements, item No. 9), if necessary	AIA/15
Substitute: Cover letter for initial application filing	Apx B-01
Attachments: Application package	
2) Disclosure	MPEP 608
- written description (Specification)	
RPA Disclosure	37 CFR 1.71 35 USC 112(a) MPEP 608.01
The following elements (in proper order) of the disclosure may include biotech-related material:	
In the Specification:	
Statement Regarding Federally Sponsored Research or Development	MPEP 310
- biotech applications often result from federally funded research; acknowledgment should be made of such funding	

Sample Statements:

STATEMENT AS TO RIGHTS TO INVENTIONS MADE UNDER FEDERALLY SPONSORED RESEARCH AND DEVELOPMENT

This invention was made with government support under Grant #8602787 awarded by the National Science Foundation. The government has certain rights in the present invention.

STATEMENT REGARDING FEDERALLY SPONSORED RESEARCH OR DEVELOPMENT

This invention was made with government support under Grant Nos. R41 AI108114, R41 AI102311, and R33 AI085548 awarded by the National Institutes of Health. The government has certain rights in the invention.

STATEMENT OF RIGHTS TO INVENTIONS MADE UNDER FEDERALLY SPONSORED RESEARCH

Not applicable.

Names of the parties to a Joint Research Agreement	35 USC 100(h), 102(c)
- a joint-research agreement allows the parties to avoid each other's prior art patent disclosures as if they were commonly owned, without assigning their patent rights to the same entity	37 CFR 1.71(g), 1.9(e) MPEP 804.03, 2156
- particular attention should be paid to any existing research agreements, as biotech R&D is often a collaborative effort between entities, such as industrial-academic partnerships	

Sample reference language to a joint research agreement:

JOINT RESEARCH AGREEMENT

The presently claimed invention was made by or on behalf of the below listed parties to a joint research agreement. The joint research agreement was in effect on or before the date the claimed invention was made and the claimed invention was made as a result of activities undertaken within the scope of the joint research agreement. The parties to the joint research agreement are (1) the ABC Corporation and (2) the Regents of XYZ University.

Reading:

US Patent Law And Cross-Border R&D

https://www.chinabusinessreview.com/us-patent-law-and-cross-border-rd/

Reference to a Sequence Listing	
- applications disclosing nucleotide and/or amino acid sequences are required to include a Sequence Listing as a separate part of the disclosure	37 CFR 1.77(b)(5) MPEP 608.01(a)
- refer to sequence listings submitted via EFS-Web (ASCII text) or on a compact disc and an incorporation-by-reference of the material on the compact disc (see 37 CFR 1.52(e)(5)). The total number of compact discs, including duplicates and the files on each compact disc, should be specified	
- see Sequence Listing discussion for details	
Exemplary references	Apx B-02
Reference to Biological Deposit	
- references to biological deposits under the Budapest Treaty are typically embedded in the Detailed Description, or a reference may appear under a separate heading at the beginning of the specification; for example, before the Brief Description of the Drawings	37 CFR 1.802(a), 809(d) MPEP 2404.03, 2406.01, 2411.05
- include statement that suitable sample has been deposited at authorized depository in accordance with Budapest Treaty	
- include nature of sample, date of deposit, name of depository, accession no.	
- see Biological Deposit discussion for details	
Exemplary references	Apx B-03

Detailed description of the invention

- biological material deposited under the Budapest Treaty and nucleotide/amino acid sequences recorded in the official sequence listing must be referenced in the disclosure:
  i. Biological Deposits
     - embedded in the description, include references to biological deposits with, at least, name of depository, and accession no.

Exemplary references:

- the *Blautia* Strain A is *Blautia massiliensis* Strain A (ATCC Deposit Number PTA-125134)
- the Bifidobacterium animalis ssp. lactis is Bifidobacterium animalis ssp. lactis Strain A (ATCC Deposit Number PTA-125097
- the bacterium is a *V. cholerae* strain having ATCC deposit number PTA-125138.
- the CNB476 strains of "*Salinospora*" sp. were deposited on Jun. 20, 2003, pursuant to the Budapest Treaty on the International Deposit of Microorganisms for the Purposes of Patent Procedure with the Patent Culture Depository of the American Type Culture Collection, 12301 Parklawn Drive, Rockville, Md. 20852 U.S.A. under ATCC Accession No PTA-5275.
- The *Bacillus* and *Paenibacillus* strains disclosed herein were deposited with the American Type Culture Collection (ATCC), located at 10801 University Boulevard, Manassas, Va. 20110, USA, on April 19, 2012.
- A mouse cell line designated T1-A, deposited under the ATCC accession number PTA-123697.

ii. Nucleotide/Amino Acid Sequences (37 CFR 1.821(d))
   - embedded within the description, sequences are referred to by their designated sequence identifiers ("SEQ ID NO.") as entered in the official Sequence Listing

Exemplary usage of Sequence Identifiers:

- Exemplary primer (SEQ ID NO: 6) and its complementary strand (SEQ ID NO: 7)
- the linear DNA of any one of (6) to (8) in which the terminator sequence is an entire length or a portion of a sequence shown in SEQ ID NO: 1 or SEQ ID NO: 2

- (about 6 kbp HindIII-XhoI fragment of SEQ ID NO: 18)
- antibody that specifically binds to SEQ ID NO: 9 polypeptide or a truncated peptide comprising an epitope of SEQ ID NO: 9,
- encoded by sequences comprising SEQ ID NO: 1 or complement thereof through SEQ ID NO: 83523 or complements thereof,
- where said nucleic acid sequence is selected from (i) a nucleotide sequence of SEQ ID NO: 1, SEQ ID NO: 2, SEQ ID NO: 3, SEQ ID NO: 4, SEQ ID NO: 5, SEQ ID NO: 6, SEQ ID NO: 33, SEQ ID NO: 36, SEQ ID NO: 37, or SEQ ID NO: 68
- comprising a sequence CXXXRCXXXHSRVPFP (SEQ ID NO: 1), in which X signifies an amino acid residue, such as a sequence selected from the group consisting of: SEQ ID NO: 2 to SEQ ID NO: 18
- region comprising the amino acid sequence of SEQ ID NO: 5, a light chain CDR2 region comprising the amino acid sequence of SEQ ID NO: 6,
- The present disclosure provides for a nucleic acid sequence encoding two or more amino acid sequences selected from the group consisting of SEQ ID NO: 1, SEQ ID NO: 2
- using SEQ ID NO: 5, 6, 7, or 8 as a probe, indicates the presence of *Escherichia Coli.*
- enzyme having an amino acid sequence of SEQ ID NO: 18
- element selected from SEQ. ID NO: 2 through SEQ. ID NO: 24, SEQ. ID NO: 22
- SEQ ID NO: 3 SEQ ID NO: 4, SEQ ID NO: 5 and SEQ ID NO: 6 or any sequence having . . .

Drawing Sheets — 35 USC 113

- generally, sequences included in the Sequence Listing should not be presented in the drawings (*see* 37 CFR 1.83(a); MPEP 2422.02 for details) — 37 CFR 1.83(a) MPEP 608.02, 2412.06, 2422.02
- if sequences are disclosed in the drawings, sequence identifiers (SEQ ID NO. x) should be included

b. Accompanying Papers as Needed/Appropriate

Certification and Petition to Make Special Under the Cancer Moonshot Expedited Examination Pilot Program — SB/465

- expedited application processing of applications disclosing inventions in the field of oncology and smoking cessation

Biosequence Disclosures
[37 CFR 1.52; MPEP 608.05(c)]
[ST.25: 37 CFR 1.821–25; MPEP 2420–26]
[ST.26: 37 CFR 1.831–35; MPEP 2412–19]
Applications disclosing specific nucleotide and/or amino acid sequences are required to include a formal sequence listing (aka, "Official Sequence Listing"), in accordance with WIPO conventions. The compliance standard for presentation and submission of biosequence listings transitioned from ST.25 ("Sequence Listing") to ST.26 ("Sequence Listing XML") on 1 July 2022 (*see* MPEP 2415.01); however, the ST.25 protocol remains in effect for all applications filed on or before 30 June 2022. Updated rules for ST.26 are found at 37 CFR 1.831–835 and MPEP 2412–2419.

Sequence Listing [37 CFR 1.52, 1.821–.825; MPEP 608.05(c), 2420–26]
Specifically defined biosequence disclosures must adhere to guidelines set forth at 37 CFR 1.821–.825 and MPEP 2420–26. A digest of the salient sequence rules is presented here. Practitioners should, however, familiarize themselves with the regulations in their entirety to gain a full understanding of disclosure requirement details.

(P) [Note: Provisional applications filed under 35 U.S.C. 111(b) need not comply with 37 CFR 1.821 through 1.825; nonetheless, applicants are encouraged to file a sequence listing as defined in 37 CFR 1.821(c) for ST.25, or a "Sequence Listing XML" (ST.26) under 37 CFR 1.831–834, for ease of identification of the sequence information contained in the provisional application. Complying with sequence rules is also advisable if international filing is planned, in order to ensure a valid priority date (*see* MPEP 2415.02).]

Disclosures Subject to the Sequence Rules (37 CFR 1.821(a), 1.831; MPEP 2422.01)
[Note: The compliance standard for presentation of biosequence listings transitioned from ST.25 to ST.26 on 1 July 2022; however, ST.25 standard remains in effect for all applications filed on or before 30 June 2022]

All nucleotide and/or amino acid sequences of specific residue composition and order, and of at least threshold length, ***whether claimed or not***, must be included in a "Sequence Listing" submitted as a separate part of the application (37 CFR 1.821(c); MPEP 2412.03, 2421.01, 2422.02)

- pursuant to 37 CFR 1.821(a), applications disclosing **one or more unbranched sequences of *four or more amino acids* and/or one or more unbranched sequences of *ten or more nucleotides*** must conform with 37 CFR 1.821.–825

- definition/attributes of nucleotides/amino acids falling under the rules (37 CFR 1.821(a)(1) & (2))
    - "specifically defined" means those amino acids defined in accordance with the World Intellectual Property Organization (WIPO) Handbook on Industrial Property Information and Documentation, Standard ST.26: Recommended Standard for the Presentation of Nucleotide and Amino Acid Sequence Listings in Using XML (Nov. 2021; hereinafter WIPO Standard ST.26 (2021)) (*see* Annex I). Available online at https://www.wipo.int/export/sites/www/standards/en/pdf/03-26-01.pdf

ST.25 remains in effect for all applications filed prior to 1 July 2022

[Note that the ST.25 standard was revised in December 2009, and the current version is available online at https://www.wipo.int/export/sites/www/standards/en/pdf/03-25-01.pdf]

Nucleotides/Amino Acids Subject to Sequence Listing

Nucleotides: includes only those nucleotides that can be represented using the symbols set forth in WIPO Standard ST.26 (2021), Annex I, Sections 1–2.

Amino Acids: includes those L-amino acids commonly found in naturally occurring proteins and are listed in WIPO Standard ST.26 (2021), Annex I, Sections 3–4.

For additional information, see:

Are You Ready for WIPO Standard ST.26?
https://www.wipo.int/pct/en/news/2022/news_0039.html

FAQ: Implementation of WIPO ST.26
https://www.wipo.int/standards/en/sequence/faq.html

WIPO Standard ST.26 News
https://www.uspto.gov/patents/apply/sequence-listing-resource-center/wipo-standard-st26-news

Sequence Listing Basics
https://www.uspto.gov/patents/apply/sequence-listing-resource-center/sequence-listing-basics

Sequence Listings Under ST.26 and New USPTO Rules
https://www.uspto.gov/sites/default/files/documents/Patent-Quality-Chat-ST26-June15.pdf

WIPO ST.26 Overview
https://www.harnessip.com/blog/2022/09/07/wipo-st-26-overview/

"All Change! All Change!" for WIPO Standard ST.26
https://www.marks-clerk.com/insights/articles/all-change-all-change-for-wipo-standard-st-26/

Overview of the New Standard ST.26 for the Filing of Sequence Listings
https://www.clarkemodet.com/en/articles/overview-of-the-new-standard-st-26-for-the-filling-of-sequence-listings/

Sequences presented as prior art and referred to only by name and a publication, or accession number, are not required to appear in the Sequence Listing (MPEP 2224.01(III)). However, prior art sequences appearing as strings of specific nucleotides or amino acids must comply with the sequence rules.

Content and Format of the Sequence Listing (37 CFR 1.822.–823, 831–832; MPEP 2412, 2422.03, 2423–25)
[Note: Existing MPEP and 37 CFR rules pertain to ST.25 only; updated MPEP and 37 CFR rules for ST.26 are forthcoming from the USPTO]

37 CFR 1.822.–824 set forth detailed descriptions of the requirements that are mandatory for the presentation of sequence data

Format and symbols for representing nucleotides and amino acids are set forth at 37 CFR 1.822.–823, 37 CFR 1.832; MPEP 2412.05(b)–(e), 2422(I), 2423

Sequence Identifier "SEQ ID NO." (37 CFR 1.821(c), 1.831(c), 1.832(a); MPEP 2412.04, 2422.01(V))
37 CFR 1.821(c), 1.831(c), and 1.832(a) require that each disclosed nucleic acid or amino acid sequence in the application appear separately in the sequence listing, with each sequence further being assigned a sequence identifier, referred to as "SEQ ID NO." The sequence identifiers must begin with 1 and increase sequentially by integers. The requirement for sequence identifiers, at a minimum, requires that each sequence be assigned a different number for purposes of identification.

Each sequence disclosed must appear separately in the "Sequence Listing." Each sequence set forth in the "Sequence Listing" shall be assigned a separate sequence identifier. The sequence identifiers shall begin with 1 and increase sequentially by integers. If no sequence is present for a sequence identifier, the code "000" shall be used in place of the sequence. The response for the numeric identifier <160> shall include the total number of SEQ ID NOs, whether followed by a sequence or by the code “000” (37 CFR 1.821(c)).

37 CFR 1.823(b) lists the items of information that are to be included in the sequence listing in the order in which those items are to appear. The numeric identifier for each item of information shall not include the explanatory information included in 37 CFR 1.823(b) (*see also* MPEP 2424).

The “Sequence Listing” shall, except as otherwise indicated, include the actual nucleotide and/or amino acid sequence, the numeric identifiers and their accompanying information. The numeric identifier shall be used only in the “Sequence Listing.” The order and presentation of the items of information in the “Sequence Listing” shall conform to the prescribed arrangement. Each item of information shall begin on a new line and shall begin with the numeric identifier enclosed in angle brackets. The submission of those items of information designated with an “M” is mandatory. The submission of those items of information designated with an “O” is optional. Numeric identifiers <110> through <170> shall only be set forth at the beginning of the “Sequence Listing” (37 CFR 1.823(b); MPEP 2424).

Where the description or claims of a patent application discuss a sequence that is set forth in the “Sequence Listing” in accordance with paragraph (c) of this section, reference must be made to the sequence by use of the sequence identifier, preceded by “SEQ ID NO:” in the text of the description or claims, even if the sequence is also embedded in the text of the description or claims of the patent application (37 CFR 1.821(d)).

Sample Sequence Listings:
Standard ST.25:
https://www.bitlaw.com/source/mpep/2431.html

Standard ST.26:
https://www.wipo.int/standards/en/xml_material/st26/st26-annex-iii-sequence-listing-specimen.xml

Submission of Sequence Listing—Form and Format
Standard ST.25 Format (37 CFR 1.823.–824; MPEP 2422.03–.04)
Applications disclosing nucleotide and/or amino acid sequences must include, as a separate part of the disclosure, a Sequence Listing (aka “Official Sequence Listing”) conforming to established format guidelines (37 CFR 1.821(c); MPEP 2421.01, 2422.03).

The Official Sequence Listing may be submitted in one of the following forms:

1. Paper;
2. Compact disc (CD);
3. PDF filed via EFS-Web; or
4. ASCII plain text (.txt) file on CD

In addition, 37 CFR 1.821(e) requires a copy of the sequence listing to be submitted in computer readable form (CRF) as an ASCII text file via any of the media formats under 37 CFR 1.824(c), or via EFS-Web

The Official Sequence Listing may be submitted:

1. *On paper* [37 CFR 1.821(c), 1.823(a)(1)]
If submitted on paper, the sequence listing is a separate part of the disclosure which must begin on a new page within the specification and must be titled "Sequence Listing." The pages of the "Sequence Listing" preferably should be numbered independently of the numbering of the remainder of the application. Each page of the "Sequence Listing" shall contain no more than 66 lines and each line shall contain no more than 72 characters. The sheet or sheets presenting a sequence listing may not include material other than part of the sequence listing. A fixed-width font should be used exclusively throughout the "Sequence Listing" (37 CFR 1.823(a)(1)).

2. *On compact disc* [37 CFR 1.52(e), 1.821(c)]
If the "Sequence Listing" required by § 1.821(c) is submitted on compact disc: The "Sequence Listing" must be submitted on a compact disc in compliance with § 1.52(e). The compact disc used to submit the sequence listing may also contain table information if the table has more than 50 pages of text. See 37 CFR 1.823(a)(2) and 1.52(e)(1)(iii). The specification must contain an incorporation-by-reference of the Sequence Listing as required by § 1.52(e)(5). The presentation of the "Sequence Listing" and other materials on compact disc under § 1.821(c) does not substitute for the Computer Readable Form that must be submitted on disk, compact disc, or tape in accordance with 37 CFR 1.824 (37 CFR 1.823(a)(2)).

Any compact disc must be submitted in duplicate unless it contains only the "Sequence Listing" in computer readable form required by § 1.821(e). The compact disc and any duplicate copy must be labeled "Copy 1" and "Copy 2," respectively. The transmittal letter which accompanies the compact disc must include a statement that the two compact discs are identical. If the two compact discs are not identical, the Office will use the disc labeled "Copy 1" for further processing (37 CFR 1.52(e)(4); *see also* MPEP § 608.05).

If submitted on compact disc, the specification must contain an incorporation-by-reference of the material on the compact disc in a separate paragraph (37 CFR 1.77(b)(5)), identifying each compact disc by the names of the file(s) contained on each of the compact discs, their date of creation ,and their sizes in bytes (37 CFR 1.52(e)).

If the sequence listing under 37 CFR 1.821(c) is submitted on compact disc, applicant is still required to submit a separate CRF of the sequence listing pursuant to 37 CFR 1.821(e) and 37 CFR 1.824. If the CRF is also submitted on compact disc, applicants will need to submit a total of three copies of the sequence listing (one pursuant to 37 CFR 1.821(c), and two pursuant to 37 CFR 1.821(e)). The compact disc with the CRF of the sequence listing may be identical to the compact disc submitted under 37 CFR 1.821(c) if the latter compact disc includes only the sequence listing (i.e., no additional content, such as tables).

3. *As a PDF submitted via EFS-Web* [37 CFR 1.821(c)]

Submission of the sequence listing in a PDF file on the application filing date is not recommended. Applicant must still provide the CRF required by 37 CFR 1.821(e), and the sequence listing in the PDF file will not be excluded when determining the application size fee. The USPTO prefers the submission of a sequence listing in an ASCII text file via EFS-Web on the application filing date because as stated above, if applicant has not filed a second copy of the sequence listing in a PDF file (or on paper) on the same day, the text file will serve as both the paper copy required by 37 CFR 1.821(c) and the CRF required by 37 CFR 1.821(e). Any sequence listing submitted in PDF format (or on paper) on the application filing date is treated as the paper copy required by 37 CFR 1.821(c).

If applicant submits a sequence listing in both a PDF file and an ASCII text file via EFS-Web on the application filing date, a statement that the sequence listing content of the PDF copy and the ASCII text file copy are identical is required. In situations where applicant files the sequence listing in PDF format and requests the use of the CRF of another application under 37 CFR 1.821(e), applicant must submit a letter and request in compliance with 37 CFR 1.821(e) and a statement that the PDF copy filed in the new application is identical to the CRF filed in the other application (*see* MPEP § 2422.05).

4. *As an ASCII text (".txt") file on compact disc* [37 CFR 1.821(c)(1); MPEP 2422.03(II)]

If the official copy of the sequence listing as required by 37 CFR 1.821(c) is submitted on compact disc, the specification must contain an incorporation by reference of the material on the compact disc in a separate paragraph, identifying each compact disc by the names of the file(s) contained on each of the compact discs, their date of creation and their sizes in bytes (37 CFR 1.52(e)).

In addition to the Official Sequence Listing, a copy of the Sequence Listing must also be submitted in computer readable form (CRF) (37 CFR 1.821(e), 1.824; MPEP 2422.04)

Form and Format of CRF (37 CFR 1.824)

- the CRF may be submitted via various electronic media approved under 37 CFR 1.824(c); *see also* MPEP 2425, or via EFS-Web

5. *As an ASCII text (".txt") file via EFS-Web* [37 1.824(a)(2)–(6)&(b); MPEP 608.05(I)(A), 2422.03(I)]

The PTO advises applicants against filing the Official Sequence Listing by PDF. If a new application is filed via EFS-Web with an ASCII text file sequence listing that complies with the requirements of 37 CFR 1.824(a)(2)–(6) and (b), and applicant has not filed a sequence listing in a PDF file on the same day, the text file will serve as both the paper copy required by 37 CFR 1.821(c) and the computer readable form (CRF) required by 37 CFR 1.821(e) (*see also* MPEP 2433.03(a)(I)&(IV)). Thus, the following are not required and should not be submitted: (1) a second copy of the sequence listing in a PDF file; and (2) a statement under 37 CFR 1.821(f) (indicating that the paper copy and CRF copy of the sequence listing are identical) (MPEP 2422.06).

Note that the specification must contain a statement in a separate paragraph that incorporates by reference the material in the ASCII text file identifying the name of the ASCII text file, the date of creation, and the size of the ASCII text file in bytes. *See* MPEP § 2422.03(a) for additional information pertaining to EFS-Web submission of sequence listings.

If the sequence listing is filed on paper (or PDF) pursuant to 37 CFR 1.821(c) and also by CRF via EFS-Web, 37 CFR 1.821(f) requires a statement that the content of the paper and computer readable copies are identical, at the time when the computer readable form is submitted. (MPEP 2422.06)

- see MPEP 2428 for sample statement language Apx B-04

Standard ST.26 Format (37 CFR 1.833–834; MPEP 2413)

Applications filed on or after 1 July 2022 and disclosing nucleotide and/or amino acid sequences must include, as a separate part of the disclosure, a Sequence Listing XML (eXtensible Markup Language format) conforming to established format guidelines.

Sequence Preparation Software
For Standard ST.26

- WIPO Sequence (Version 2.2.0): software for facilitating the preparation of patent applications containing nucleotide and/or amino acid sequences; generates sequence listings that comply with all domestic and foreign disclosure format requirements (i.e., ST.26); available on the WIPO website at: https://www.wipo.int/standards/en/sequence/index.html (see MPEP 2418)

Reading:
Structure of a Sequence Listing in XML (WIPO ST.26 Format)
https://www.smartbasedip.com/st26-insights-blog/structure-of-a-sequence-listing-in-xml-wipo-st26-format

PatentIn Instructions and Software
https://www.uspto.gov/patents/basics/types-patent-applications/utility-patent/checker/patentin

For Standard ST.25

- **PatentIn** (Version 3.5.1)(MPEP 2430); available at https://www.uspto.gov/patents/basics/types-patent-applications/utility-patent/checker/patentin
- **Checker** (Version 4.4.6): software for checking biotechnology Sequence Listings for compliance with format and content rules, available on the USPTO website at: https://www.uspto.gov/patents/basics/types-patent-applications/utility-patent/checker-version-446

Reading:
Errors in Patent Application Sequence Listings
http://www.craic.com/documents/Reprint_NBT_10_2003.pdf

Sequence Listings Webinar
http://www.canadylortz.com/wp-content/uploads/2018/02/20180109-Sequence-Listing-Webinar-Updated-w-Hyperlinks.pdf

Sequence Listing for Biotechnology Patents: A Beginner's Guide
https://sagaciousresearch.com/blog/sequence-listing-biotechnology-patents/

Preparing a Sequence Listing for the USPTO
https://www1.udel.edu/research/doc/SequenceListing.doc

What/Where/When/Why/How Do I Include This Sequence in a Sequence Listing
https://newsletter.bpla.org/spring2016-whatwherewhenwhyhow

Sequence Compliance Soup to Nuts
https://www.aipla.org/docs/default-source/committee-documents/bcp-files/rwax_sc.pdf?sfvrsn=f4be09bd_2

Sequence Listing Errors Can Rob You of Patent Term Adjustment
https://www.natlawreview.com/article/sequence-listing-errors-can-rob-you-patent-term-adjustment

Proposed Rule Changes by the USPTO Aim to Improve Large Data Submission by Patent Applicants
https://www.crowell.com/files/20210602-IP-Alert-proposed-rule-changes-by-the-uspto-Morgan-White.pdf

Time for Submitting Sequence Listing [MPEP 2414.01, 2422.07; 37 CFR 1.821(g), 1.835]

- applications must be in full compliance with the sequence rules at time of filing (37 CFR 1.821(g)). Deficient applications will be given opportunity to comply in order to avoid abandonment. Responses to any notice to comply must include a statement that the submission contains no new matter (*see* 37 CFR 1.121(f); MPEP 608.04)

Request for a Transfer of a Computer Readable Form Under 37 CFR 1.821(e)	SB/93 37 CFR 1.821(e)
- request to use CRF sequence listing from parent application in subsequently filed application; asserts that current paper or PDF listing is identical to previously filed CRF and contains no new matter	MPEP 608.05; 2422.05
Substitute: draft request to incorporate Sequence Listing from parent application into new application	Apx B-05

If the computer readable form of a new application is to be identical with the computer readable form of another application of the applicant on file in the Office, reference may be made to the other application and computer readable form in lieu of filing a duplicate computer readable form in the new application if the computer readable form in the other application was compliant with all of the requirements of this subpart. The new application must be accompanied by a letter making such reference to the other application and computer readable form, both of which shall be completely identified. In the new application, applicant must also request the use of the compliant computer readable "Sequence Listing" that is already on file for the other application and must state that the paper or compact disc copy of the "Sequence Listing" in the new application is identical to the computer readable copy filed for the other application (37 CFR 1.821(e)).

Where the computer readable form (CRF) of the sequence listing of a new application is to be identical with the CRF of another application of the applicant on file in the Office, 37 CFR 1.821(e) provides a mechanism for applicant to request a transfer of the CRF from the application already on file to the new application in limited circumstances. Instead of submitting a transfer request of a previously filed CRF, however, the Office strongly recommends that applicant submit a sequence listing in ASCII text format in the new application, which will serve both as the sequence listing part of the disclosure, as well as the CRF.

D. Application Submittal

EFS-Web

- the PTO advises that applications with Sequence Listings should be submitted via EFS-Web (MPEP 2422.03(a))

If Sequence Listings are filed on CD, see 37 CFR 1.52(e) for mailing instructions

[see Part One for full details]

E. Post-Filing

1. Pre-Exam

a. Office-Initiated Actions

Notices to Correct Defects in Application Papers

[Note: correspondence related to sequence rules compliance should be addressed to "Box SEQUENCE"] MPEP 2422.09

Notice to Comply with Requirements for Patent Applications Containing Nucleotide and/or Amino Acid Sequence Disclosures	37 CFR 1.821(g), 1.825 MPEP 2414.01, 2421.03
- Sequence Listing disclosure in computer-readable form (CRF) fails to comply with 37 CFR 1.821.–825	
Applicant Response: submit preliminary amendment with required parts per Notice	Apx B-06
- amendment should request entry into the application, and include a statement that the sequence listing information recorded in computer readable form is identical to the written (on paper/PDF or compact disc) sequence listing and, where applicable, contains no new matter, as required by 37 CFR 1.821(e–g), 1.825(b) & (d)	

Amendments to or replacement of sequence listing	37 CFR 1.825, 1.835; MPEP 2414.02–03, 2422.07, 2426
When applicant files an amendment to comply with the requirements of 37 CFR 1.821(g) and that amendment adds or amends a compact disc(s) or ASCII text file submitted via EFS-Web, applicant is required to update or insert in the specification an appropriate incorporation by reference statement describing the compact disc and the files contained thereon or the description of the ASCII text file submitted via EFS-Web (*see* 37 CFR 1.77(b)(5) and 37 CFR 1.52(e)(5)). Submissions in reply to requirements under 37 CFR 1.821(g) must be accompanied by a statement that the submission includes no new matter (37 CFR 1.121(f)) or matter which goes beyond the disclosure in the application as filed (*see also* 35 USC 132).	
1. Paper or electronic text copy (CRF; *see* 37 CFR 1.824) of Sequence Listing	
2. Amended reference to Sequence Listing in Specification (37 CFR 1.52(e)(5)); request for entry of amendment Statement in support of substitute CRF Sequence Listing; content of CFR listing is identical to the written listing (paper or compact disc), and contains no new matter	Apx B-07
Computer-Readable Form (CRF) for Sequence Listing Defective	37 CFR 1.825(d)
"Sequence Listing could not be accepted."	
- lists errors in submitted listing	
Applicant Response: submit corrected CFR per Reviewer Comments on listing	

b. Applicant-Initiated Actions

Declaration of Biological Deposit	Apx B-08
- asserts that deposit has been made pursuant to Budapest Treaty	37 CFR 1.808
Attachments: Deposit Receipt	
Amendment Under 37 CFR 1.71(g)	37 CFR 1.71(g)
- amendment to disclose the names of the parties to a joint research agreement as defined in 37 CFR 1.9(e)	
Attachments: processing fee may apply if not timely filed (*see* 37 CFR 1.71(g)(2))	AIA/17i

[Note: This point in the procedure generally marks the conclusion of practice specific to biotech application; beyond this point, biotech applications are prosecuted substantially the same as any other utility application. Refer to Part One for details on the remaining procedure.]

III. International Biotechnology Patent Applications

Overview

This section will deal with biotechnology applications under the EPC, PCT, and Paris Convention. Only those elements relevant to biotechnology will be presented in this supplement. For complete details on these foreign applications, see Part Two.

Countries vary in what they consider patentable biotechnology. United States patent policy is relatively expansive concerning patent-eligible subject matter; however, what is patentable in the United States may not necessarily be patentable abroad. For instance, the EPO does not grant patents on random polynucleotides or polypeptides with no demonstrable function or use, nor for plant varieties developed through conventional selective breeding methods. Applicants should consult the laws of each individual nation to determine if the claimed invention is deemed patent eligible.

Biotech applications filed under the aforementioned accords require sequence listings and deposit of biological material, if necessary. Formatting procedures for sequence listings are substantially standardized across jurisdictions; if a sequence listing is implemented correctly for a priority U.S. national application, this requisite should be generally acceptable in foreign jurisdictions. Likewise, an original biological deposit made in a Budapest Treaty member nation is recognized in all other party nations. Applicants should be mindful, however, that certain countries (e.g., Taiwan) are not signatories to the Budapest Treaty, and deposits must be made individually in these countries if patent protection is desired.

A. PCT Application

1. Laws and Rules of Practice [Note: for general PCT rules of practice, see Part Two]

MPEP Chap. 1800, Sec. 1823 (PCT Rule 5)

Sec. 1823.01: Reference to Deposited Biological Material

Sec. 1823.02: Nucleotide and/or Amino Acid Sequence Listings, and Tables Related to Sequence Listings

Sec. 1848 Sequence Listings (PCT Rule 13ter)
Sec. 1877 Nucleotide and/or Amino Acid Sequence Listings During the International Preliminary Examination

35 USC Part IV, Chs. 35–37
Administrative Instructions Under the Patent Cooperation Treaty (1 July 2022)

Annex C—Standard for the Presentation of Nucleotide and Amino Acid Sequence Listings in International Patent Applications under the PCT. https://www.wipo.int/pct/en/texts/ai/annex_c.html
Sec. 208 Sequence Listings
209 Indications as to Deposited Biological Material on a Separate Sheet
513 Sequence Listings

Regulations Under the Patent Cooperation Treaty (1 July 2022)
- Rule 5.2 (MPEP 1823.02) Nucleotide and/or Amino Acid Sequence Disclosure
- Rule 13bis (MPEP 1823.01, 1848, 1877) Inventions Relating to Biological Material
- Rule 13ter (MPEP 1823.02) Nucleotide and/or Amino Acid Sequence Listings

Guide for Applicants; PCT procedure before the EPO (Euro-PCT Guide)
- Ch. 5.6

EPO as PCT Authority
- Part F, Ch. II, 6

2. Pre-Application Activities and Considerations

The PCT places no restrictions on patent eligibility of biotechnology subject matter; each member state is permitted to decide what it considers patentable. The description, however, should state how the invention is "capable of exploitation in industry" (PCT Rule 5.1(a)(vi)), implying that the claimed subject matter should possess some commercial application. For more information, see Part Two. Applicants should consult the policies of each elected country for details.

Applicants should be especially mindful to implement any requisite biological deposit in compliance with the Budapest Treaty ahead of the priority date or the PCT filing date to ensure priority (MPEP 2406.03).

3. Filing

a. Application Preparation and Assembly

1) Requisite Parts Pertaining to Biotech (PCT Articles 3 & 11; 37 CFR 1.431; MPEP 1812)

PCT Request	Apx B-09
PCT standard application form	PCT/RO/101 Article 4 Rules 3, 4 37 CFR 1.434 MPEP 1821

Complete Request form as follows:
Items relevant to biotech applications:

Box No. IX (9)—Checklist for EFS-Web filings

Attention: Items (f)&(g), 7, 8, 9

- for international applications (PCT), the checklist of the PCT Request filed with the international application must contain an indication that the sequence listing forms part of the international application. See MPEP § 2422.03(a), subsection IV, for information specific to filing sequence listings in international applications (PCT) via EFS-Web.

Invention Disclosure [Application Body as Filed]

In the Description:

Biological Deposit

- reference should be made in the description to any biological deposit (*see* Rule 13bis.3 for content)

Sequence Listing Part of the Description (if necessary)

- included as separate part of the description
  - if the "Sequence Listing" required by 37 CFR 1.821(c) was submitted in ASCII text format in an international application, indicated on the Request as part of the international application, and published as part of the international application for which national stage is entered under 35 USC 371, then no further submission or incorporation by reference into the specification is necessary (MPEP 2422.03).

Sequence Listing [MPEP 2422(II), 2422.03(a)(IV)]

- when required, reference must be made in the description to a Sequence Listing submitted as a separate part with the international application	PCT Rule 5.2, 13ter PCT Admin Inst. Annex C MPEP 1823.02

For Standard ST.26

- WIPO Sequence (Version 2.2.0): software for facilitating the preparation of patent applications containing nucleotide and/or amino acid sequences; generates sequence listings that comply with all domestic and foreign disclosure format requirements (i.e., ST.26); available on the WIPO website at: https://www.wipo.int/standards/en/sequence/index.html

For Standard ST.25

- 37 CFR 1.821 incorporates by reference the World Intellectual Property Organization (WIPO) Handbook on Industrial Property Information and Documentation, Standard ST.25 (1998)

Note that the standard was revised in December 2009, and the current version is available online at https://www.wipo.int/export/sites/www/standards/en/pdf/03-25-01.pdf

PatentIn Version 3.5.1 software (*see* MPEP § 2430) generates sequence listings that meet all of the requirements of WIPO Standard ST.25. The requirements of 37 CFR 1.821 through 37 CFR 1.825, however, are less stringent than the requirements of WIPO Standard ST.25 (*see* PCT Rule 13ter; PCT Admin. Inst. 208, Annex C). Thus, applicants who wish to file in countries which adhere to WIPO Standard ST.25 should consider the following when not using PatentIn Version 3.5.1.

Reading:

Changes to Sequence Listing Format at WIPO in 2022
https://forresters-ip.com/changes-to-sequence-listing-format-at-wipo-in-2022/

Sequence Listings in International Applications
https://www.ipnewswire.blog/blog/2018/6/4/sequence-listings-in-international-applications

WIPO Sequence and Standard ST.26
https://e-courses.epo.org/pluginfile.php/86815/mod_label/intro/PU81-2021%20VC2%20presentation.pdf

Time for filing sequence listing

- requirements pursuant to 37 CFR 1.821(b–f) must be satisfied at time of filing the international application where the USPTO is the designated Search Authority or the Examining Authority (37 CFR 1.821(h)). Applications not in full compliance at time of filing will be given time to comply. Submitted elements must be accompanied by a statement declaring that no new matter has been added.

Declaration in Support of Sequence Listing	Apx B-10,
- asserts that sequence listing in CRF is identical to written form and contains to new matter	*see also* B-04
Transmittal Letter to the U.S. RO	PTO-1382
Attention: Itemized List	
- sheets of sequence listing (paper or PDF)	
- sequence listing txt. File (CD or EFS-Web)	

2) Additional Documents as Needed

Reference to Biological Subject Matter Deposit (if necessary)	PCT Rule 13bis MPEP 1823.01
- if reference not given in description, submit indications on separate sheet (use of form PCT/RO/134 is preferred)	PCT Admin Inst. 209
Indications Relating to a Deposited Microorganism	
i.) file via PCT-Safe; or	Apx B-11
ii.) submit fillable form RO/134	Apx B-12
- (**Attention:** Box No. IX, check item No. 7 on the PCT request form). This form must, likewise, be used if the applicant wishes samples to be made available only to an expert	PCT/RO/134 PCT Rule13bis
- itemize Form 134 in check list attached to Request	
- if omitted from application, applicant is given 16 months from priority date to submit biological deposition information	Rule 13bis.4
Submission of Additional Indications	Apx B-13
- transmittal of information pursuant to Rule 13bis, if necessary	
Declaration of Biological Deposit	Apx B-08
- asserts that deposit has been made pursuant to Budapest Treaty	PCT Rule 13bis
Attachments: Deposit Receipt	

b. Application Submittal

- see Part Two

4. Post-Filing

a. Enter International Phase

Office-Initiated Actions

If any of the requirements of 37 CFR 1.821(b)–(f) are not satisfied at the time of filing an international application under the Patent Cooperation Treaty (PCT), which application is to be searched by the United States International Searching Authority or examined by the United States International Preliminary Examining Authority, applicant will be sent a notice necessitating compliance with the requirements within a prescribed time period.

Submissions in reply to requirements under this paragraph must be accompanied by a statement that the submission does not include matter which goes beyond the disclosure in the international application as filed (37 CFR 1.821(h); MPEP 2422.07).

Invitation to Furnish Nucleotide and/or Amino Acid Sequence Listing and to Pay, Where Applicable, Late Furnishing Fee	PCT/ISA/225 PCT Rule 13ter.1(a)–(d)
- request for applicant to submit proper sequence listing information pertaining thereto	Admin. Instr. 208, Annex C
Applicant Response: submit information per notice	Apx B-14

b. Enter National Phase

Applicant-Initiated Actions

Preliminary Amendment	Apx B-15
- often filed to make disclosure compliant with 37 CFR 1.821–1.825, such as, adding sequence identifiers and references to Sequence Listing and priority document	

Office-Initiated Actions

Notice to Comply with Requirements for Patent Applications Containing Nucleotide and/or Amino Acid Sequence Disclosures	MPEP 2414.05, 2421.03
- Sequence Listing disclosure in computer-readable form (CRF) fails to comply with 37 CFR 1.821–.825	

Applicant Response: submit preliminary amendment with required parts per Notice	Apx B-16
- Paper or electronic text copy (CRF; see 37 CFR 1.824) of Sequence Listing	
- Amended reference to Sequence Listing in Specification (37 CFR 1.52(e)(5)); request for entry of amendment	
- Statement in support of substitute CRF Sequence Listing; content of CFR listing is identical to the written listing (paper or compact disc), and contains no new matter	Apx B-07
Notification of Missing Requirements Under 35 USC 371 in the United States Designated/Elected Office	PCT Art. 3, 11 35 USC 371
- notification to submit missing parts of application	37 CFR 1.431, 1.495 MPEP 1812
Applicant Response: submit requested parts per Notice to avoid abandonment	Apx B-17

B. European Patent Convention (EPC) Application

The EU takes a generally liberal approach to the patentability of biotechnology, with some notable exceptions. Although it is permissible for U.S. domiciles to file an initial EPC application, it is advisable to consult with a EU-registered agent regarding the patenting process in Europe, especially for highly technical biotech applications.

Reading:
Biotech Inventions and Patentable Subject Matter
https://lawexplores.com/biotech-inventions-and-patentable-subject-matter/

1. EPC Biotechnology Patent Laws and Rules of Practice [Note: for general EPC rules of practice, see Part Two]

EPC [17th ed., Nov. 2020]
Articles 52, 53

Implementing Regulations to the Grant of European Patents [last amended 15 Dec. 2020] Part II, Ch. V Biotechnological Inventions (Rules 26–34)

EPO—Guidelines for Examination in the European Patent Office [Mar. 2022 ed.]
Part A, Ch. IV(4–5)
Part F, Ch. III(6)
Part G, Ch. II(5), Ch. III(4)

European Patent Guide—How to Get a European Patent [21st ed.; updated to Oct. 2021]

Chap. 3 Patentability
Chap. 4.2.010-011 Nucleic acid/amino acid sequences
Chap. 4.2.012-017 Depositing biological material

Case Law

(II)(C.)(7.6) Deposit of Living Material

2. Pre-Application Activities and Considerations

a. Patentability: (EPC Rules 27-29; Guidelines for Examination, Part G, Ch. II(5))

- As with all other technologies, inventions in biotechnology are generally considered patentable under the law and the same general patent examination rules and processes apply to all inventions.
- refer to EPC Rules 27-29 and Guidelines for Examination, Part G, Ch. II(5.2) for definitions of patentable biotech inventions, and exceptions
- The EPO grants patents in strict accordance with its legal basis, the European Patent Convention (EPC) and takes ethical considerations into account when granting patents. Inventions whose exploitation is deemed to be contrary to Article 53 EPC are not patentable. The law lists exceptions to patentability for ethical reasons, among them human cloning, modification of the human genome, and commercial uses of human embryos.
- For patents in biotechnology the rules of the EU's Directive on the legal protection of biotechnological inventions ("Biopatent Directive") also apply. The Directive for instance clarifies that human genes, plants, and animals are patentable when all conditions for a patent are fulfilled. The Directive became part of the EPC in 1999.
- Plants that have been purposefully altered to carry a new characteristic, such as resistance to pests or droughts, or enhanced yield, are generally considered patentable under the law. Such inventions usually concern modifications introduced by genetic engineering ("GM plants"), but other technical processes are also used to obtain such changes. To be patentable, these plants need to be novel and inventive.
- Patents for a human gene often form the basis for many life-saving drugs. The EPO does not grant patents for genes without a known

activity, or for unidentified gene fragments. For a patent to be granted for a human gene, its activity must have been described in the patent application and not be obvious. Patents for human genes do not confer any rights to the human body.

- In the area of human genes, numerous applications were refused because the function of the gene had not been convincingly demonstrated in the application.
- Like plants, animals are patentable according to the law. The patent applications filed with the EPO mostly concern transgenic (genetically modified) mice and rats used in medical research. However, the EPO takes ethical considerations into account: If the transgenic invention is found to make the animal suffer, it may only be patented if it brings a substantial medical benefit to humans (or animals).
- As with plants, conventional breeding methods for animals are not patentable. No patents for farm animals produced by such conventional breeding methods have been granted by the EPO.

Art. 53: exceptions to patentability

European patents shall not be granted in respect of:

- inventions the commercial exploitation of which would be contrary to "ordre public" or morality (ethical principles);
- such exploitation shall not be deemed to be so contrary merely because it is prohibited by law or regulation in some or all of the Contracting States;
  - (a) plant or animal varieties or essentially biological processes for the production of plants or animals; this provision shall not apply to microbiological processes or the products thereof

Inventive step in the field of biotechnology (Guidelines for Examination, Part G, Ch. VII(13))

Inventive step of antibodies (Ch. II(5.6.2))

Reading:
Can Living Beings Be Patented?
https://abg-ip.com/living-beings-patented/

EPO: Plants and Plant Materials Not Patentable If Exclusively Obtained by Essentially Biological Process
https://www.cooley.com/news/insight/2020/2020-05-29-epo-plants-and-plant-materials-not-patentable-if-exclusively-obtained

b. Sequence Listing [EPC Rule 30; European Patent Guide 4.2.010–011]

EPO rules for submitting a sequence listing are substantially similar to U.S. rules. Sequence listings must be submitted in electronic format, complying with WIPO Standard ST.26.

Applicants are advised to use "WIPO Sequence" online filing tool. The EPO urges applicants against filing sequences on paper or PDF.

- specify on Request
- sequence submission software
    - BiSSAP (version 1.3.6)

Reading:

Sequence Submission Tools—BiSSAP
https://www.epo.org/applying/online-services/online-filing/auxiliary/bissap.html

Standard ST.26 (ST.26) Changes and the Big Bang
https://www.vennershipley.co.uk/insights-events/standard-st-26-st-26-changes-and-the-big-bang/

Sequence Submission Tools
https://www.epo.org/applying/online-services/online-filing/auxiliary/bissap.html

Global Changes to Sequence Listings from 1 July 2022
https://www.lexology.com/library/detail.aspx?g=d67d9a0b-bb6d-4285-af2c-58ef89bccadc

Sequence Listing:

Sequence Listings in Patent Applications
https://e-courses.epo.org/wbts/bissap_module/epo-bissap-1.1.3/pages/en_page_1_2.html

WIPO Sequence Listings Standards for PCT Applications
https://thesequencelistingcompany.com/sequence-listings-standards-pct-applications/

Brand New Requirements for Patent Applications with Biological Sequence Listing
https://ssrana.in/articles/requirements-patent-applications-biological-sequence-listing/

Administrative Instructions under PCT, Annex C, Standard for the Presentation of Nucleotide and Amino Acid Listings in International Patent Applications under the PCT
https://www.wipo.int/pct/en/texts/ai/annex_c.html

WIPO Sequence Suite
https://www.wipo.int/standards/en/sequence/index.html

Significant Changes to Sequence Listings for Biotech Patent Applications Are Approaching in 2022
https://www.gje.com/significant-changes-to-sequence-listings-for-biotech-patent-applications-are-coming-in-2022/

Changes for Patent Applications With Biological Sequence Listings
https://www.gov.uk/government/publications/changes-for-patent-applications-with-biological-sequence-listings

A New Standard for Submitting Protein and Nucleic Acid Sequences—"ST.26"
https://www.schlich.co.uk/a-new-standard-for-submitting-protein-and-nucleic-acid-sequences-st-26/

New WIPO Software Tool—WIPO Sequence
https://inpi.justica.gov.pt/en-gb/INPI-News/New-WIPO-software-tool-WIPO-Sequence

Biotech Patent Attorneys, Have a Look at Your New Sequence Listing
https://www.bereskinparr.com/doc/biotech-patent-attorneys-have-a-look-at-your-new-sequence-listing

Changes to Sequence Listing Format at WIPO in 2022
https://forresters-ip.com/changes-to-sequence-listing-format-at-wipo-in-2022/

c. Biological Subject Matter Deposit [EPC Rule 31–34; European Patent Guide 4.2.012–017; Guidelines for Examination Part F, Ch. III(6)]

Under EPO rules of practice, biological deposits must be made in advance of filing, and deposit information, such as name of the depositary and accession number, should be furnished with the application (*see* Rule 31). However, a grace period of sixteen months after the EPO application or any priority application is provided to submit this information. Applicants are advised to file a deposit receipt with the application.

The disclosure should include any relevant information regarding the characteristics of the deposited material, such as, *inter alia*, classification of the material and significant differences from known biological material (*see* Guidelines for Examination, Part F, Ch. III6.3)).

- indicate on Request

European Union: Introduction to Biological Deposits at the European Patent Office and Under the Budapest Treaty
https://www.mondaq.com/uk/patent/1096980/introduction-to-biological-deposits-at-the-european-patent-office-and-under-the-budapest-treaty

3. Filing

a. Application Preparation and Assembly

Request for Grant (Form 1001) Apx B-18
Attention: Items 34–38 relate to biotech applications

Notes on the Request for Grant of a European Patent
http://archive.epo.org/epo/pubs/oj97/6_97/e1001.pdf

b. Application Submittal
EPO Online Filing Basic Tutorials http://docs.epoline.org/onlinefilingdocs/version5/OLF5_TutorialBasic_EN_100407.pdf

C. Paris Convention Application

The Paris Convention takes no express position on biotechnology as patent-eligible subject matter; member nations reserve discretion regarding what they consider patentable in the biological arts. Accordingly, applicants should review the rules of practice for individual countries, or consult in-country legal agents.

Biotechnology Patentability in Selected Paris Convention Members [consult patentability rules in individual countries for details]

Canada
Canadian Intellectual Property Office
https://www.ic.gc.ca/eic/site/cipointernet-internetopic.nsf/eng/home

For details on what can be patented, see Chapter 17: Statutory Subject-Matter in the Manual of Patent Office Practice (MOPOP), available on Canadian Patent Office website.

Patent-Ineligible Subject Matter

- higher life forms by virtue of their not being either manufactures or compositions of matter
- method or process of surgery or therapy on living humans or animals

For details on what cannot be patented, see Chapter 17.03: Excluded Subject-Matter in the Manual of Patent Office Practice (MOPOP).

Republic of Korea (South Korea)
Republic of Korea Intellectual Property Office
https://www.kipo.go.kr/en/MainApp?c=1000

Under the Korean Patent Act and Korean Intellectual Property Office's (KIPO) Requirements for Patentability, the following are not patentable in South Korea:

- biotech subject matter is generally patent eligible, except where the invention has no specific, substantial, and credible utility
- any invention detrimental to public order, morality, or public health
- scientific discoveries
- animal and plant varieties
- methods for medical treatment of the human body

For more detailed information, see the Korean Patent Act and KIPO's Requirements for Patentability (available on KIPO website)

Japan
Japan Patent Office
https://www.jpo.go.jp/e/index.html

According to the Japan Patent Act and the JPO's Examination Guidelines for Patents, the following subject matter is not patentable in Japan:

- inventions not using the laws of nature (e.g., economic laws, mathematical methods, etc.) For more information, see the Japan Patent Act and the JPO's Examination Guidelines for Patents
- any invention that is liable to injure public order, morality or public health
- laws of nature
- scientific discoveries
- inventions not using the laws of nature (e.g. economic laws, mathematical methods etc.)
- inventions contrary to a law of nature
- methods for medical treatment of the human body

For more information, see the Japan Patent Act and the JPO's Examination Guidelines for Patents and Utility Models (available on JPO website)

Australia
Australian Intellectual Property Office
https://www.ipaustralia.gov.au/patents

Patent protection can be applied to a wide range of biological inventions, including micro-organisms and other biological materials

Non-patentable subject matter includes:

- human beings or the biological process for their generation

India
India Intellectual Property Office
https://ipindia.gov.in/index.htm

The Patent Act of 1970 defines what is patent eligible.

Patent-Eligible Subject Matter

- DNA sequences and gene sequences having disclosed functions
- micro-organisms and microbiological procedures

Patent-Ineligible Subject Matter

- discovery of living things occurring in nature; discovery of living things or non-living substances or materials in nature
- plants and animals in whole or any part thereof, including seeds; varieties
- genetically modified multicellular organisms including plants, human beings, animals and their parts
- human beings and embryonic stem cells
- methods of medical treatment
- any essentially biological processes for the production or propagation of plants and animals
- any process for the medicinal, curative, surgical, prophylactic, diagnostic or therapeutic or other treatment of human beings or animals to render them free from a disease or to increase their economic value or that of their products
- specific methods of agriculture or horticulture
- traditional knowledge
- inventions against public order or immoral, harmful to the animal, human or plant life or harmful to the environment

Taiwan (Republic of China) [Note: Taiwan is not a signatory to PCT or Paris Convention]

Taiwan Intellectual Property Office
https://www.tipo.gov.tw/en/mp-2.html
Patent-Ineligible Subject Matter

Pursuant to Article 24 of the Patent Act, the following subject matter is not patentable:

- animals, plants, and essential biological processes for the production of animals or plants, except for processes for producing micro-organisms
- diagnostic, therapeutic, and surgical methods for the treatment of humans or animals
- an article that is detrimental to public order, morality, or public health

Index

Q

R

Index of Statutes and Regulations

Index of Forms

Index of Petitions and Requests